THE SMALL
SHALL BE STRONG

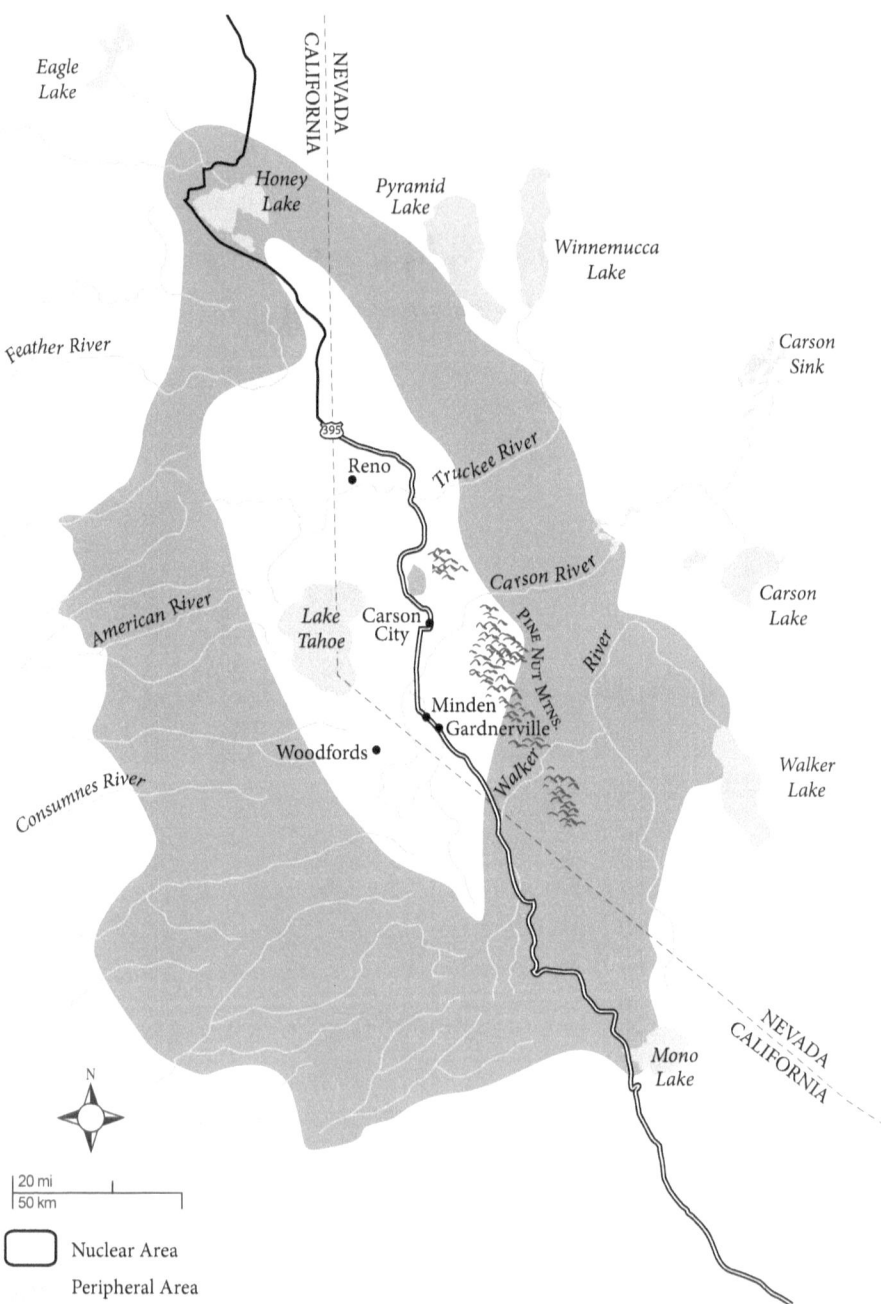

FIGURE 1. The Washoe homelands. Notice Lake Tahoe sits near the center of the nuclear area. Also notice Highway 395 skirting the western edge of the Pine Nut Lands. The road sign for Simee Dimeh Summit sits just south of Gardnerville. Map by Tracy Ellen Smith and Ted Avila.

THE SMALL SHALL BE STRONG

A HISTORY OF
LAKE TAHOE'S
WASHOE INDIANS

MATTHEW S. MAKLEY

University of Massachusetts Press
Amherst and Boston

Copyright © 2018 by University of Massachusetts Press
All rights reserved
Printed in the United States of America

ISBN 978-1-62534-347-5 (paper); 346-8 (hardcover)

Designed by Sally Nichols
Set in Minion Pro
Printed and bound by Maple Press, Inc.

Cover design by Kristina Kachele Design, LLC

Cover art: (Top) Adonis Villanueva, detail from photo *Emerald Waters, Lake Tahoe,* Shutterstock.com. (Bottom left) detail from photo of Datsolalee posed with two baskets from her final visionary "masterpieces" series: "Light Reflected" (left) and "Hunting Game in a Proscribed District" (right), courtesy of the Nevada Historical Society. (Bottom right) Canyon Florey, *Continuing traditions: Ethan Wyatt placing a willow trap for fall fish runs, 2013,* copyright © Women of the Mountain, courtesy of the photographer.

Library of Congress Cataloging-in-Publication Data

Names: Makley, Matthew S., 1974–author.
Title: The small shall be strong : a history of Lake Tahoe's Washoe Indians / Matthew S. Makley.
Other titles: History of Lake Tahoe's Washoe Indians
Description: Amherst, MA : University of Massachusetts Press, [2018] | Includes bibliographical references and index. |
Identifiers: LCCN 2017050254 (print) | LCCN 2017053854 (ebook) | ISBN 9781613765869 (e-book) | ISBN 9781613765876 (e-book) | ISBN 9781625343468 (hardcover) | ISBN 9781625343475 (pbk.)
Subjects: LCSH: Washoe Indians—History. | Lake Tahoe Region (Calif. and Nev.)—History.
Classification: LCC E99.W38 (ebook) | LCC E99.W38 M35 2018 (print) | DDC 979.3/57—dc23
LC record available at https://lccn.loc.gov/2017050254

British Library Cataloguing-in-Publication Data
A catalog record for this book is available from the British Library.

For Washoes: past, present, and future

CONTENTS

Preface   ix
Acknowledgments   xiii
A Note on the Washoe Language   xvii

Introduction   1

CHAPTER 1
The People from Here   18

CHAPTER 2
Newcomers   38

CHAPTER 3
Violent Transformations   46

CHAPTER 4
The Chaos of Destruction   60

CHAPTER 5
Survival   76

CHAPTER 6
Washoe Colonies   94

CHAPTER 7
Prejudice and Persistence   119

CHAPTER 8
Carrying It   141

CHAPTER 9
The Journey Home   164

Afterword   185

Notes   189
Index   227

Illustrations follow page   140

PREFACE

History is about place more than time.
—A. Brian Wallace, Washoe Tribal chairman, 2005

The rumors were true. There, on an outcropping beneath them, sat three men. Desperate, weather beaten, and dangerous, the foreigners heralded the beginning of a new era for Washoe Indians. It was the late spring of 1827. Those doing the observing, a small group of Washoes, are silent to history. Their presence, recorded by one of the strangers, stands alone as testimony to their existence.

Long protected by the towering Sierra Nevada on their western boundary and the desolate, alkaline Great Basin to the east, Washoes had been hearing about foreign people for decades—light-skinned outsiders who spoke a strange tongue. It is likely that Washoes had observed other early travelers who had not noted their presence. That is how the Washoe preferred it. Their isolated nature meant that they maintained a precolonial lifestyle well into the nineteenth century, much later than most other North American Native communities. However, the California gold rush (1848) and the Comstock silver rush (1858) brought a tidal wave of newcomers to Washoe country and ushered in a prolonged period of dramatic transformations. Washoes met the challenges associated with these changes as best they could; they were hopelessly outnumbered, and war was a losing proposition. The first priority was simply to survive. In the process of surviving, they contributed to the growth of a new society. Washoes have maintained an active and important presence in the Lake Tahoe region. Their history helps to prove the notion that small western Indian communities have pasts that, when factored into the larger history of the American West, add dimensions to our understanding of that past and by extension the present.

The Washoe homeland cuts a wide swath along the eastern Sierra Nevada and the western Great Basin. At the center sits Lake Tahoe, a body of water internationally famous for its beauty and recreational opportunities. The word *Tahoe* comes from the Washoe word *DaɁaw* or the phrase *DaɁaw Ɂaga,* which means the "Edge of the Lake." The Washoes' ancestors began living part of each year at Tahoe thousands of years ago. Archaeologists and anthropologists believe they are the oldest human community to continuously occupy the Tahoe region, putting the arrival of their ancestors somewhere close to ten thousand years ago. Many Washoes believe they were created there.

Families lived on Tahoe's shores in the snowless seasons. From a Washoe perspective, the water "breathed life" into humans, plants, and animals; it was, and for many still is, a center of their world. Washoe elder Susie James explained that traditionally, when a family first arrived on the lake's shores in spring, they "blessed the water and themselves because they had come to a sacred place."[1]

Anthropologists have had trouble trying to fit Washoes into a Native American cultural region, debating whether they belong in the California or Great Basin cultural region. The answer is both or neither. They are unique. They are the only speakers of the Hokan language in the region. Historians, for their part, have mostly ignored Washoe history.

Washoe custom placed a high value on modesty. They were not, and are not, a "flashy" or "showy" people. These geologic and cultural traits help to make their history unique. Like many of the small, isolated nonequestrian western tribes, their history has not received the attention larger groups or those that engaged in imperial wars with Europeans and later Americans typically receive. The pages that follow seek to change that, while simultaneously suggesting there are more small tribal histories, particularly in the American West, waiting to be told.

I came to this history through both personal and professional interest. Born on the south shore of Lake Tahoe in the early 1970s, I grew up in the Tahoe basin and the adjacent Carson Valley, today the seat of the Washoe Tribal government. I went to school and played sports with Washoes. I formed lasting friendships with tribal members. The people and the area form a part of my identity. That made my research and writing both easier and more difficult. I made a conscious decision to go "light" with historical and academic theory in the book. While that might be disappointing to some of my professional colleagues, it is nevertheless more important to me that the history being told is accurate, sensitive, and rich with the voices of Washoe people when possible.

I recall interviewing Washoe Tribal chair Brian Wallace as an eager doctoral student. I was transcribing everything he said. At one point he commented, "You know, in Washoe country we think when you write something down, you intend to forget it." I wrote that down. After a moment I stopped writing and *listened*. Chairman Wallace then told me that for Washoe people, history is about place more than time.

The place has changed dramatically over the past 150 years, and so too have the Washoes; they transformed themselves in order to continue living in their ancestral home. That adaptation was painful and often still is. But the people remain, connected to their ancestral lake and lands in new ways. Despite overwhelming forces of transformation, massive land loss, disease, and conflict (at times violent), they persist.

ACKNOWLEDGMENTS

Many Washoe community members gave generously of their time over the past ten years while this book took shape. Former Hangalelti community chairman Mahlon Machodo has been an especially helpful resource and a better friend. Thank you to Art George Jr., whose knowledge of Washoe culture and history is impressive. Former tribal chairman Brian Wallace made time for interviews and several informal conversations. More recently, tribal historic preservation officer Darrel Cruz has dedicated much time and effort to this work. He edited drafts of the manuscript with a special eye toward making sure all Washoe bands received representation. Culture/resources director for the Washoe Tribe Herman Fillmore helped enormously with the final stages of this book.

The staff at the Woodfords Indian Education Center provided critical support, especially Beverly Caldera, who helped with language questions. My onetime high school geometry buddy Angela Jones provided advice and helped me photocopy hundreds of historical documents. Katie Keliiaa's scholarship has been helpful and inspiring. Thank you, Katie, for bringing elders, community members, and scholars together at the University of California at Berkeley in the spring of

2015. Special appreciation goes to the elders who made that trip: Melba, Rakow, Jo Ann Nevers, Rocky Jim, and Wanda Batchelor. Community members included Mischelle Dressler, Lisa Enos, and Kristin Burtt, all of whom have worked hard to preserve and teach Washoe history. Thanks to Beau and Cloud Medicine Crow, Barbara Jones, Rob Jones, Linda Shoshone, Danny Wyatt, Willard Bennett, Frank Pitts, Dena Pitts, Kerri Pitts, Tony Kizer, Kevin Jones, Gwen James-Fair, and Cecil Wyatt. I also benefited from the help of former Washoe Tribal attorneys Timothy Seward and Robert Greenbaum. Elder Jo Ann Nevers published a history of the Washoe people in 1976 that served as the authoritative guide when I began work on this manuscript.

Thank you to my mentors in graduate school. Lisa Emmerich was the first to encourage me to begin this history. She along with Mike Magliari and the late Mike Gillis provided rigorous edits of the earliest versions. Waziyatawin Angela Wilson, thank you for pushing me to think critically about the continuing effects of colonization on Native communities. I am pleased to count Donald Fixico as a valued mentor and friend. Martha Knack graciously stepped into this project, in its dissertation form, at a late date and made invaluable suggestions.

Professor Peter Iverson's influence permeates this work and all of my professional life. Those of us who were his students know the value of his mentorship; he is a giant in our field. My now grown sons remember fondly swimming in Dr. Iverson's pool.

Any student of Washoe history owes a tremendous debt of gratitude to the late anthropologist Dr. Warren d'Azevedo. Dr. d'Azevedo spent much of his career working with Washoe families, tirelessly accumulating and cataloging Washoe history and knowledge, and he generously donated his research materials to the Special Collections Department at the University of Nevada, Reno.

At the University of Massachusetts Press, Matt "Becks" Becker has been a steadfast champion of this work for more than ten years, and I thank him for his patience and his friendship. Thank you as well to the two anonymous reviewers whose critical edits and suggestions made this a better book. A hearty thank-you goes to Annette Wenda, one of the best copy editors in the business. Thanks to Canyon Florey and Rebecca Byerly for help with photographs.

I have benefited from generous institutional and intellectual support at Metropolitan State University of Denver. Stephen Leonard and Joan Foster have provided valuable support. Jim Drake and Meg Frisbee have been a constant source of ideas, feedback, and camaraderie. Thank you as well to all of my current and former students, especially Jonathan Lussier, Jennifer Harrelson, Devin Strauch, and Jordan Kowalenko.

Last, my family: Carole Michelsen, who is unwavering in her commitment to all of her children and grandchildren; Ron Michelsen, whose work ethic and artistic abilities set a high standard for all those around him; Randi Makley, who never seemed to tire from my last-minute requests for help with faxes, forms, or finances; Lloyd and Vicki Odegard, who always welcome me into their home in Reno when I have research or writing to do; Mikiah and Alijah, who keep me rooted to all that is good; and Alea Makley, my partner in life and frontline editor. Finally, thank you to historian Michael J. Makley, without whose enthusiastic support this book would not exist.

A NOTE ON THE WASHOE LANGUAGE

Some members of the Washoe community prefer to spell *Washo* without the *e*. Others, in particular Native speakers, might prefer *Wašiw*. I have chosen to use the *Washoe* spelling because that is the spelling the community used when they incorporated in 1934 and that is the name most people outside of the community are familiar with.

For many years members of the Washoe community have been working hard to keep their language alive in both written and spoken form. Linguistics professor William H. Jacobsen produced a number of works on the Washoe language. Over several decades, Jacobsen, with the help of community members, created a Washoe orthography.

I have chosen throughout the book that follows to use the formal Washoe orthography when presenting key Washoe words, as opposed to the alternative phonetic rendering. I have provided a brief symbol key below, based on one published by Jacobsen, to help readers with pronunciations. Here are the words that occur most frequently:

SYMBOL KEY

ORTHOGRAPHY	MEANING	PHONETIC RENDERING
Waši·šiw	The People from Here	Wa She Shu
Wašiw	Washoe	Washoe
DaʔAw	Lake Tahoe	Da ow
DaʔAw ʔaga	The Edge of the Lake	Da ow a ga
Welmelti	Northern Washoes	No difference
Pʼa·walu	Central Washoes	Pawalu
Hangalelti	Southern Washoes	No difference
Maʔaš	Family lands	Ma ash
Deʔek Wadapuš	Rock Standing Gray (Cave Rock)	De ek Wadapush
Tʼa·gɨm	Piñon pine nut	Tah gum
Tʼa·gɨm ʔaša	Pine Nut Lands	Tah gum a sha
Tʼagɨm Gumsabayʔ	Pine nut harvest ceremony	Da goom sa bye

Interested readers can consult William H. Jacobsen, *Beginning Washo*, Nevada State Museum Occasional Papers no. 5 (Carson City: Nevada State Museum, 1996).

š	make the sh sound, like *ship*
ʔ	glottal stop; this signals a quick, short stop in the throat
ɨ	sounds like u in just
ɨ·	sounds like ee in see
ɨw	sounds like ew in sinew
Pʼ	glottalized p, sounds like pb

THE SMALL
SHALL BE STRONG

INTRODUCTION

> I am part of everything just like my old people were. I am part of this plant, I am part of the sky, I am part of the dirt, I am part of what you do not see, I am a part of it.
>
> —Art George Jr., Washoe, 2006

He came from Cimé Dimé, Double Springs Flat, within the T'a·gim ʔaša, Pine Nut Lands. Relatives and close friends called him Epesuwa. Others knew him as Gumalanga. To whites he was Captain Jim. He embodied the traditional Washoe virtues of modesty, generosity, and kindness. He did not seek to wield authority, but his years of experience and gentle nature drew others to him. By 1892 Epesuwa had seen enough of his people's suffering. He set out for Washington, D.C. According to Washoe tradition, when he met President Benjamin Harrison, he extended a handful of piñon pine nuts and said, "My brother this food from the pine nut trees is what my people eat.... [I]t is the same as our mother's milk when it is made into soup.... [Y]our people are destroying our trees and our food.... [W]e ask you to help us so we can live."[1]

Epesuwa made his journey at a time when Washoe people were suffering. For more than thirty years, American mining, milling, lumbering, fishing, farming, and ranching had been transforming the Lake Tahoe region. Tahoe itself had become the center of large commercial timber and fishing operations. Because Washoes had lived in such an isolated environment, protected to the west by the Sierra range and to the east by the Great Basin, they did not encounter significant foreign disruption until a number of years after the discovery of gold in California in 1848. This point frames Washoe history in significant ways.

Washoe isolation in the Sierra is different from, say, Ute isolation in the Rockies. This is true for several reasons. Perhaps the most important is geography. While the Rockies have many waterways, canyons, and corridors that open up to large, sprawling intermountain valleys and grasslands, the Sierra Nevada do not. The Rocky Mountain openings encouraged far more exploration early on. The towering Sierra, with fewer significant gaps, are not easy to get across.

One scholar of the American West puts it this way: "The Sierra lacks the Rockies' great grassy 'holes' and 'parks' and miles-wide valley bottoms that in the past supported large populations of native ungulates, and that were capable of sustaining thousands of horses and mules for weeks at a time between spring and fall. . . . [T]here is little in the American Rockies that could have prepared cordilleran trappers for the toil and deprivation they would face in a crossing of the Sierra." Because the Washoes occupied a high mountain sanctuary, not easily reached or breached, and because they did not enter the horse trade, they remained mostly untouched by early European explorations, diseases, and colonial efforts. Even when the initial gold rush brought thousands of Argonauts trekking across Washoe lands, the small size of Washoe communities combined with their mobility allowed them to remain unseen and largely undisturbed.[2]

They could not, however, evade the massive human migration that followed the unearthing of the Comstock Lode near Virginia City, Nevada, in 1858. Family members watched in horror as their critically important Pine Nut Mountains became overrun with fortune seekers and loggers. Soon colonial activity spilled out into the river valleys, the forests surrounding Lake Tahoe, and the lake itself. In less than two decades, dozens of commercial logging and fishing operations had begun operating at Tahoe, harvesting the bounty of cutthroat trout that Washoes had carefully stewarded for thousands of years.

A common misconception of hunter-gatherer peoples paints them as "miserable" occupants of harsh landscapes. Some have argued that against bleak and forlorn landscapes, hunter-gatherers have wandered, foraged, and starved. Every semester for the past ten years I have conducted the following exercise in my university history classes. I ask students to jot down the words or images that come to their minds when I say the term *hunter-gatherers*. We then populate the whiteboard with the words students come up with. Words that make the board every semester include *primitive, nomadic, simplistic, violent, dirty, bows and arrows, stones, wanderers, foragers, war,* and *Stone Age*. Far from scientific, this exercise is nevertheless useful in gauging the perceptions students have about indigenous peoples labeled "hunter-gatherers."

It is not just students who hold inaccurate perceptions. *The Encyclopedia of Nevada Indians*, published in 2000, suggests that Washoes and other Nevada Indians "had no permanent villages." In the desolate Great Basin, "All the Natives wandered . . . foraging for seeds, nuts, bulbs and other wild vegetables." This statement is wrong on several counts. Washoes, Paiutes, and Western Shoshones did have year-round village sites, often tended by elders or community designees during the hunting and harvesting seasons that would have drawn the majority of villagers away for varying lengths of time. The hundreds of edible and medicinal vegetables used by Nevada Natives were not "wild" to those who had tended and harvested them for countless generations. And those who hunted and harvested certainly were not "wandering." They had established patterns that included care and maintenance rounds to improve crops' health. Hunters regularly took reconnaissance trips to monitor particular deer or antelope herds before coordinating a group hunt.

The ethnobotanist M. Kat Anderson, in her book *Tending the Wild*, notes that the California environment Euro-Americans thought to be virginal and Edenic appeared that way because it had been tended and cared for by Native peoples for thousands of years. Washoes have been making this point for at least the past half century. In 1963 tribal member Manuel Bender put it this way: "Young hunters and fisherman were thoroughly indoctrinated in the importance of leaving 'seed' for next year. . . . [I]t was drilled into all providers of food that from one pool with 5 only 2 fish could be killed. . . . The practice was observed in game. So well established was this rule and so well observed that the white people merely took it for granted that the fish and game were just prolific without any means to perpetuate the source." This well-known rule among the Washoes is often expressed by the phrase "Take one, leave two."[3]

The rush to the Comstock led to the disruption or thorough destruction of every major ecosystem Washoes had been tending and using. Without the benefit of their resources, they carved out a tenuous existence. As the twentieth century began, individuals did what they could to survive, which often meant entering the growing wage market as ranch hands, domestic servants, and laborers. In these capacities Washoes became crucial contributors to the early economy of northwestern Nevada and northeastern California. Without their work the tourist industry at Tahoe would not have grown the way it did; likewise, ranches and farms in the Carson Valley would have had to look elsewhere for the labor necessary to support their growing operations.

Many enterprising Washoes became entrepreneurs, hiring themselves out as fishing and hunting guides to tourists at Lake Tahoe. Others sold fish and game to growing markets in Carson City, Reno, and Virginia City. Some women, like Louisa Keyser, also known as Datsolalee, became exceptionally successful by selling woven baskets. Keyser is credited with creating the degikup style of basketry, a mix of tradition and innovation, which in turn influenced generations of Indian weavers in the American West. One of her baskets, named "Beacon Lights," sold in 1914 for $2,000, some $47,300 in current value. Today, collections around the world feature her work, including the Smithsonian's National Museum of the American Indian, in Washington, D.C.

The nature of Washoe survival following the arrival of outsiders shaped their unique expressions of sovereignty in the twentieth and twenty-first centuries. When traced, those adaptations add a significant piece to the history of the eastern Sierra, the Lake Tahoe region, and the broader American West.

The steadfast insistence that Washoes would not leave their ancestral lands formed the core from which all community survival efforts extended. Even at the height of their dispossession and suffering, Washoes refused the federal offer to relocate them to Pyramid Lake, where they could live with their neighbors the Northern Paiutes. Several years later, when federal politicians again urged them to move, this time even farther away to the Humboldt River valley, they again emphatically declined. This truth about Washoes' connection and commitment to their home provides a firm foundation for the history that follows. Washoe history converged with American history when Washoes had their first consequential contact with an American federal official.

The well-known American explorer and politician John C. Frémont, on his trek to the California coast in 1844, wrote about his encounters with several Washoe groups at the base of the eastern Sierra, in the Carson River valley. His journal emphasizes Washoe hospitality and their consistent warnings to him and his men not to attempt to cross the snow-laden Sierra. Individuals who offered Frémont pine nuts and advice participated in historically significant meetings. As soon as Frémont's journals were published and read, Washoe people became part of the American lexicon; they were "known." Their territory no longer existed in what the historian Ned Blackhawk labels a "cartographic phantasmagoria."[4] In the wake of the Frémont encounter, Washoes, with no way of knowing what was to follow, may still have felt safe in their traditional lands. Conversely, in all likelihood, they had heard enough stories from trading partners about the Spanish, Mexicans, and Americans to give them serious pause. Whatever they believed, their course as a people had been irrevocably altered by the encounter.[5]

Most of what happened in Washoe history before the confluence of Washoe and American history has been lost. How they lived, what they believed, what individuals did on a daily basis, and what their form of government looked like are all subject to debate. This fact should not suggest that Washoes lived static, unchanged lives over countless generations before Euro-Americans arrived. The oral tradition, along with the archaeological record, indicates that the Washoes had been adapting and innovating for thousands of years.

All humans regardless of time or place depend on things that can, and do, change and eventually come to an end. The near extinction of bison and subsequent transformations of Plains peoples such as the

Lakotas, Crows, Cheyennes, and Arapahos have been well documented by historians. Washoes relied on deer, antelope, rabbits, trout, piñon pine nuts, and hundreds of seasonally edible and medicinal plants. Similar to the bison, and other resources used by Plains peoples, these resources were impacted and in some cases severely depleted after the arrival of newcomers. Yet unlike demographically larger equestrian Plains groups, and similar to many small indigenous communities, Washoe history has not received professional historical attention.[6]

Multiple factors contribute to the oversight. First, small communities seem less important from a demographic perspective. Second, Washoes never adopted horses, and as the historian Steve Fountain notes, "Indians without horses are Indians without histories." Europeans and later Americans looked down on Indians who did not use horses. Horseless Great Basin Indians suffered particular scorn, leading to a persistent belief that the Great Basin was "essentially empty of people, history, or value." There were many practical reasons Washoes did not adopt horses, foremost among them being the environmental constraints dictated by the vertical region they occupied. Small, narrow, precipitous trails in the rugged Sierra proved difficult for horses to navigate. Third, Washoes did not fight any large-scale significant battles against Americans. And finally, forgetting Washoes and their rights to ancestral lands makes it easier to justify their dispossession.[7]

With the odds stacked against them, Washoes could have vanished. This book tells the history of a people who refused to disappear, and when they stabilized following the initial devastating wave of American arrivals, they began to wage legal battles to recover and protect their homeland, their sovereign rights, and their culture. That process continues to this day. The following brief examples ranging from the late 1880s to 2017 will be examined in subsequent chapters. They are mentioned here to underscore the point that far from going away, Washoes have continued to influence the culture, society, and physical space of the eastern Sierra.

In the 1880s, following Epesuwa's journey to Washington, D.C., Washoes successfully used the Dawes Act of 1887 to protect more than eighty thousand acres of culturally significant yet nonirrigable Pine

Nut lands. This outcome flew in the face of federal policymakers, who wanted the Dawes Act to help assimilate Indian people by turning them into ranchers and farmers. But Epesuwa, and the community he represented, insisted that they wanted to use the Dawes Act to protect their piñon groves, and they did so against the wishes of powerful federal legislators. Today, a road sign on Highway 395 (a major north–south artery connecting Southern California and the Canadian border) sits adjacent to a large section of Washoe Pine Nut lands. It reads, "Simee Dimeh Summit, Elev. 5,987." This is a Washoe phrase meaning "Double Water," a reference to a nearby double spring. The phrase is also connected to violent events that unfolded during the gold-rush era in this region. How many thousands of travelers pass the sign and summit in a given year? How many people, at least subconsciously, process a Washoe phrase in the heart of Washoe lands? But like the Washoes' history, the phrase itself remains unknown to most outsiders, just as does the realization that the vast piñon forests around the sign might not exist had it not been for Washoe efforts in the late 1800s.

Washoes were not the only small, landless western community to use the Dawes Act to acquire lands. But many of these histories remain to be told. As the historian Khal Schneider points out, "Thanks to the scholarship of the past quarter century we have a rich understanding of 'how the Indians lost their land.' We know much less about how Indians got some of it back."[8]

Several decades after protecting the pine nut groves, tribal members voted to unify themselves under the provisions of the Indian Reorganization Act (IRA) of 1934, writing a constitution and officially becoming the "Washoe Nation." The Washoe government evolved over the next fifty years, engaging in struggles over land protection, cultural integrity, and sovereignty. By 1997 the government was in a strong-enough position to enter into an impactful dialogue with the federal government. That year federal leaders, including President Bill Clinton, Vice President Al Gore, and Senator Harry Reid, convened a summit to discuss the future of Lake Tahoe. Tribal members played a crucial role in the summit. After days of meetings and proceedings, Washoes and the federal government signed several memorandums of understanding. One of the MOUs established an interagency partnership that consisted of the Washoe Tribe along with the secretaries for the Departments of Agriculture, Interior, Transportation, and Defense. It also included the Environmental Protection Agency (EPA). Together this group was charged with creating a plan for the long-term protection of Lake Tahoe. A second MOU stated that federal entities involved in protecting Lake Tahoe would recognize Washoe rights to use and access their ancestral lake. A third and critically important MOU was signed between the Forest Service and the Washoe Tribe to formally recognize a government-to-government relationship.

Directly after signing this last MOU, the Forest Service and the Washoe Tribe entered into a project agreement that resulted in the tribe stewarding 350 acres of meadowland at Meeks Bay, on the west shore of Lake Tahoe. The location had traditionally been an important harvesting and fishing site. Lumber operations during the late 1800s had denuded the land. By the late 1900s the site had been significantly impacted by the growth in tourism and development. Native plants and animals had all but disappeared. Granted management rights, the tribe initiated a comprehensive watershed plan aimed at restoring the meadow and granting access to community members to study traditional cultivation and harvesting techniques. As a result of the presidential summit, the MOUs, and the Meeks Bay agreement, it is accurate to say that Washoe land-management practices and environmental philosophy have had a real and direct impact on federal management practices at Lake Tahoe.[9]

The same year as the presidential summit, Washoe Tribal attorneys pressed the EPA to investigate and begin cleaning up a toxic site close to Washoe reserved lands in the Carson Valley. The former sulfur mine had been worked extensively in the 1950s and 1960s. When the Anaconda Mining Company sold it, the new owner did nothing to control the waste that when mixed with snow and rain became sulfuric acid. The acid leached toxic contaminants, such as arsenic, which flowed into the East Fork of the Carson River and onto tribal lands. Federal officials proved reluctant to undertake mitigation efforts, but the Washoes pushed until the government created a Superfund cleanup site.

In 2007, after a twenty-year struggle, the Washoes won the right to prohibit rock climbing at one of their most sacred sites on the eastern shore of Lake Tahoe: Deʔek Wadapuš, or "Cave Rock." The saga ended in the Ninth Circuit Court of Appeals and resulted in federal protection of an Indian sacred place. It was one of the first times in American history that a sacred site was given precedence over public recreational use of federal lands. Moreover, the outcome emphasized a distinctly Washoe cultural view of land management at one of the American West's great tourist centers.[10]

At the end of the twentieth century, the Washoe community had become actively engaged in working to protect the Washoe language and to reclaim traditional lands. Language-preservation efforts were nurtured by two dedicated individuals who organized a nonprofit and established Washiw Wagayay Mangal, "the house where Wašiw is spoken." Originally aimed at children from ages three to five, it soon became one of only a few full-immersion language schools in the United States. Graduates of that program have since grown into adulthood, and a few of them have returned home to help spark a newly invigorated language and cultural preservation movement. These endeavors have contributed to the regional sociocultural and political composition. The degree to which they contribute can be debated, but it cannot be denied—they have contributed.[11]

Professional historians have only recently begun turning to stories like these. While the book that follows is not steeped in a particular theory, or historical paradigm, it is nevertheless worthwhile to briefly map out historical approaches that have contributed to the form this work takes.

A distinct line of inquiry and research related to small Indian communities expanded following the tumultuous 1960s, but anthropologists, not historians, primarily undertook these approaches. Those anthropologists produced in many cases excellent volumes, but their disciplinary focus and priorities were different from those of historians. There are many reasons historians are late in getting to these stories. There are more historical records available for large communities and those who had violent relations with Euro-Americans. In particular, tribes positioned on the fringes of the North American continent along the Atlantic slope, the Gulf Coast, the southwestern corridor, and the Pacific Coast encountered Europeans much earlier than interior communities, due to their proximity to accessible deep-water ports, centers of trade, and trading routes. Thus, Algonquian- and Iroquoian-speaking peoples along the Atlantic slope and in the Great Lakes region, Pueblos in the Rio Grande country, and many diverse tribes along the California and Gulf coasts had dealings with Europeans for centuries before the Washoes had direct contact with Euro-Americans.

These sustained relations produced relatively bountiful documentation that, combined with Native oral traditions, have contributed to richer historical treatment of these regions and communities. It must also be acknowledged that researching, writing, and publishing histories are no small undertakings. Part of the absence can be explained by the vast number of small communities versus the relatively small number of professional historians dedicated to American Indian history.[12]

In addition to the question of records and human power, larger Indian communities just seemed more important. They appeared to wage the most vigorous wars and negotiated prominent treaties. Textbooks on the histories of California and Nevada, when they include Native peoples, often leave out the smaller groups. A notable exception is the recent history of Nevada written by historian Michael Green. Green's second chapter goes a long way toward recognizing the rightful place of Washoes, Paiutes, and Shoshones as the first occupants and stewards of the land that would become Nevada. Even books specifically dedicated to America's first peoples give Washoes and other "minor" communities short shrift.[13]

At the end of the 1970s, when histories of many larger communities had been written and historians might have been tempted to turn their focus to smaller ones, the idea of writing tribal histories became passé in some academic circles. There was a movement away from telling one community's history toward critical analysis involving multiple tribes and diverse regions. A concern for overly simplistic, and often romanticized, tales of defeat and victimization prompted one scholar to argue by 1979 that tribal histories had become an "obsolete paradigm."[14]

In the years that followed, practitioners of a "new Indian history" challenged that assertion by producing histories emphasizing the agency and resilience of Native communities who strategically adapted to survive. The new Indian history also led to the widespread examination of Indian adaptations and new understandings of their relationship to the cultural and economic development of the United States.

Recently, scholars like Nicholas Rosenthal have encouraged historians to push their inquiries further by fully acknowledging how Indians have contributed "to the creation of complex societies and cultures." Rosenthal's suggestion helps to frame parts of this book, which show how Washoes have helped shape the eastern Sierra and Tahoe region.[15]

Ned Blackhawk's book *Violence over the Land: Indians and Empires in the Early American West* goes a long way in bringing much-needed historical focus to the understudied Great Basin. Blackhawk's work argues that Ute Indians on the eastern fringe of the Great Basin ultimately "helped to create and sustain, as some might suggest, 'a middle ground' outside the reach of imperial [European] power." Utes "endured by adopting the new technologies initiated by Spanish colonization, eventually carving out profitable roles within the colonial world. They became courted, feared, and powerful actors along this edge of empire and soon dictated the pace and scale of colonial expansion to the northwest."[16]

Blackhawk is quick to point out that many nonequestrian Basin peoples suffered at the hands of Ute, Spanish, and later Mexican slave raiders because they did not hold power roughly equivalent to the other groups. While there is no clear evidence that Washoes were significantly impacted by the slave trade, Blackhawk's point that small nonequestrian peoples had less opportunity to shape the rapidly changing world certainly applies to the Washoe. The scope of Blackhawk's work extends west to include Southern Paiutes and Western Shoshones, but it stops just short of Washoe country. While much of what Blackhawk finds among Western Shoshones and Southern Paiutes parallels Washoe history, there are significant differences. With the Euro-Americans' arrival, the uneven balance of power dramatically affected the Washoe people.

While Utes and other equestrian groups such as the Comanches and Lakotas were able to defend themselves and challenge European and American dominance in their respective regions, at least for a while, the Washoes had to rely on different methods to survive and adapt. Robust scholarship on the "middle ground" where Native peoples, Europeans, and Americans met has proved that "Indian-white frontiers . . . were messy, eclectic contact points where all protagonists are transformed—regardless of whether the power dynamics between them are evenly or unevenly balanced." However, up to this point, most of the scholarship has focused on those groups who are, in the words of Pekka Hämäläinen, "embedded in collective American memory," groups such as the Iroquois, Lakotas, and Comanches, who held, for a time, power roughly equivalent to the newcomers. Initially, in 1844, the Washoes outnumbered Frémont and his band of weary travelers, and although they had no firearms, they were likely more powerful. However, that dynamic shifted swiftly following the gold and silver rushes; after 1860 Washoes never held equivalent or even close to equivalent power. Scholarly currents coming out of new Indian history have informed the work that follows. So too has one of the most recent compelling intellectual shifts related to the writing of Indian history: the decolonization school.[17]

Decolonization moves the study of Native peoples away from written Euro-American sources and toward indigenous centers of knowledge and interpretation. Decolonization studies often point out that historians and their craft have at times been complicit in the subjugation of indigenous forms of knowledge and remembering. While the work that follows is not strictly a decolonization history, it certainly has been informed by many of the practices and sensibilities embodied in that approach.

The term *colonization* is used in this book to connote the appropriation and destruction of traditional Washoe resources. Colonization studies have led to the creation of distinct categories of colonialism. The two categories that broadly scaffold this history are settler colonialism and extractive colonialism.

Settler colonialism has to do, first and foremost, with an incoming colonial group's access to and desire to permanently hold land. A leading scholar on settler colonialism, Patrick Wolfe, explains, "Land is life—or, at least, land is necessary for life. Thus contests for land can be—indeed, often are contests for life." Wolfe further suggests that settlers engaged in colonizing a new place, like Washoe country, were connected to a larger state or national apparatus, which was further tied into "a global chain of command linking remote colonial frontiers to the metropolis. Behind it all lay the driving engine of international market forces."

Wolfe's analysis certainly applies to the silver pulled from the Pine Nut Lands during the Comstock era. The nearly $300 million worth of silver harvested during the two decades the Comstock flourished ensured Nevada's connection to international market forces, while hastening the pace of colonization and increasing the sheer number of new arrivals. This connection to international markets brought influences and practices to Washoes from places they had yet to even learn about. Indeed, their name, "Washoe," became synonymous with the rush to the Comstock Lode. Anyone involved in mining, finance, or mineral processing in the American West during the 1860s and 1870s knew the word *Washoe*, although they might not have had any idea that the name came from Nevada's earliest Native community. While many of the miners and financiers might have left following the Comstock's decline, the farmers, ranchers, millers, ferriers, railroaders, and many others had no intention of leaving. The former Washoe homelands had now become their home.[18]

The second form of colonialism, extractive colonialism, connotes a practice in which colonial interests center specifically on a natural resource or raw good—for example, the beaver pelts that drew the French to the St. Lawrence River region or the gold that drew the Spanish up through Latin America and into the American Southwest. In the case of the Washoes, precious metal, specifically silver, certainly influenced extractive colonialism, as did timber in the Lake Tahoe basin and the Pine Nut Range along with the protein-rich cutthroat trout. The primary difference between settler colonialism and extractive colonialism is that extractive colonialism does not necessarily include perpetual residence of the colonists—that is, people come, harvest the resources, and leave. Obviously, there is significant overlap between these two forms of colonialism, and the point here is only to mention the concepts in order to fully frame the use of the terms *colonial, colonists,* and *colonization* as they are employed in this book.[19]

Colonization is clearly evident during the intense eras of resource extrapolation in Washoe country, and it was a mix of the extractive and settler forms. Some remained only a short while and left, while others stayed. *Colonization,* for the purposes of this book, has an intellectual component as well. It signifies the arrival of people whose worldview cast Washoes and other western Indians as "savages."

Great Basin and California Natives became the target of a particularly vicious strain of colonial racism. Some of the first federal reports prove that the American use of racial categories placed Great Basin Indians and their neighbors among the lowest forms of human life in the West. In 1861 the territorial governor of Nevada, James Nye, described Washoes as "miserable people." He claimed they were "but one remove from the brutes." In 1875 a visiting ethnographer labeled them a "lower race."[20]

This form of colonialism, this flawed view of humanity, must be acknowledged because it shaped the relationship between Washoes and Americans, and in some instances it continues to do so. It became part of the human calculus that allowed Americans to systematically dismiss Washoes' and other Great Basin Indians' concerns as unimportant. It regularly served as a useful tool to blame Natives for being "incapable" of helping themselves for their own condition. This intellectual colonization had real and devastating impacts that continue to this day.

While the terms *colonize* and *colonization* have come to describe the dispossession of indigenous peoples and the impositions wrought through that process, these terms are not reserved to the distant past. Bobbi Sykes, the late Australian poet and indigenous scholar, once asked, "What? Post-colonialism? Have they left?" This expresses a growing sentiment among indigenous peoples around the world.[21]

Americans today, living in what formerly was Washoe country, do not regard themselves as "colonists," but Washoes and other Native peoples in Nevada might still think of themselves as "colonized." Dakota scholar Waziyatawin Angela Wilson describes continued colonization as "the constant denigration of our [Native] intellectual, linguistic, and cultural contributions to the world." This colonization has led to the belief that Native stories, histories, languages, and "cultural contributions are insignificant." Washoe history helps to prove the significance of small western tribal histories.[22]

In turning to these histories, it is important to acknowledge that they matter in their own right. The stories of loss, suffering, struggle, and survival demand attention. It is also noteworthy, and in many ways remarkable, to recognize that many of these groups have been at the forefront of important contests over land, resources, and Native rights. Their efforts have contributed to Indian identity and sovereignty writ large.

For example, the small California Cahuilla bands, known as the "Cabazon Indians," waged a legal battle in the 1980s for their right to operate gambling operations on tribal lands. The Supreme Court ruling in the 1987 case *California v. Cabazon Band of Mission Indians* led to an expression of Indian autonomy that has in turn helped create a multibillion-dollar Indian gaming industry across North America.[23]

The Ak-Chin community, in central Arizona, provides another example. A small, often overlooked group, they lobbied for and gained the first Native federal water settlement in the United States. Their current tribal chairman, Robert Miguel, described the water settlement as "one of the great settlements in the country." Moreover, their growth as an agricultural producer is a notable factor in the broader economic, social, and cultural fabric of central Arizona.[24]

Established by executive order in 1912, the Ak-Chin reservation provides a home base for members of both the Tohono O'odham (Papago) and Akimel O'odham (Pima) tribes. The term *Ak-Chin* refers to the precolonial method of farming practiced by O'odhams. Despite centuries of land loss, forced assimilation, and cultural transformations similar to the Washoes, O'odham people fought so that they could remain in the lands of their ancestors. Once established on the Ak-Chin reservation, they began building a self-sustaining agricultural community.

In 1962 community members created Ak-Chin Farms. Owned and operated by tribal members, Ak-Chin Farms generated enough income for them to become almost entirely financially self-sufficient. Ak-Chin Farms today is one of the biggest farming communities in North America, producing barley, corn, cotton, pecans, potatoes, and wheat on around sixteen thousand acres.

In the arid reaches of the Sonoran Desert, competition for water is fierce, though. In the 1960s non-Native irrigation interests began draining groundwater sources that had been supporting the Ak-Chin Farms. Watching wells dry up, the community lobbied for a legislative solution that, in 1978, resulted in the passage of a law providing them eighty-five thousand acre-feet of water annually. The original compact had to be amended several times over subsequent decades, and at each turn the O'odhams have been resolute in defense of their rights. The matter is still not settled. In the spring of 2017, the Ak-Chin community again filed suit because the largest municipal water corporation in Arizona began reducing the amount of water delivered to them.[25]

Another as yet unresolved conflict with implications regarding natural resources involves the Makah people on the Olympic Peninsula—the farthest western continental reach of the United States. Their struggle to protect and promote ancient rights, rituals, and practices is associated with harvesting whales. With about twelve hundred community members today, the Makahs' oral tradition and material culture prove they have been hunting whales for thousands of years.

When international commercial whaling operations brought the Pacific whale population to near extinction in the early 1900s, the Makahs stopped whaling. In the early 1990s, when the gray whale was removed from the endangered species list, the Makahs set out to resume their harvests. This ignited a firestorm between animal rights groups, Native lobbyists, the federal government, and governments of other countries involved in whaling.[26]

The case went in and out of the courts until 2002, when the Ninth Circuit Court put the hunts on hold. In the interceding years, the Makahs successfully held one hunt that served to dramatically energize the culture and morale of the Makah people. And in the spring of 2015, the National Oceanic and Atmospheric Administration issued a draft environmental impact statement that indicated there could be a continuation of Makah whaling in the near future. Makah history, including the question of whale hunting, has recently been interpreted in the historian Joshua L. Reid's book *The Sea Is My Country: The Maritime World of the Makahs*. Reid's work proves that the Makahs played a critical role in shaping the economic, social, and cultural world of the Pacific during the period of heightened European and later American exploration and trade. Their struggle to retain access to their traditions associated with whale hunting demonstrates that they continue to influence the region.[27]

Washoes, Cahuillas, O'odhams, and Makahs, in fighting to strategically adapt, found footholds where they could. Weighing their efforts and successes, it is clear that many small tribes actually shaped the course of twentieth- and twenty-first-century Indian sovereignty while fighting out of a corner. This is not to suggest that "all's well that ends well." Washoe, Cahuilla, O'odham, and Makah suffering has been traumatic, their losses steep. Among the Washoes, poverty, violence, alcoholism, and disease have been a stable presence. This reality adds critical context to their continued struggle to survive in the lands of their ancestors.

This book is intended to dovetail with the other histories of Great Basin Indians: Martha Knack's histories of the Northern and Southern Paiutes, Steve Crum's history of the Shoshones, and Blackhawk's work. Collectively, these narratives go a long way toward explaining the human history of the region. When we consider the Washoes' efforts to retain and protect their piñon pine forests, their acquisition of land at Lake Tahoe, their struggle against toxic contamination, and the precedent-setting Cave Rock decision, we are compelled to wonder, what other stories are out there?

CHAPTER 1

THE PEOPLE FROM HERE

> Washoes believe Lake Tahoe is a part of them. Whatever happens to the lake is going to happen to us.
> —Mahlon Machado, Washoe Community Council member

On a summer day in 2008, I joined a small group for a journey into Lagomarsino Canyon, deep in the western Great Basin. Along the eastern slope of the Virginia Range, due west from Lake Tahoe, we approached a slight draw; wild horses dotted nearby hillsides. On a broad, sweeping south-facing cliff, I saw what we had come for: 2,229 petroglyphs. Their strength of imagery makes a distinct impression. They include lines, dots, circles, spirals, and symbols. Human and animal forms—bighorn sheep, lizards, and birds—appear as well. These glyphs provide a window into a distant human past. But the view is clouded.[1]

Who made the drawings? When and why? What do the patterns and symbols signify? Was this a teaching place, a ritual gathering space for ceremonies of abundance and successful hunts? Was it a border crossing where many distinct travelers felt compelled to leave their mark? Archaeological study indicates some of the carvings might be up to ten thousand years old; others could have been completed just before the arrival of Euro-Americans in the region in the 1800s. Other than that, answers take the form of opinion. Similarly, no one can say exactly when humans first started occupying the western Great Basin.

Washoe tradition tells of their creation in this region. Tribal elder

Jean Dexter shared a concise version of the Washoe creation story: "The Maker of All Things was counting out seeds that were to become the different tribes. He counted them out on a big winnowing tray in equal numbers. West Wind, the mischievous wind, watched until the Maker had divided the seeds into equal piles on the basket. Then he blew a gust of wind that scattered the seeds to the east. Most of the seeds that were to have been the Washoe people were blown away. That is why the Washoe are fewer in number than other tribes."

This brief account is one of a much longer and complicated set of narratives that include encounters between forces of nature, a powerful woman creator named Nentushu, weasel brothers called Pewetseli and Damalali, spiders, giants, coyotes, and humans. One version of the creation story recounts Nentushu creating people by burning the fuzz off cattail seeds. Once the seeds were ready, Nentushu said of the Washoes that though they are small, they shall be strong. The stories are always set against a familiar backdrop that includes Lake Tahoe, along with its surrounding rivers, streams, mountains, and piñon trees. The degree to which the stories have changed over the past two hundred years is impossible to know. Translated into English and collected by anthropologists in the early and middle twentieth century, these narratives contain echoes of a distant past that has always included Washoes living in the region.[2]

In 1955 Omer Stewart, a distinguished anthropologist, testified in a federal court that Washoes have occupied the Tahoe region "for at least several thousand years." More recently, Susan Lindstrom, the archaeologist who has done the most work with Washoes in the twentieth and twenty-first centuries, indicated that ancestral Washoes took up residence in the Tahoe region eight or nine thousand years ago.[3]

Washoes did not live the same way all that time; their practices grew and changed over thousands of years, reflecting changes in the environment, weather patterns, and available food sources. They engaged in intensive land-management practices, caring for and harvesting hundreds of edible and medicinal plants. They observed and managed regional deer and antelope herds along with fish and rabbit populations. They studied the night sky and developed stories about constellations, seasons, and the movement of planets.

The chapter that follows does not seek to promote a version of a precolonial "Garden of Eden." Owing to the great period of time living in the same place, it is certain Washoes faced cycles of hardship and suffering. Climactic shifts, technological advancements, human migrations, and border disputes consistently influenced the nature of their survival, long before Europeans set foot in North America.

The evidence of the earliest human beings in the western Great Basin and eastern Sierra Nevada consists mostly of projectile points and lithic, or stone, remains, along with the petroglyphs. One spectacular archaeological find in 1940, however, turned up some of the oldest human remains ever discovered in North America. Near present-day Fallon, Nevada, employees of the Nevada State Parks Commission uncovered a burial site inside a cave. The location contained a well-preserved man, later named the "Spirit Cave Mummy," wrapped in intricately woven textiles with leather moccasins. The site also held the remains of a woman covered by a sturdy woven mat. Fifty years later, advances in science enabled biological anthropologists to test the remains. They determined the woman lived about ninety-three hundred years ago, while the man, who was deeper in the cave, lived about ninety-four hundred years ago. There is no clear evidence to suggest who these people were ethnically or who their descendants might be. It is nevertheless stimulating to imagine a time ninety-three hundred years ago when civilizations we know almost nothing about made their homes in the western Great Basin. Did these people leave a mark at Lagomarsino?[4]

Grinding tools, projectile points, manos, metates, pestles, and petroglyphs are the far more common physical items that prove humans lived in and around the Lake Tahoe basin up to ten thousand years ago. Anthropologists and archaeologists have labeled these early human communities "paleo-Indians," often categorizing them as part of the "Martis archaeological complex." While scholars debate whom these first people were, Washoes steadfastly claim them as ancestors.

It is clear that groups of humans were making a living in the Tahoe basin and adjacent valleys as the environment began to shift between the geologic epochs of the Pleistocene to the Holocene, ten to twelve thousand years ago. During the late Pleistocene, all archaeological evidence points to a highly mobile lifestyle for these communities. The environment was markedly wetter and cooler than today; many Great Basin valleys would have been filled with wide wetlands. People lived on the edges of these numerous shallow lakes abutting the foothills. From here they could fish, hunt waterfowl and small game, and harvest plants while maintaining access to reliable water sources.[5]

Archaeologists and geologists have determined that around the mid-Holocene, eighty-three hundred to forty-five hundred years ago, the Great Basin environment became extremely dry. Ancient tree stumps line the shallows of Lake Tahoe's south shore beneath the water's surface, proving that the lake's level dropped significantly during this period. The abundant resources that had been available when the extensive shallow lakes populated the region were significantly reduced. Washoe ancestors would have had to seek out new food opportunities and become careful observers of growing cycles for edible grasses and nut-bearing trees. The proliferation of grinding sites identified and dated to this period proves that human communities did in fact begin to rely more heavily on small seeds and nuts. At roughly the same time, piñon trees began to spread from the southern Great Basin to the north, and this very well could have been the initial period in which Washoe culture began a heavy dependence on and therefore reverence for the piñon pine nut.[6]

Most archaeologists agree that by about forty-five hundred years ago, during the late Holocene epoch, human communities lived in ways easily identifiable with tribal communities in the Basin today. For one thing, the archaeological record becomes far more active during this period, suggesting a larger population density. The spreading of the piñon and the fact that many of the water sources had been replenished undoubtedly abetted the increase. By this time, Basin communities, including the Washoes, had begun to rely on a consistent seasonal cycle to take full advantage of the resources becoming available at different times of the year.[7]

Washoes speak a language called Hokan. It is one of the oldest language groups in America. By the time Euro-Americans arrived in the western Great Basin, the Hokan-speaking Washoes were bordered to the east by Numic speakers, the name given to six groups who speak a form of the umbrella language Uto-Aztecan. The Numic group includes Northern Paiutes and Western Shoshones, who are the Washoes' closest Great Basin neighbors. California communities to the west spoke a variety of languages.[8]

The date of the arrival for the Washoes' neighbors in the Great Basin has been debated by archaeologists and linguists since at least the 1950s. The dates range anywhere from three thousand to one thousand years ago. Regardless of when they came, new neighbors meant new opportunities and new challenges. The oral traditions and the archeological record indicate that over the past one thousand years or so, Washoes, Paiutes, and Shoshones figured out how to live in their respective areas with only periodic, mostly localized incidents of violent confrontation. Far more common would have been diplomatic encounters.

In border regions it became common for Washoes, Paiutes, and Shoshones to intermarry, thereby cementing alliances. Thus began what we might term the recent "historic" period when Washoe lands would have included pine forests, rivers, streams, and lakes along with rich fertile river valleys that would look familiar to people in the area today. Members of distinct Washoe communities met annually, in the snowless seasons, on Lake Tahoe's shores, where they renewed kinship ties, cemented political relations, celebrated births, mourned deaths, and feasted on fresh trout and forest game, along with seasonal fruits and vegetables. Washoe elders remember summers on the shore as a "big time," the return to a sacred place.[9]

Washoe settlements dotted the eastern Sierra landscape. Their territory stretched from what is today Susanville, California, to the north to Sonora Pass, California, to the south. The Sierra Nevada provided something of a fluid western boundary, depending on relations with neighboring California tribes, while the Pine Nut Range delineated a similarly mutable eastern border. Families maintained permanent homes in valleys near water and areas of plentiful game. They also kept specific summer home sites on the shores of Tahoe.

Across this immense landscape, Washoe people moved in coordination with a seasonal cycle, a connection to the first Basin peoples who cycled from wetland valleys to higher-elevation pine forests. Washoes lived in the valleys during the winter, at Tahoe during the snowless months, and in the Pine Nut Range during fall harvests. Loosely affiliated familial units created distinct regional communities. The Welmelti occupied the northernmost quadrant, while the Hangalelti populated the South. The P'a·walu occupied the lands in between.[10]

Kinship groups were matrilocal (mother centered), patrilocal (father centered), or both. Washoe families, the backbone of their society, included extended relations and sometimes friends. Kinship groups provided a foundation that ensured cooperation for group hunts, martial action, and religious practices. A complex web of relations bound people together. Children learned quite young that they were a small part of a larger group that demanded respect for time-honored protocols. These proprieties had been defined over thousands of years, based on survival needs. At the center of the web was the value placed on cooperation. One family might survive on its own for a time, but families had to band together for defense, hunting, fishing, and harvesting.

Political structures tended to be local. Washoes did not have an overarching government or one presiding leader, although esteemed elders from each community would be recognized by the larger groups. And it is likely that councils of elders helped govern the day-to-day life of a local community. However, each group also featured multiple leaders serving in diverse capacities. Individuals called animal "bosses" monitored herds, led hunting rites, and set hunting limits. Warriors, curers, and medicine people, or *Domomali*, also held varying degrees of authority. So too did women who had mastered the massive encyclopedia of edible and medicinal plants in the eastern Sierra.[11]

Families maintained specific hereditary resource areas called *MaʔaÅ¡*. These could include lands for plant procurement, fishing, hunting, pine nut collecting, and spiritual practices. One Washoe man described *MaʔaÅ¡* lands as a "body of tools—resources." Tribal members or families could move across the land on their own, as long as they respected established territorial and familial boundaries. Permission had to be granted in order to cross or use another family's lands.[12]

Spiritually significant lands and sacred spaces existed throughout the eastern Sierra. Washoes believed (and many continue to believe) that a power or energy they called *wegéleyú* animated the universe. This neutral force permeated all things, including people, animals, plants, the land, and its features. Washoes feared, respected, and honored power, which could be channeled in higher concentrations through a select few individuals and places. Some sites, like Deʔek Wadapuš, "Cave Rock," on Tahoe's eastern shore, required special ministrations by a shaman. If ever a sacred place was misused or desecrated, the offenders could suffer injury or death and might condemn their kinship group to dire fates as well.

Shamans occupied an exclusive role among the Washoes. They were often mysterious individuals who cultivated specialized and private knowledge. There existed a clear distinction between curers and shamans. Curers, usually older females, prepared and prescribed cures for diverse sicknesses. Shamans, because of their acquisition of power, were different. Their healing involved elements beyond the knowledge of curers.

Power chose the person who would become a shaman usually in their childhood. Unlike other Native communities where an individual could actively seek out power through ceremonies, fasts, or rituals, Washoes claimed no control over the acquisition of power. Power first visited a person in the form of a dream. Power dreams could take many forms, but typically visitations from animals and water beings of the eastern Sierra world brought power to the dreamer. Out of respect for the taboo associated with using the name for these water beings publicly, this book refers to them simply as "water beings." Washoes believed (and many still do) that these small beings lived in the lakes, rivers, streams, and springs of the western Great Basin. Washoes are not alone in this belief; many Great Basin groups, including Paiutes and Utes, shared a common view that mysterious and powerful supernatural creatures inhabited Great Basin waters. In the Washoe world, underground passageways linked surface waters to a central hub near Deʔek Wadapuš, "Rock Standing Gray," today known as Cave Rock.[13]

The guidance and training of an experienced shaman were critical to a young novice, for power came with a great risk. Developed improperly, it could sicken and kill an individual. Power could also be wielded maliciously. Washoes considered power used in such a way to be witchcraft. Another shaman could kill those accused of evil work, or in more recent times they could be banished.[14]

One story tells of Detutudi, a southern Washoe shaman. On a trip to Dangberg Hot Springs, Detutudi encountered central Washoes who treated him with scorn. He returned home and fixed up a killing spell. He broadcast the spell some thirty miles from his home to the hot springs, and in its wake the spell left a trail of dead trees, grasses, weeds, and people. Central Washoes recognized the scarred trail for decades afterward. Bones have been discovered at the site, and to this day many Washoes avoid that area.[15]

Whether an individual was destined to gain power or not, the path to adulthood began with lessons from parents, aunts and uncles, and especially grandparents or elder members of a kinship network. Boys and girls entered gender-specific courses of training early in life. Girls began with the lessons learned while assisting older female relatives. Washoe elder Belma Jones remembered grandmothers as the ones "you learn everything [from] as you go along . . . so you would know." Her grandmother told her, "You have to know these things, 'cause someday you'll grow up." Women, with girls in tow, cared for and harvested plants, processed foods, fished, sometimes hunted, and made meals. They also produced many of the tools and utensils needed for daily living, which included seed beaters, woven baskets, fish traps, hunting nets, and digging sticks.[16]

Weavers created baskets in diverse forms to serve many purposes. Some were narrow, tightly woven, rounded at the bottom, and cured with sap to hold water. Larger baskets with a tight weave could be used for cooking, food storage, or serving. Others of a looser weave and flat shape served for collecting nuts and plants and also for winnowing seeds. Women harvested and prepared willow for the frame of their baskets. They used the inner bark of willow to create threads for lashed baskets. Redbud provided the raw material for red-hued thread, while fern roots dyed in black mud offered a dark contrast. Women with their young apprentices gathered necessary materials year-round and spent long winter months weaving. Depending on their design and function, baskets might take several months to complete. After the arrival of Euro-Americans in the late 1800s, some, including Louisa Keyser (Datsolalee), turned weaving into high art (which will be discussed in chapter 6).[17]

As young girls matured, their studies focused on the hundreds of edible and medicinal plants of the eastern Sierra. A mature woman, complete in her training, could have at her command hundreds of edible and medicinal plants. The dense catalog of vegetal stock allowed for tremendous diversity in diet. Edibles included sunflower seeds, pine nuts, wild rye, wild mustard, wild onions, Indian potatoes, watercress, camas, bitterroot, and sego lily, to name a few. In addition, berries such as buckberry, chokecherry, elderberry, wild strawberry, serviceberry, currant, Sierra plum, and Sierra gooseberry contributed to the Washoe diet. Berries could be eaten raw, but more often they were added to dishes or mixed with flour to make baked goods. Pine nuts and acorns were regularly ground into flour that would be used for making soups, stews, and bread.

The management of this abundance required encyclopedic knowledge and diligent care. Women knew that crops like the cattail could be harvested and used in multiple ways. Cattails grow in wet, marshy areas below sixty-five hundred feet. In spring women harvested the green shoots, which could be peeled and served raw or used in soups and stews. Later in the year, close to the summer solstice, women collected cattail pollen and seeds by burning the outer layer off the fuzzy heads. They then milled the seeds into flour, which they used to make dough. Cattail pollen served as a sweetener for many Washoe dishes.

Some nuts, such as the black oak acorn, required leaching to remove poisonous tannic acid. Women first ground the nuts into flour. Next they placed the flour on a woven tray or cloth, which they set in a shallow pit and strained with hot water.

Because of their vast understanding of plants and herbs, women were skilled healers. The most accomplished knew the locations and properties of some 250 plants as well as when and how to harvest and process them for prescriptive uses. Most could treat maladies like the common cold, allergies, skin irritation, headaches, and stomach ailments. They procured and administered rose hips for the common cold, dogwood-bark tea to bring down a fever, and willow-bark tea for aches and pain. Moss was used to stanch blood flow. Sore throats and toothaches could be treated with various roots.

Badópo, corn lily in English, had multiple medical applications. The root could be heated and then ground and mixed for use as a poultice for flesh wounds. Alternatively, it could be made into a tea for stomachaches or cramps. Knowing the Sierra flora and complicated processing techniques was not enough. Young students also studied the diverse growing environments to ensure croplands stayed healthy and productive.

There was a spiritual dimension associated with plant care as well. Before significant work, a woman, usually an elder, prayed for the success of their collective venture; she also prayed in honor of the plants to be taken and asked a blessing upon the harvesting tools. Girls' education took years to complete, and families honored their progression to womanhood with an important ceremony.[18]

In the days leading up to the ceremony itself, the candidate entered a period of fasting and exercise. Mornings began with a walk or jog, and during the day the candidate worked on preparing a special elderberry staff decorated with red bands to be used in her ceremony. In order to cultivate the Washoe value of generosity, the girl was required to make the products of her gathering and processing available to family and friends in her community. After three days of fasting and sharing the fruits of her labor with her community, the girl and her family lit a fire on a mountain or nearby hill to officially announce the ceremony.

It took place at night and opened with ceremonial singing by female relatives and friends. The girl handed out small gifts to attendees, who would dance, sing, and celebrate throughout the night. A feast prepared by the candidate's family would be provided. Near dawn everyone gathered around the initiate and her female sponsor; the sponsor offered prayers and painted her charge with ashes. A basket of water was then used to bathe her. Finally, her father took the specially prepared elderberry staff and planted it in a secret place nearby where it would remain upright and unbroken, like his daughter. The ceremony ended with some light dancing, visiting, and breakfast. This new woman would later initiate and help train another generation of girls so that the ecological, pharmacological, and ritual wisdom of the elders would never be lost.[19]

Similar to girls, boys began their training early in life. They had to master effective weapons, tools, strategies, and religious rites to take advantage of the diverse Sierra animal, fish, and bird populations. They learned about the power of animals and how to respect them. In the traditional Washoe worldview, animals were no different from humans. They had their own communities, languages, and essence of being that demanded esteem. Bows and arrows were used for deer hunting, while clubs, nets, and stone knives could be used for other game. Small quarry, often the object of the novice, was taken with a short, sturdy bow made of pine, yew, or other tight-grained woods. Larger game, not hunted until a boy had demonstrated his ability and preparedness, could be taken with a bigger bow, often backed with sinew to add strength. Bowstrings consisted of deer sinew that had been cured. Rosewood, reed, and willow provided the raw material for arrow shafts.

Craftsmen planed arrows between pumice slabs. Obsidian or flint points served as piercing tips. The preferred Washoe shooting technique was unique. It consisted of a clutch between the first and second fingers, aided by the thumb.[20]

Most hunters had a general knowledge of flint knapping, shaping arrowheads in diverse sizes for distinct purposes, and some developed their skills to a degree that qualified them as specialists. They used a punch tool made from a specially shaped piece of buckhorn close to half a foot long, roughly the circumference of a pinkie finger. The buckhorn was lashed to a longer wooden handle, some eighteen inches in length. The craftsman held this tool in one hand and brought the force of the punch down on the flint, which he held in the opposite hand. With each punch tiny bits of flint flaked off. This was a painstaking process.[21]

Large prey consisted of mule deer, pronghorn antelope, and mountain sheep. Smaller prey included rabbits, porcupine, chipmunks, gophers, squirrels, woodchucks, and badgers. Quail, grouse, and doves were commonly sought birds. Among numerous waterfowl, Canada geese and mallard ducks were especially prized. A select few men became skilled crafters of duck decoys using tule reeds.[22]

When elderly hunters were no longer able to sustain the rigors of large game hunting, they prepared, set, and checked traps. They also assumed the primary role in training boys. Lessons began by the age of six or seven, often with target practice and pursuit of small animals.[23]

The lessons for young boys included observation of various quarries' traits. Boys also spent years learning how to control their movements so that they could creep up on an unsuspecting herd. The student would be required to learn the ceremonies connected to large hunts as well. A hunter that traveled to the high country and successfully killed a bighorn gained special recognition.

All hunting depended on the maintenance of healthy herds. In the case of deer and antelope, that meant regulating hunting and recognizing tribal individuals as leaders or "bosses." Often the boss's ability included an element of *wegéleyú,* tied to dreaming and ceremony. The boss positions could be but were not necessarily hereditary. Bosses typically specialized in one type of animal and would learn the habits, population numbers, and migration patterns of local herds. A few of these leaders possessed the ability to "charm" game like deer and antelope.[24]

The ability to charm animals usually came in the form of dreams suggesting a specific location where herds might be found. The charmer then visited the dream place, and if he saw antelope or signs of them, he advised others to build a corral, encompassing up to an acre of land. The corral, composed of sagebrush walls, was constructed to allow a narrow opening. The charmer stood behind the corral and coaxed the antelope in. If the charm worked correctly, the antelope entered the corral "like sheep driven into a pen." While only select trainees would become leaders, all initiates had to learn the methods that adhered to the established customs and study their prey.[25]

The ideal time to hunt the *memdewe,* or mule deer, was the late fall, after they had fattened from summer grazing. Washoes had observed that the local herds formed two principal groups, those that moved west for the winter and those that wintered in the Pine Nut Range to the east. Hours and sometimes days of preparation preceded a *memdewe* hunt. Participants readied themselves by performing a ritual cleansing in a creek and scrubbing with roots and plants to disguise their scent. They offered prayers for a successful hunt and thanks for the deer that would give up its life.[26]

The most accomplished deer hunters used a stalking technique that required imitating a deer's movement. The practitioner draped a preserved deer head, including a partial hide, over his own head and shoulders, thus taking the form of a buck. Disguising oneself demanded strict adherence to protocols. Hunters respected the bones of their prey and observed taboos related to their handling. Bones had to be prayed over and placed in water so that scavenging animals could not pick them clean. Instead of using real horns for the deer disguise, hunters fashioned horns out of manzanita. Once disguised, a skilled hunter could put a herd at ease through movements and gestures characteristic of an unknown buck approaching a new herd. But moving into a herd was risky. A false movement could send the herd into flight and jeopardize the entire hunt. There was also the danger of being attacked by a buck, which could weigh as much as two hundred pounds and used antlers and hooves as weapons. Another hunt that held a life-threatening risk was the rarely attempted bear hunt.[27]

Bears, along with their physical prowess, had the ability, like some shamans, to read people's minds. In the words of one Washoe man, "If you talk about bear to anyone, the ground communicates your intentions to bear or the bear reads your mind. He concentrates on what you're thinking and knows." Only "fearless" hunters attempted to kill a bear. The owner of a bear hide maintained special prestige; the hide was often buried with its owner at death.[28]

Hunters in training began with easier tasks, like the use of brush blinds strategically located near water sources and salt licks, to get deer. This method required patience, timing, and, like all others, luck.[29]

The butchering and preparation process required that every part of the animal be handled properly. Hunting parties composed of five to ten men often butchered the meat at the kill site and distributed the cuts evenly. Each hunter could transport up to two hundred pounds of meat, some of which would be dried for winter storage. Nonedible animal parts were usually processed by women and used for threads, needles, clothes, moccasins, and blankets.[30]

The ceremony for boys becoming men, similar to the girls', emphasized the community standard of generosity. As a boy progressed from small game to large, tradition demanded that he eschew the products of his hunt, distributing them instead among his kin group. When a boy killed his first large buck, a ritual of advancement took place. Immediately after the successful hunt, his father and grandfather gave him a ceremonial bath. Next the buck's antlers were placed point side down on the ground. The young hunter then attempted to belly crawl beneath the horns. If he was able to crawl through, he had attained the status of manhood, and there would be a celebration.[31]

As girls became women and boys men, family members took an active role in coordinating marriages. Relatives of prospective couples exchanged small gifts for as long as a year prior to marriage. Even after an appropriate match had been determined, the potential bride had the final say and could negate the arrangement. Newly wedded couples could choose to live in either of their kinship groups. In the event of a divorce, mothers and fathers had an equal claim to the children.[32]

The training of boys and girls, indeed the entire fabric of community life, was set against the backdrop of the seasonal cycle. Honed over many hundreds of years, the cycle allowed each Washoe community to maximize their food yields by accessing diverse resource bases. In the early spring, when plants like watercress began transforming stream banks and hillsides from brown to green and the Watasému, "the main river," now the Carson, rose, tribal members began moving from valley floors to home sites at Lake Tahoe.[33]

The young and healthy started their ascent to the six-thousand-foot-high mountain lake as early as possible. Later in spring the throughways became more passable, and those who had difficulty traveling, like new parents, infants, and elders, could join the others. The Welmelti, the northerners, maintained sites on the northern end of the lake; P'a·walu, from the central region, lived on the eastern shore; and Hangalelti were on the south shore.

Upon arrival at the lake, individuals "blessed the water and themselves because they had come to a sacred place, Da ow was the giver of life; it fed fish, animals and humans." The water "breathed life" into the Washoe ecosystem; it was the cultural, spiritual, and ecological center of their world. The lands around Tahoe contained rich forests of ponderosa, Jeffery, and sugar pine; Douglas fir; cedar; and mountain hemlock. Important quarry, like deer, lived in the mountains, and Tahoe, along with smaller lakes and streams, provided a variety of fish.[34]

Washoe men and women were skilled fishers, and they tailored their techniques to suit different environments. They used nets woven of plant fiber framed with willow rods to trap fish. A method called *belashi* consisted of green willows bundled together and anchored on the bottom of a creek or stream. Once fish got caught in the willow bundles, fishers pushed them up the bank. The water drained, leaving the fish.

Along densely lined waterways, fishers bound the tops of trees across the water to create shady areas that attracted fish. Streams were diverted to create small pools, and dams were built in swift-moving water, forming ponds, so fish became more visible. Dam-like weirs were also used. Stretched from bank to bank, the weirs were lined with shredded sagebrush on the upstream side to slow the water's flow and force fish up over the top. A specially crafted basket in the shape of a trough caught the falling fish on the downstream side of the weir and channeled them to a larger catch basket.[35]

In deeper bodies of water, individuals used barbed hooks shaped from a swan's clavicle. Four or five hooks could be strung along a line and baited with minnows, worms, or fish eggs. A person might bait three hooks with worms to catch minnows and a fourth hook with minnows to catch trout. In that way, one pole could simultaneously catch bait and food. Some Washoes also became proficient using two-pronged spears, launched from a fishing platform built above the water.[36]

Communities monitored trout populations and worked to maintain them. Spring fishing centered on the cutthroat, or *imgi,* runs; white fish, *mutushahoo,* dominated the fall runs. During spring runs women seined suckers or parasitic fish out to protect young trout populations. Female fish distinguishable from the red-jawed males were released if caught. Fishing leaders regularly designated harvesting areas and established a reasonable limit on the number of fish to be taken. The careful management provided such abundance that when Americans arrived, the supply of fish was believed to be illimitable.[37]

During the mid- and later stages of the summer, families spread out, and many traveled to the western slopes of the Sierra to collect acorns and to trade with neighboring tribes. Small groups traveled to Maidu and Miwok country in the western Sierra foothills or to Nissenan territory, present-day Colfax and Grass Valley, California. Their network of trade was large and intricate. Goods acquired in California, such as skins, seashells, and acorns, could be traded to Nevada's Great Basin communities.[38] Generally, families traveled alone, but they may have camped in groups in the western foothills. There are stories of members getting caught on the western slopes by early storms and having to spend some part of winter away from home.[39]

Warfare between the Washoes and neighboring tribes was not common, although territorial skirmishes did occur. A widely repeated story tells of a battle against the Maidu near Honey Lake. Two Washoe shamans, whose power was associated with weather, summoned a north wind. It brought hail, and the lightly clad enemy froze to death.[40]

Surrounded by Numic speakers to the north, south, and east, along with Miwok, Maidu, and Yokuts to the west, Washoes were effectively insulated from the growing influence of the Spanish, French, English, and for a significant time Americans. Communities in the Snake River country of south-central Idaho, including Bannocks and Northern Shoshones, chose to adopt horses; so too did the Utes in the southeastern Great Basin. That choice brought them into the wider world of European trade and commerce. The Washoes did not. It made no practical sense for them to abandon a system of living that had served them well for thousands of years. Due to the difficult vertical Sierra environment, keeping horses would have been impractical. As historian Steve Fountain puts it, "The horse held little utility in hunting rabbits, antelope, or deer" in the eastern Sierra. Moreover, it would have been difficult to keep horses fed year-round. While it is true that without horses, the Washoes missed the opportunities and power that came with horse culture, they also were able to largely avoid the "harrowing world of raid and counter raid." Fountain astutely points out that this exclusion contributed to the staying power of Washoe culture. Utes and Southern Paiutes in the southeastern Great Basin absorbed the greatest impact of Spanish colonization and the spread of horses. While it is impossible to say how directly colonial jockeying and the spread of the horse affected Washoes, it is certain that they could effectively retreat from the principal trading routes skirting their territory. Consequently, they remained extremely isolated and therefore autonomous all the way up until the arrival of Americans in the 1800s. Time spent in the trading camps of the western Sierra provided Washoes a window into the world of trade and raid, and they likely made a strategic decision not to get heavily involved.[41]

As autumn days grew shorter, families began to return to their homes on the valley floors below the Sierra basin in order to prepare for winter. This eastern region included piñon pine, sagebrush, and Utah juniper land and provided fertile hunting grounds for antelope, mule deer, and small game such as the black-tailed jackrabbits and the cottontail. *T'a·gim*, piñon pine nuts, the staple of the Washoe diet and culture, flourished in this zone, most notably in the region called T'a·gim ʔaša, the Pine Nut Lands. Waterfowl, plants, small game, and fish thrived in and around the valleys, wetlands, and streams.[42]

Fall meant time to hunt, but it also signified the season of the T'agim Gumsabayʔ, the all-important first pine nut festival. Elders monitored piñon trees year-round, taking note of growth indicators in order to forecast the upcoming harvest, and families actively worked to maintain their *Maʔaš*, or areas of the groves. They groomed trees and cleared or burned underbrush to protect the stands, using only dead and fallen timber for firewood. Families cared deeply about the health of the groves. Indeed, so close is the association between the people and these trees that the Washoe phrase for "my pine nut lands," *di Maʔaš*, is extremely similar to the phrase for "my face," *di mash*. Language teacher Herman Fillmore explains it this way: "The only thing separating the two words is the stress and vowel length of the second vowel." He continues, "Wašiw people treated the pine nut lands as an extension of themselves, almost like it was one's face. This meant that live trees were not cut down, or burned. That the branches in the trees were not broken and that none of what was gathered was wasted." A person recognized as having special power usually decided when pine nuts were ready to be picked.[43]

The harvest festival meant a gathering of families and friends, just as spring did on the shores of Tahoe. First pine nut festivals lasted four or five days. While it included lighthearted visiting, game playing, and gambling during the day, it also featured ceremonial dancing that lasted through each of the four nights. The festivities closed with a prayer, in which a spiritual leader reminded people to share food, think kindly of their neighbors, and honor the pine groves as well as the Creator by leaving some food.[44]

It is likely that the northern, central, and southern bands held their own first pine nut festivals, but many elders recall a large, possibly intercommunity, annual celebration taking place near Double Springs Flat in P'a·walu, in central Washoe country. The pine nut forests in this region are some of the most important. Leaders, distinguished elders, or spiritual figures announced the large ceremony after careful scrutiny of pine nut groves or perhaps a significant dream. To invite distant villages, the leader dispatched a runner, usually a young boy, who carried a hide rope tied in knots. The number of knots indicated the number of days until the celebration. The runner untied one knot each day of his journey.[45]

Elders in the late twentieth century remembered the festival as a time to "give thanks for the food, to thank the creator for supplying it." Bernice Auchoberry recounted: "[People] talk[ed] directly to the pine nuts [and asked them] to help us, to make us strong, to help us grow." Another elder, Belma Jones, emphasized, "No self respecting Washoe would dare ever pick Pine Nuts before [the ceremony and prayers] took place." In good years bountiful pine nut harvests contributed to a well-supplied winter food cache. But pine nut yields are sporadic—some years bountiful, other years sparse. The T'agim Gumsabay?

served as an annual reminder of how important the protein-rich nut was to Washoes.[46]

After the ceremony the harvest began. Everyone in the community participated. Men used the *beyú'gum,* a long stick with a hook on the end, to shake pinecones loose. Women and children collected the cones in baskets. Harvested cones were slow-roasted in sagebrush-lined cooking pits and then left to dry for a week to help open the cones and separate the seeds from the sticky sap. Women cracked shells by rolling a handheld mano over nuts on a granite metate. The nuts would then be winnowed on a woven tray to isolate the kernels. After preparation of the nuts, families transported them to caches near their home sites for winter storage; caches were built off the ground on stilts to protect them from rodents.[47]

Nuts could be ground into a fine powder and mixed with seasonal meats or vegetable and fruit products to create hearty meals. A favorite winter dish consisted of pine nut flour, herbal seasonings, and fresh or dried meats cooked and mixed to form a nourishing stew.

In the fall rabbit pelts were especially thick. Families joined together to hold cooperative rabbit drives. They tied nets of plant fiber together to create one large net into which a line of people drove the rabbits. Once the rabbits were snared, hunters used an arrow or a club to kill them. Individuals might also place snares, made of wiry grass, on rabbit trails. Rabbit meat could be eaten right away or dried for later use. The thick pelts made warm blankets and wraps.[48]

By late fall families would be settled in their winter homes on the eastern valley floors. Belma Jones recalled the importance to her grandparents of preparation. "My grandpa was always getting ready for winter. . . . [H]e was always thinking ahead."[49] The winter home, *galis dungal,* consisted of *himú* (willow) or sometimes the sturdier lodgepole-pine poles up to sixteen feet long, fastened together at the top, creating a conical (sometimes round) structure insulated with bark and a second layer of brush. The top of the *galis dungal* held an opening for smoke, which allowed for a fire pit in the middle of the shelter. Families could either dismantle these homes in springtime or maintain them for use the following year.[50]

When winter conditions made outside work impossible, individuals passed their time indoors, pursuing handiwork, visiting, and storytelling. Men made arrows and fishing tools, while women wove baskets made from willows collected earlier in the year. Winter, which might last six months, could be difficult, as families awaited the signs that would mark spring and the renewal of their seasonal cycle.[51]

CHAPTER 2
NEWCOMERS

They say that when the white man entered this country, they brought civilization to the Indian people. Oftentimes, I wonder whether this is so or not, whether the Indian people had a better, civilized world.
—John Dressler, Washoe elder, 1972

Strong winds and heavy, wet snow showers swept across the eastern Sierra during the last week of May 1827. Washoes were accustomed to late-spring storms. They took refuge in their sturdy winter homes. An American fur trapper, Jedediah Smith, and two of his companions were not so lucky. They struggled through a mountain pass in southern Washoe lands. The lure of new trapping grounds and the possibility of finding a Pacific port had brought them here. The storm's violence convinced Smith that his party was "marked out for destruction." He wrote in his journal that May 26, 1827, was "one of the most disagreeable" days of his life. Two horses and a mule froze before his eyes.

The next day a valuable horse gave out as it labored through more than a foot of fresh snow blanketing four feet of Sierra snowpack. After thirteen miles, on a slope beneath a high bluff, the snow receded, exposing good grass for the horses. Smith and his men spent the night and the next day trying to recover.

Washoes chose to observe quietly from a distance. Close to noon on May 28, a group of about a dozen Washoes appeared on top of the rocky outcropping and began shouting; Smith believed they were trying to scare him off. When that did not succeed, they rolled large rocks toward the encampment and then vanished.

The following morning Smith happened upon two Washoe women at work. Startled, the women quickly assumed defensive positions, wielding harvesting sticks as weapons. Smith likened their actions to a "frantic mother rushing to scare away some beast that would devour her child."[1] His description was apt. From the women's perspective, the explorers were a type of "beast." Washoes used the terms *da ba ah* and *mushege* when speaking of the newcomers. *Da ba ah* meant "dangerous men," and *mushege* is defined as "wild due to madness." This meeting with Smith is significant. It is the first documented account of Americans meeting Washoes. Smith did not know them to be Washoes; he did not know which tribe they belonged to.[2]

Their actions make sense. It is certain that Washoes had been hearing rumors about light-skinned foreigners from their neighbors and trade partners in the western Sierra. Their Paiute neighbors also probably shared news coming out of the southeast, as well as from the Columbia Plateau to the north.

By the 1840s Washoes would have the opportunity to observe more of these strange faces as immigrants began to cross the Sierra Nevada. In the summer of 1842, a few watched the Bartleson-Bidwell party follow a mountain pass into California. The first encounter with an American federal official took place on the morning of January 17, 1844. A surveying expedition led by John Charles Frémont stumbled upon a Washoe family settled in their winter homes. Most of the family disappeared into the nearby foothills, but the Americans grabbed a lone woman who, owing to her vigorous defense, was quickly released.[3]

The family had probably heard about a group of white men exploring the region from their Northern Paiute neighbors, with whom they shared, according to Frémont, a "facility of communication." During the days before their arrival in Washoe country, the group spent time with Northern Paiutes on the shores of a desert lake Frémont named "Pyramid." Pyramid Lake is a beautiful oasis in a sprawling desert. The Truckee River, the lone river that drains Lake Tahoe, carries Tahoe water down the eastern Sierra, meandering through meadowlands, before finally turning north toward its terminus in Pyramid. Paiute families came together at Pyramid Lake during the late fall and winter, much like Washoe families did at Tahoe in spring and summer. Cutthroat trout from the river and lake nourished Paiute families. Paiute fishers, like their Washoe neighbors, used weirs, platforms, nets, and traps.[4]

The Americans, who had been short on food, welcomed Paiute generosity. Frémont's journal recounts the abundance and quality of the fish being harvested. The Frémont group left Pyramid Lake well fed, reinvigorated, and determined to find the mythical river that drained the Rockies into the Pacific, connecting western and eastern worlds of commerce. They followed the Truckee in a southwesterly direction toward the looming Sierra peaks and unwittingly entered Washoe lands.[5]

On January 24 a lone Washoe man approached the group using the Washoe language, which the Americans did not recognize. The man offered them a few pounds of pine nuts, a traditional welcome. He may well have been an ambassador representing a larger kinship network; the next day a group of twelve visited the Americans, offering more pine nuts. The offerings underscore the Washoe cultural practice of generosity. The act of diplomacy demonstrates a desire on their part to engage these foreign men. Frémont and his group appreciated the gesture; he noted in his journal the nut's pleasant flavor when roasted. To Frémont, the Washoes appeared guarded yet hopeful of exploring the potential benefits of a relationship. He had no idea how deeply imbedded in Washoe culture these protein-rich nuts were or how valuable a commodity they were in the regional economy.[6]

The encounters continued. On January 28 a group circled the Americans on snowshoes, gliding easily on top of the snow "like birds." Frémont described the snowshoes as circular hoops about a foot wide, woven with a bark lattice. These snowshoes worked quite effectively so that Washoes could travel to some degree in the higher elevations during the winter months.

The group on snowshoes kept their distance and would not let the foreigners approach. When they tried, the Washoes broke into laughter and in Frémont's words "skimmed off over the snow, seeming to have no idea of the power of firearms, and thinking themselves perfectly safe when beyond arm's length." The above passage reveals the chasm between the Washoe and American worlds in 1844.[7]

Frémont's reflection on the Indians' "safety" throws into relief an American ethos built around the idea that firepower dictates control. His assertion seems only partially correct. Because they had been protected from Spanish colonization by the Great Basin to the east and the jagged Sierra to the west, Washoes likely did not have firsthand experience with guns. They probably had heard through their trade network about such things, but Frémont and Smith before him did not witness firearms among the Washoes. What Frémont missed that we can see with the benefit of hindsight is that the snowshoers that day might also have felt secure because the Americans were in *their* territory. The newcomers had pack-weary animals and depleted food stores. Given the Washoe knowledge of the land, their skill with bows, and their ability to move almost silently across the snow, had they so desired they could have struck a terrible blow to the foreigners. The American leader's assertion provides an eerie foreshadowing to the relationship between America and the Washoes that would follow.

The following day Frémont set out on an "Indian trail" and soon found himself amid a large group of Washoes. He noted that they arranged themselves "like birds on a fallen log on the hillside above" his head. He again added his perception that their positioning led the Washoes to believe they were "safe" from harm.

Through friendly gestures, the Americans assured the observers of their peaceful intentions; in return, people came forward with "handfuls of Pine Nuts." Frémont now realized that this represented an act of "hospitality" and accepted the offering. He then signaled with hand gestures his intention to cross the Sierra Nevada; Washoes responded with discouraging body language. Two "pointed to the snow on the mountain, and drew their hands across their necks, and raised them above their heads, to show the depth."[8]

Members of the Washoe group suggested instead that Frémont should head south, where he might find an easier route across the

Sierra. Not dissuaded, the Americans managed to secure a guide who led them as far as he felt comfortable and then disappeared. On January 31 the Americans made camp near what they hoped to be the "central ridge of the Sierra Nevada." The group had been following a river that the Washoes called the Watasému River, "the main river." Today, the Watasému bears the name Carson, after Christopher "Kit" Carson, who accompanied Frémont as a guide.[9]

The river led the party into southern Washoe territory, near present-day Markleeville, California. That night Washoes joined the Americans and, using signs, again advised against a Sierra crossing. Frémont offered cloth and other "trinkets" to anyone willing to guide his group. An elder entered a home and came out with a young man Frémont described as very intelligent in appearance. Gifts, including leggings, clothing, moccasins, and a large green blanket, were given and his services secured. They called him Mélo, a Washoe word the Americans had heard frequently and took to mean "friend." With their new guide they continued pushing west. Progress slowed as the snow deepened.[10]

The night of February 4 brought a powerful cold wind. The beleaguered group huddled around a fire near the base of an enormous pine. Two Washoes appeared from the trees. The elder began to speak. Americans interpreted the "unintelligible" speech as a dire warning not to continue into the snow-laden Sierra. The non-Washoe explorers dismissed the advice, as they had the two previous admonitions.[11]

Frémont woke the next day to find Mélo gone. Although his journals heretofore recorded only acts of hospitality from the Washoes and Paiutes, he now adjudged Mélo's actions as treacherous and "in perfect keeping" with his estimate of "Indian character."[12]

This would not be the last time that incoming foreigners unfamiliar with Washoes would characterize them in a negative way. Historian Ned Blackhawk points out that one of America's most celebrated figures, Mark Twain, who cut his literary teeth reporting on life in the Comstock Lode area, cast Washoes and other Great Basin Indians as miserable savages. As Blackhawk puts it, pity and disdain informed Twain in just about equal measure. Subsequent arrivals picked up the disdain often without the pity. The first territorial governor of Nevada, James Nye, referred to Washoes as "miserable people," who were "but one remove from the brutes." These racial characterizations eventually formed an important part of American colonial practices. The stereotype helped to justify Indian dispossession and mistreatment.[13]

One could speculate what the Washoes thought of the Americans based on the interaction. They likely saw wayward travelers in need of help. Both Smith and Frémont noted Washoes' discomfort and unfamiliarity with light-skinned foreigners. Although the newcomers had strange and new technologies, they were ill-equipped to traverse the Sierra in midwinter. They lacked practical knowledge of the area and rejected advice to travel south. Instead, they were determined to risk their lives to "conquer" the mountains. The degree to which the Washoes perceived these newcomers as a long-term threat is impossible to gauge. The alien weapons, use of large stock animals, and desperate determination of the Americans must have had a lasting impression nevertheless.

One month later, an experience more in concert with what Frémont thought white-Indian relations should be occurred. On March 6, 1844, his party reached the western Sierra foothills and met a group of Native vaqueros. A "well-dressed" Native greeted them with excellent Spanish. The man explained that he worked for John Sutter and pointed the way to Sutter's compound, just over the next hill. Frémont's journal illustrates the stark contrast between the Indians he encountered in the western foothills and the Washoes he encountered. He found western Sierra Natives in the employ of Sutter to be helpful and capable. Frémont's journal provides the definitive proof that up to 1844, Washoes had indeed lived isolated, protected lives. Their Sierra asylum bounded to the east by the Great Basin provided ample opportunity for families to simply disappear when necessary, thereby avoiding the lasting impacts of early European and later American colonization.[14]

"Sutter's Indians" who met Frémont were the product of interactions dating back to Spain's early colonial endeavors in California. Franciscan missionaries had established the first California mission in 1769, and seventy-five years later missions and military garrisons were scattered across Spanish, later Mexican, lands. Religious conversion, military compulsion, and strategic deliberate assimilation led to the Hispanicization of many California Indians. Simultaneously, many Indians fled the Spanish centers of influence, taking up residence with more isolated mountain communities, while others chose armed resistance.[15]

Spain intended for the missions to last ten years, after which time "improved" lands and tools of industry would become the property of assimilated Indians, now hopefully loyal citizens. The secularization of missions did not occur until 1834, when the young Mexican nation liquidated church lands for money. Mexico, however, did not turn the property over to the Natives. Instead, the lands ended up in the hands of wealthy Mexican families, leading to the rise of Mexican cattle empires and the ranching Californio culture.

Mexico, similar to Spain, suffered from the lack of citizens in their northern lands; to combat this they offered large grants of land to foreigners. Sutter represented an early wave of Euro-Americans moving to Mexican California, where they found vast fertile stretches of land distant from both American and Mexican oversight.[16]

By the time Frémont reached California, Sutter had developed irrigation ditches, grain fields of mostly wheat, and a large fort made of sun-dried bricks. All work had been carried out by California Indians, who toiled for "moderate compensation." If they gave Sutter any "trouble," he responded with, in Frémont's words, "well-timed authority." The Washoes had not known the sting of a Franciscan's whip or the "well-timed authority" of a ranchero boss. But colonization would move closer to Washoe territory with each passing year. Frémont's journey presaged the American movement.[17] Like earlier explorers, he described California as an untapped resource. He either did not see or chose to ignore the improvements made by generations of indigenous ownership. The Euro-American impressions of Native land use, or lack thereof, helped eventually to justify widespread Native dispossession.[18]

In the summer of 1844, following Frémont's visit, a group of trappers set up camp at Honey Lake in northern Washoe territory. Because Honey Lake exists close to the northern border, it not clear whether the trappers met Washoes, but they did interact with Indians. Their relationship turned violent when members of the trapping party killed five Indian people, whom they accused of taking traps. The trappers burned the bodies before leaving to "set an example."[19]

Two years later, in the fall of 1846, another group of Americans ventured into Washoe country but did not meet the by now reticent Natives. This ill-fated group, the Donner party, encountered a terrible early Sierra storm. A number of Washoes saw the snowbound party and again wondered why people were entering the Sierra as winter approached. Some apparently felt sorry for the Americans and left deer jerky near the camp. But none risked getting close. Observers later reported that these foreigners were eating their dead.[20]

On February 2, 1848, Mexico acknowledged their defeat to the growing United States and signed the Treaty of Guadalupe Hidalgo. The treaty ceded a large portion of northern Mexico, which subsequently became the present-day states of California, Nevada, Utah, New Mexico, and Arizona. Unbeknownst to Washoes, their ancient territory had become the focus of international wars and transnational claims. With no real idea about a distant government in Washington, D.C., Washoes nevertheless became part of the American domain. Their country had changed colonial hands again. This time, lured by gold and silver, the newcomers would arrive in Washoe lands to stay.[21]

CHAPTER 3

VIOLENT TRANSFORMATIONS

> The women were out cutting willows while the menfolk were fishing hen someone said there were lots of horses coming their way and before they knew it, these men on horses opened fire on us, killing everyone.
>
> —Helen Nevers Enos, Washoe elder, 1974

Washoes watched their approach. The foreigners had likely been traveling for months, perhaps on their way to the California goldfields. On a hill, among piñon pines, junipers, and sage, they found a spring. Shortly thereafter, chaos ensued. If there were any survivors, they fled and are unknown to history. One of the casualties was a white man with a white beard. Washoe individuals cut off his head and posted it on a rock by the spring to serve as a warning to other would-be trespassers. Today, near the site of the encounter, a road sign sits atop a rise on Highway 395. It reads, "Simee Dimeh." The phrase means "Double Springs." Many Washoes have a different name for the place: "Tzimél Dimé," which means "Whisker Water."[1]

To Americans in the nineteenth century, the West meant open lands and new opportunities. When they pushed "forward," they crowded in on Native communities who struggled to maintain their homelands. Washoes' long isolation meant they would meet American colonization without the skills years of association could provide. They did not speak English and had very little knowledge of American economic practices or nineteenth-century technologies. And they had no idea how many people would be coming or how violent the eastern Sierra world would become. Confronted by a mass of gold seekers, ranchers, capitalists, tradesmen, and day laborers, Washoes did the only thing they could: they retreated.[2]

Avoidance offered only temporary respite, as rumors of gold in California turned to fact. Several routes to the California diggings emerged, the main stem passing through Washoe lands. In the midst of southern Washoe territory, the west fork of the Carson River carved a deep, winding bed. Granite cliffs towered over stands of willow, aspen, and Jeffery pine. Before the gold rush, Washoes used the canyon as a route to access the mountain pass, leading to western acorn-collecting lands. Non-Natives quickly recognized the canyon and the pass as the best course to California and began referring to it as the "Carson Route." At first foreigners stayed close to the developing road. But it was not long before people began to create way stations along the trail and then homes, farms, ranches, and, in a remarkably short time, towns.[3]

Members of the Mormon Church had a head start in setting up supply stations along the trail. Their exodus from Illinois beginning in 1844 led to the creation of a refuge at the Great Salt Lake. They intended to establish a theocratic state separate from the United States, which led to the creation of Deseret on March 18, 1849. Their claim included the present-day states of Utah and Nevada, along with portions of New Mexico, Arizona, Colorado, Wyoming, Idaho, and Oregon. For the Native populations of the Great Basin, the arrival of the Mormons heralded significant changes.[4]

Church members held a particular view when it came to Indian people. The Book of Mormon tells the story of a Jewish prophet, Lehi, who traveled to the Americas around 589 BC. His sons, Nephi and Laman, fathered the people of North America. Laman gave rise to a rebellious society, the "Lamanites," who competed with the Nephites for dominance. The "civilized" Nephites prevailed, and the Lamanites survived to become American Indians. From Deseret, church members went forth to convert "lost" brethren. Missionary work earned the church access to valuable lands.[5]

The establishment of a Mormon trading post in 1851 led to the first permanent American colony in Washoe country. John Reese led sixteen people with ten supply wagons from Salt Lake to establish the western supply post. He crossed the Great Basin to the home of the central Washoes, the P'a·walu. In a valley that, like the mountain pass beyond it, would later be named after Christopher "Kit" Carson, the Carson Valley, Reese established a way station. Situated at the base of the eastern Sierra, it was commonly called Mormon Station. The station was later named Genoa, becoming Nevada's oldest non-Indian town. Far from Salt Lake's immediate jurisdiction, the small town, and the Carson Valley around it, established a local government consisting of a justice of the peace and four associate justices. The justices appointed a surveyor, and by 1853 seven American land claims had been recorded in the middle of Washoe lands. Less than a decade after Frémont first met with Washoes, portions of their lands had become "private property," and whites began to complain about Washoe "trespassing."[6]

In his first year at the way station, Reese fenced a garden that produced a healthy crop, demonstrating the fertility of Washoe lands. The deceptively benign act of planting a garden set in motion a colonial transformation. The garden represented a symbolic and physical expression of a new ethos applied to the eastern Sierra. Reese's enclosure provided an example of what Americans believed to be the justifiable use and occupation of Native soil.[7]

Americans in the nineteenth century embraced ideas put in place by the earliest European colonists, who developed a raison d'être that "justified" taking Indian lands. In the early seventeenth century Massachusetts Bay Colony governor John Winthrop issued a critical observation of Indians: "They enclose noe [sic] land."[8]

In 1868 Gilbert Malcolm Sproat, who would become Vancouver's colonial representative to Parliament, claimed, "The particular circumstances which make the deliberate intrusion of a superior people into another country lawful or expedient are connected to some extent with the use which the dispossessed or conquered people have made of the soil."[9] To Europeans and later Americans, land uncultivated meant land unclaimed. The use of fences, gardens, and livestock represented reasoned seizure of "unutilized" property. Natives had no right to land they did not cultivate or put to pasture. One recent scholarly assessment puts it this way: "European cultivation was the measure by which all other practices were judged." The Euro-American understanding of land use became an "ideology of conquest."[10] This "justification" reached full articulation in the late nineteenth century as federal officials crafted Indian policy. Commissioner of Indian Affairs J. D. C. Atkins claimed that agriculture represented the "highest intellectual and moral development" of the human race. Those people who did not practice Euro-American agriculture were "ignorant of almost everything else."[11] Reese's garden then became a symbol of conquest, a tangible expression of the American colonial system that would eventually strip Washoes of all but tiny remnants of their once vast country.

With newcomers continuing to claim Washoe lands, a continent away in Washington, D.C., the federal government took steps toward controlling western Indian communities. The federal government had established the Office of Indian Affairs shortly after the American Revolution. Because the United States faced the threat of constant Indian wars, from Shawnees, Miamis, Hurons, and Odawas in the Ohio River Valley to Creek and Seminoles in the South, the OIA became an arm of the War Department.[12] On March 3, 1849, the OIA moved from the War Department to the newly created Department of the Interior. Thereafter, the OIA and its officers worked under the supervision of the secretary of the interior. In March 1849, the OIA established the Salt Lake Indian Agency, and in 1850, with the congressional formation of Utah Territory, the Utah Superintendency began to administer Indian affairs.[13]

Superintendents and agents constituted the two forms of field jurisdiction within the OIA. Superintendents monitored Indian affairs in a large state or territory and reported directly to the commissioner, whose subsequent reports appeared in annual publications. Agents, assigned to specific communities or areas, reported to the superintendent, and their roles changed over time to reflect the interests of the expanding United States. Initially, they worked as diplomats, enticing "hostile" tribes to move to reserved lands and to cede traditional lands. Gradually, as Native communities relocated, agents began to carry out an agenda set forth by Congress: Americanizing Native communities.[14]

Jacob H. Holeman became an agent for Utah Territory in March 1851. Two months later, he set out on a journey to inspect the western boundary of Utah Territory, today western Nevada. Holeman traveled from the agency at Salt Lake along the California Trail through the Great Basin. He encountered Western Shoshones and distributed "presents" and in return received some "promised friendship to the whites, and seemed much pleased." As Holeman continued west, he witnessed evidence of depredations committed against Natives by white travelers. Violence in the West was commonplace, and the disproportionate amount of violent acts was directed at Indian people. Holeman, in a report to Commissioner Luke Lea, claimed, "Almost the sole cause of all the difficulties—the destruction of life and property on this route is owing to the bad conduct of the whites." Some twenty years later, Major G. W. Ingalls, an OIA agent who worked in the West, described many emigrants as "reckless." Some, he suggested, "thought that the reputation of having killed an Indian would transform them into heroes." Consequently, the "depredations" occurred regularly.[15]

Violence in and around the Great Basin did not always take the form of whites versus Indians. The vigorous horse trade, dating back to the late 1600s, had created difficult human relations between groups who had horses and joined fully in the changing socioeconomic worlds of the American Southwest and Columbia Plateau. Neighbors of the Washoes like the Western Shoshones, Southern Paiutes, and diverse California communities in the West had long toiled amid the chaos of clashing worlds and the attendant violence. The Western Shoshones and their neighbors the Utes had been particularly affected by the violence born of colonial jockeying.

Holeman, now accompanied by two Shoshone guides, followed the Humboldt River to its terminus in the Humboldt Sink. He then traveled to the Carson Valley, where he had difficulty locating Washoe families. When he arrived at Mormon Station, he met small groups of people he referred to as "Pintahs" and "Washaws" engaged in hunting and fishing. He claimed that the "Washaws" had "been very troublesome" and guessed that the "many depredations which have been committed on the whites [sic] in crossing the Sierra Nevada no doubt have been by this tribe."[16]

Holeman's reference to "Washaws" certainly represents an Anglicization of *Washoe*. By "Pintahs" he, no doubt, meant the Paiutes. The agent's description raises interesting questions: Why were Paiutes hunting and fishing in traditional Washoe territory? Had Holeman's observation been made in a border area, farther north near present-day Reno, Nevada, or south near the Walker River, the comments would not be surprising, since those were borderlands. But Mormon Station sat squarely in P'a·walu territory, and Holeman offers no explanation. His difficulty in finding Washoes was a circumstance shared by other government agents and early researchers. Ethnographer J. W. Hudson, who traveled to Washoe country in 1902, observed:

> I have never had such difficulty in locating Indians. It was told me that there are over one hundred [Washoe] Indians in this valley, but I have searched all through this sage brush for miles yet found only seven arbors.... The only sure way to find them is to follow up a stream, necessarily afoot, and search for the water trail in a camp or to patiently follow the visiting Indian when in town to his lair. He will never direct you nor explain anything at any price.... The rule is for a family to build a sun shade out in the sage brush adjacent to a stream and remote from any other camp, and they may suddenly move.[17]

Holeman's designation of Washoes as "troublesome" is curious. Later American reports consistently described them as mostly peaceful. Did Holeman confuse the two groups? Early arriving Euro-Americans did not clearly distinguish between Paiutes and Washoes. Many attacks against whites took place on the eastern fringes of the Washoe territory in the Pine Nut Range, near Humboldt Sink lands, an area commonly contested or shared by Paiute and Washoe families.

There is little doubt that during the initial stages of colonization, Washoes fought to defend their homelands, but, thoroughly outnumbered, they quickly turned to other survival strategies. Paiutes, who were larger in number, had already been involved in skirmishes with Americans, and in 1860 they would engage whites in what came to be called the Pyramid Lake War. If not confused, Holeman was likely referring to one or two instances. Both American historical records and Washoe oral tradition recount isolated violent confrontations, with most being initiated by the newcomers. Perhaps the agent knew of an occurrence like that at Double Springs at the beginning of this chapter.

Only ten years after Holeman's trip to Mormon Station, in 1861, the governor of Nevada and ex officio superintendent of Indian affairs, James W. Nye, wrote, "[I] found [the Washoes] peaceably inclined." In 1870 Superintendent Henry Douglas recorded, "In intercourse with white people [the Washoes] are docile and tractable." Another contemporary observer noted that many western communities regularly attacked whites, but Washoes rarely committed "depredations or killing of the white settlers or emigrants."[18]

Irrespective of the degree to which Washoes were involved, like many other western outposts, Mormon Station became a violent place. Far from territorial and federal authority, lawlessness and "frontier justice" prevailed. In his diary, an early émigré, John Woods, portrayed an area plagued by "roguery," with high levels of livestock theft and claim jumping. Another contemporary stated, "Nearly every man either carried a gun or had one where he could readily get at it." In the early 1850s, rumors circulated about Mexican fugitives hiding out near Mormon Station. It did not take long for vigilante committees to emerge.[19]

Violence was, of course, common across the American West. In the words of the historian Ned Blackhawk, "The history of Indian-white relations, particularly throughout the eighteenth and nineteenth centuries, reads like a series of constant wars." That statement is especially true when applied to the plains and American Southwest. What occurred among the Washoes can hardly be described as wars. Small, isolated episodes of violence better characterize the nature of violence between Washoes and whites. There is a strong popular notion that violence was largely perpetuated by Native people against pioneers and American immigrants. This notion is tied to a belief that Natives were by nature prone to violence. Blackhawk argues convincingly in his work *Violence over the Land* that it was the colonial maneuverings of Europeans and Americans that led to such dramatic violence. Yes, violence existed prior to the arrival of Europeans, but the scale and purpose shifted seismically when European powers brought Old World wars, rivalries, and practices to the "New World."

In English common law, an individual had the duty to escape when possible from bodily harm. If a confrontation became violent, a person had to flee unless escape was impossible. Americans pushing the expansion of the young nation west had little use for English common law as it related to self-defense and violence. By the end of the nineteenth century, American state legislatures and judiciary bodies upheld the right of citizens to defend themselves from would-be assailants. Well-armed young men in the West, often fueled by alcohol and competition for resources, did not hesitate to commit violence, especially when the targets were Indians. There are dozens of well-documented, horrific massacres that occurred in the American West during the mid- and late 1800s. Sand Creek in Colorado (1864) and Wounded Knee in South Dakota (1890) are two of the best publicized. Closer to home for Washoes was the Bear River Massacre of 1863, in which hundreds of Shoshones were massacred on a cold January day.[20]

In the growing outpost of Genoa, complaints of Washoe raids had become a common refrain by 1852. Major Ingalls described an incident that occurred at a recently established supply station. A number of valuable American horses were stolen. The proprietor blamed a "band" of Washoes. A group of whites set out to find the band. When they found them, they noticed many women moving the group's belongings into the hills. The whites then met sixty or so Washoes prepared for battle. The leader of the whites made a hasty retreat, but two men from his party stayed. The issue was resolved when the Americans traded tobacco with them. But the stolen horses were not seen or recovered.

Horse and livestock thefts continued, and many whites believed Washoes to be the culprits. In response, leading American figures decided to hold two innocent Washoe individuals at Mormon Station until the guilty parties returned the stolen property. They took captive a powerfully built man "dressed in a full buckskin suit" and a boy around sixteen. When the man attempted to escape, a guard shot him in the back.[21]

Five years later, in 1857, tensions threatened to boil over into full-scale war. The *San Francisco Herald* ran a story that claimed residents of Carson Valley anticipated a widespread "Indian outbreak." In early September two white men, John McMarlin and James Williams, were killed while running pack trains from Mormon Station to California. Investigators found Washoe arrows at the death scene, which in turn led to quick accusations.[22]

As days passed, violent confrontations increased. Newspaper accounts reached a fever pitch. Whites signed a petition for the governor of California to provide assistance. A recent arrival, Major William Ormsby, for whom a Nevada county is named, took a principal role in trying to bring the guilty parties to "justice." Self-assured and quick to judge, Ormsby brought in two Paiute advisers to confirm the make of the arrows from the murder scene. War chief Numaga and his associate Natchez authenticated claims of Washoe craftsmanship.

Next, a Washoe headman, Lenúka, called by whites "Captain Jim" (not the same Captain Jim who traveled to Washington, D.C., in 1892; that was Epesuwa), traveled to Mormon Station. He also identified the arrows as Washoe, but vehemently denied that Washoe men had carried out the murders. Ormsby gave Lenúka one week to produce the killers; if he did not, war would be brought upon the entire community. Lenúka returned six days later with three unmarried men. A young Paiute girl, Sarah Winnemucca, who later gained nationwide fame as a Native spokeswoman, lived with Ormsby at the time. She later recorded the events, recalling that a day after the prisoners were taken into custody, a crowd gathered, and many began calling for immediate executions. Later, a large group of armed men arrived, ostensibly to take the prisoners to jail in California. Upon seeing the group of armed men, the mothers and relatives of the prisoners began to wail, swearing that the young men were innocent. Winnemucca described what happened next: "The three prisoners broke and ran. Of course they were shot. Two were wounded and the third ran back with his hands up. But, all of them died." Later that fall, Ormsby told Lenúka that the actual culprits had been caught. "They were whites who admitted using Washoe arrows to make it appear Indians had killed them." These two examples prove that it was dangerous to be Washoe in early America.

Washoes could be accused and killed whether guilty or not. There were no inquiries, no reparations paid to families of the victims. "Justice" unfolded in localized, organic, often violent ways when Washoes were concerned.[23]

Mormon Station, or Genoa, did not have a monopoly on violence. Washoe elder Helen Nevers Enos recalled a massacre that took place after the first battle in what whites referred to as the "Pyramid Lake War" between the Northern Paiutes and Americans. The opening battle had been a decisive defeat for the American volunteers, led by Ormsby, who was killed along with seventy-six others. The Americans rode into a trap set by the Paiute leader, Numaga. The quick victory encouraged white perceptions of a widespread "Indian threat." In the tense climate, soldiers began "looking for revenge" indiscriminately against Indians.[24]

Passing through what is today Washoe Valley, north of Carson City, Nevada, soldiers fell upon a group of Washoes near the base of Slide Mountain. A woman managed to save herself and her child "by hiding in the brush." She later recalled, "The women were out cutting willows while the men folk were fishing when someone said there were lots of horses coming their way and before they knew it, these men on horses opened fire on us, killing everyone."[25] By 1872 the American ethos could be glimpsed in the major newspapers of the region. The *Gold Hill Evening News* editorialized, "Let [the Indians] fully understand that they are safe while on their reservation, but when they absent themselves there from [sic] they are liable to be shot down like deer." This issuance was particularly problematic for Washoes who did not have a reservation. The choice of language here is interesting: "shot down like deer." That threat is callously telling. The newcomers could kill Washoes and other Indians with little to no compunction. They thought of them as less than human, animals, like "deer."[26]

Violence was only one manifestation of the clash of cultures in the eastern Sierra. The Washoe world became further complicated as they increasingly found themselves between two would-be rulers, the Mormon Church and the federal government.

By 1855 Garland Hunt, the new Indian agent for Utah, which still included the future state of Nevada, began to worry about the influence of Latter-day Saints (LDS) on indigenous communities. Hunt postulated that missionaries created "distinction[s] in the minds of the Indian tribes of this Territory between the Mormons and the people of the United that cannot act otherwise than prejudicial to the interests of the latter." Two years later, the commissioner of Indian affairs informed the secretary of the interior that Latter-day Saints were likely in violation of the Intercourse Act of 1834. The tension between the federal government and LDS missionaries spread rapidly.[27]

The Mormons had significantly advanced the process of Washoe dispossession. By the early spring of 1852, the Mormon government at Salt Lake imposed county lines and boundaries across Washoe lands. An act of January 17, 1854, created Carson County, which included Mormon Station, and the future counties of Washoe, Douglas, Ormsby, Storey, and Lyon. This act formalized a physical alteration of the Washoe landscape. The probate judge assigned to Carson County, a Mormon elder named Orson Hyde, surveyed Mormon Station in 1856 and renamed it Genoa. Meanwhile, the church formulated a plan to control all significant agricultural pieces of the valley.[28]

Non-Mormons sensed the inequitable distribution of power, and in 1855 a group of them petitioned for Carson County to be annexed by California. The petitioners sought a separation from the rule of Salt Lake. On July 17, 1855, the *San Francisco Herald* reported that Brigham Young had sent one hundred Mormon settlers to Carson Valley and would send five hundred more to keep it from being annexed to California.[29] The Mormons maintained firm control of the Carson Valley with the elections of August 4, 1856, which led to an all-Mormon ruling body. The county offices, including sheriff, treasurer, justice of the peace, and constable, all went to Mormons. The election caused further disaffection and frustration among the non-Mormons.[30] The fact that Genoa and the recently subdivided valley had belonged to the Washoes for millennia did not trouble the newcomers—Mormon or non-Mormon. The usurpation of land allowed no regard for tribal land claims.

In 1857 the federal government under President James Buchanan decided to assert its authority in Mormon country. Buchanan sent a contingent of troops under Albert Sydney Johnston, the highest-ranking officer who would be killed in the Civil War, to Utah. In response, LDS leaders immediately recalled church members from their western outposts to defend the homeland. This led to a Mormon exodus from Washoe land, creating a political vacuum in the valley. Public meetings among non-Mormons led to resolutions calling for the creation of the Nevada Territory.[31]

A year after the federal assertion of power in LDS country, the Utah Indian Superintendency created the Carson Valley Agency. Agent Frederick Dodge served as the first OIA official in Washoe lands. He suggested the Washoes share a reservation with the Paiutes at Pyramid Lake or on the Walker River. It would "have removed them from the heavily traveled east–west trails and reduced their contact with whites, since the proposed reservation areas had not yet been settled." Washoes dismissed the offer. They did not want to relocate or share limited space.[32]

Distant from the Mormon center of power at Genoa, small groups of miners continually combed the eastern fringes of the Sierra in search of the next "mother lode." One canyon sandwiched between the future site of Virginia City, Nevada, and the Carson River earned the name "Gold Canyon" in the early 1850s. In 1855 a group of about 180 miners realized a profit of more than $100,000. That year's take led to the creation of Johntown, a typical gold camp located two miles from the foot of the canyon. In two years the exhaustion of surface levels of gold, combined with seasonal water shortages, led to the near abandonment of mining in the canyon. The real mineral wealth sat lodged in quartz veins just north of Gold Canyon, in Six Mile Canyon.[33]

Miners who had been working Gold Canyon and others regularly encountered and discarded a dense, dark earthen material they called "blue earth." Sometime before March 1856, two brothers, Allen and Hosea Grosh, decided to have the blue earth assayed. The assay revealed the true nature of the blue stuff: it was high-grade silver ore. The brothers told no one except their father, who lived back east. In a letter to him they described the ore as "thin sheet-lead broken very finely." They explained that other hopeful miners in the area believed it to be lead, and the brothers were content to let them. Before they could cash in on their knowledge, though, both died tragically, in 1857. Not long after, others learned the value of the blue earth when a sample of the ore assayed in Grass Valley, California, revealed a projected value of up to $4,791 per ton.[34]

The discovery of silver ore created a buzz in the eastern Sierra. But two discoveries in 1859 would lead to one of the largest mineral rushes in human history. The first, which came to be known as the "Old Red Ledge," created a stir. Located in Gold Canyon, the Old Red Ledge stood right in the heart of good hunting and pine nut harvesting grounds. But the next discovery in the summer of 1859 proved to be even greater: the Comstock Lode. News of the silver ledge spread like wildfire. Fortune seekers who had rushed through Washoe lands to the goldfields of California quickly reversed course and set out for the new Eldorado. In 1859 alone, more than 20,000 miners and businesspeople rushed to Washoe lands.[35] The Comstock Lode sat just north of Gold Canyon at what quickly became the boomtown of Virginia City, Nevada. A year after the discovery, "All of California rang with the call. 'To Washoe!' it ordered. 'To Washoe, charge!'"[36] The region that would be home to one of the richest mineral discoveries in human history gained the name "Washoe." Its name might suggest newcomers understood this land to be the property of Washoes, but such was not the case. Most had no idea where the name came from and could not care less about the ancestral claims of Native people in the eastern Sierra.

The forests and valleys that had belonged to the Washoes now became hinterlands and sources of raw materials to support the growth of the greatest ore discovery the world had known. In the early days it looked like Virginia City would compete with San Francisco for economic dominance in the region. Virginia City quickly became a bustling city, with the requisite opera hall, saloons, dance halls, restaurants, newspapers, roads, and steadily growing population. Mark Twain, who lived and wrote on the Comstock as a young journalist, described Virginia City as "the liveliest town for its age and population that America ever produced." In his characteristic satirical fashion he went on about Virginia City: "There were military companies, fire companies, brass bands, banks, hotels, theaters, 'hurdy-gurdy houses,' wide-open gambling palaces, political pow-wows, civic processions, street fights, murders, inquests, riots, a whiskey-mill every fifteen steps, a Board of Aldermen, a Mayor, a City Surveyor, a City Engineer, a Chief of the Fire Department, with First Second, and Third Assistants, a Chief of Police, City Marshal, and a large police force, two Boards of Mining Brokers, a dozen breweries, and half a dozen jails and station-houses in full operations, and some talk of building a church."[37] Twain's description, while comical, is also revealing. There was indeed a lot of alcohol production, with "whiskey-mills" and "breweries," and enough people to consume the alcohol, young men mostly. Far from the "civilizing" influences of the East, Virginia City became the quintessential western boomtown. For Washoes who had encountered Frémont only twenty years before, it must have been as if the world had been turned upside down.

The presidential contest of 1860 resulted in the election of Abraham Lincoln and the Republican Party. South Carolina immediately led six other Southern states from the Union. By February 1861, disaffected Southerners had formed the Confederate States of America.[38]

With war looming, a Nevada territorial bid was given an immediate boost, and it passed both the House and the Senate on February 26, 1861. In the midst of the Civil War in the East and the gold and silver frenzy redoubling the impact on Washoe resources, authority over Indian lands again changed. Washington established the Nevada Superintendency to oversee Indian affairs in the region. Seventeen years had transpired since Frémont's arrival. Washoes could no longer afford to extend handfuls of pine nuts to newcomers; they often did not have enough for themselves. Their lands had been stolen and the physical environment altered. Their system of living was about to be destroyed. In response, Washoes would need to reinvent and adapt their traditional way of life to fit a changing world.[39]

CHAPTER 4

THE CHAOS OF DESTRUCTION

Within a fifty year period, a way of life the Washo [sic] had preserved for centuries disappeared. Abundant timber, fish, and game had been destroyed.

—Jo Ann Nevers, Washoe elder and tribal historian, 1976

In 1862 the *Pacific Coast Annual Mining Review and Stock Ledger* reported that the word *Washoe* was "in everyone's mouth." *Washoe* had become synonymous with mineral wealth and opportunity. People from all over the world flocked to the "New Eldorado." The Washoe homeland had become a "world's wonder." In 1863 alone the Comstock produced more than $12 million worth of silver and gold. Mining companies sprang up everywhere. John Ross Browne's penchant for dramatic phrasing captures the moment vividly. A travel writer and sometime government agent, Browne reported witnessing "myriads of swarthy, bearded, dust-covered men" piercing "into the grim old mountains." The newcomers cut "murderous holes" in the earth and piled "up engines to cut out [the mountains'] vital arteries." Mechanized mining tools carried out the "stamping and crushing" of traditional lands and resources, while the newcomers held "fiendish revel amid the chaos of destruction." While not writing from the Washoe perspectives, Browne nevertheless shared the horror Washoe families must have felt at the "fiendish revelry." One Washoe man reflecting on what that time must have been like told me simply that his relatives "had no place to go." The young American nation had sharpened its teeth during the gold rush in California. By the time of the Comstock, the American colonial apparatus was operating at full speed.[1]

In the early years of the California gold rush, at least some Euro-American miners acknowledged a degree of Native rights to the land they wanted. After James Marshall made the initial gold discovery on the south fork of the American River, his boss, John Sutter, entered into a treaty with a band of Nisenan Indians, the Yalesummy, whose land contained the gold. Sutter sent the treaty to the military governor of California in February 1848. The governor responded the following month: "The United States do not recognize the right of Indians to sell or lease lands on which they reside."[2]

The question of Indian landownership is complicated. This is not the place for a complete telling of that history, but it is important to note that during the English colonial period, the practice of buying land from Indians became widespread. The act of buying land from Native peoples established the de facto right of Indians to therefore "own" land. By the time the United States gained its independence, many politicians and land speculators wanted to find a way around buying land from Indians, and in 1823 the Supreme Court of the United States granted that wish. The controversial ruling in the *Johnson v. M'Intosh* case held that Native people could not own land. Their "title" to the land was effectively extinguished when Europeans "discovered" their land. Without the right of ownership, Indians could not sell land to individuals. They did have "aboriginal title," which allowed them to occupy certain lands, but the federal government through right of conquest or treaty could extinguish that title. The governor of California, who responded to Sutter's treaty with the Yalesummy, applied the *Johnson v. M'Intosh* ruling perfectly with his dismissal.[3]

With a legal basis that held Indians had no right to the land or minerals beneath them, mining in the western Sierra foothills developed at a breakneck pace. Foreshadowing what would happen just ten years later in Washoe country, the California goldfields absolutely devastated the ecosystems Indians had cultivated for generations. The early mining practices in California centered mostly on rivers. The practice of "washing" the sands through use of a pan or rocker was soon replaced with larger-scale practices. Investors began pooling resources and applying new technologies to move rivers. Dams and diversions quickly popped up on almost every river or stream draining the western Sierra. The disrupted river in turn negatively impacted the freshwater muscle and trout populations so important to California Natives. Hydraulic mining, the practice of training massive powerful jets of water on a mountainside to force erosion and therefore expose gold veins, was even more destructive. As more people poured into the goldfields, Natives continued to steadily retreat higher and higher into the western Sierra, where their resource bases were severely limited. Pushed to desperation, some resorted to stealing from the newcomers, while others began attacking the foreigners. These were the acts of people who had been driven to the brink. In return for the small-scale theft and isolated acts of violence, many in California began to mobilize in militias and makeshift gangs to punish the Indians.

California became extremely violent. Massacres were common. Thousands of California Natives died due to violence related directly to mining. Some counties in California instituted scalp bounties, which legalized and paid for the murder of Indian people. The sheriff of Mariposa County pronounced the "Indian outlawed." His decree stated, "Everyone is permitted to kill the Indians he encounters anywhere in the county of Mariposa."[4]

Many who had rushed to California soon set their sights on Nevada and the Comstock Lode. Mining activity on the eastern slope of the Sierra operated in the heart of the sacred Pine Nut Lands. The swath of the range used by Washoes stretched north to south from what is today Reno, Nevada, to Antelope Valley, just across the California border. Before the arrival of foreigners, Washoes situated homes and their seasonal camps near streams and springs in the Pine Nuts. Because of its scarcity in the range, water was always a central concern. One elder remembered her grandmother, who was a midwife, giving newborns a drop of water with her finger, because "she said all living things have to have water." Mining, industrial, and agricultural interests quickly developed an insatiable thirst for Sierra waters, commandeering most of the springs and waterways. The Carson River became a coveted source of power for mills connected to mines and for agriculturalists hoping to irrigate fertile Sierra valleys. Overlapping claims and overallocation on the Carson led to disputes that led to decades of bitter litigation, with Washoe interests not even considered, until the late twentieth century.[5]

Driven from their lands, families watched as pine groves fell to American axes. They experienced a special dread when newcomers dug out even the stumps and roots of piñon trees, which were then "hacked to pieces . . . loaded on donkey and toted to town for firewood." Washoes viewed these trees as part of their heritage, and their eradication ominously announced the emergence of a new society.[6]

Destruction would not be confined to the Pine Nut Lands. Soon it reached into the Lake Tahoe basin as well. Virginia City's development created a voracious appetite for wood. Much of Virginia City's ore was locked in quartz veins in deep, damp, unstable ground. Digging down to the veins proved a dangerous task, and in the early days cave-ins occurred frequently.

In 1860 the director of the Ophir Mining Company hired Philip Deidesheimer, a young engineer fresh from the California goldfields. Deidesheimer designed a wooden support mechanism to make tunneling safer. His design employed two massive 18-by-18-inch, 5- or 6-foot-high vertical supports joined at the top by a horizontal brace about 4 feet long. These "square sets," as they came to be called, were linked together to provide support for tunnels that bore hundreds, and eventually thousands, of feet into the earth.

The efficacy of Deideshimer's invention became clear immediately, and the need for wood increased exponentially. Eager capitalists turned their attention to Tahoe's forests, the same that had supported Washoe families during the snowless months for thousands of years.[7] The famous Comstock journalist, and associate of Mark Twain, Dan DeQuille, once described Virginia City mines as the tombs of Tahoe's forests. They were equally symbols marking the end of a Washoe way of living in the Sierra.[8]

The forests of Tahoe featured massive Jeffrey, lodgepole, and sugar pine trees. One observer in 1859 recorded trees towering up to 150 feet, some with diameters as large as 10 feet around. Nascent lumbering activities began at Lake Tahoe as early as 1859. The subsequent lumber boom, followed by the rise of commercial fisheries, clearly demonstrates the destructive nature of extractive colonialism that transformed the Washoe homelands. By the 1870s large-scale logging companies had taken over. The development of an infrastructure capable of delivering Tahoe's wood from high in the Sierra, out of the mountains, across a desert basin, and up to the Comstock, situated on Mount Davidson, 6,150 feet above sea level, required organization and tremendous amounts of capital. The most successful Tahoe lumbering companies' ownership rosters read like a "who's who" of bankers, mining magnates, and capitalists from the Comstock and San Francisco.

In 1873 powerful Comstock men came together to form the Carson Tahoe Lumber and Fluming Company (CTLFC) at the behest of William Sharon, a mining and banking titan. They headquartered their operation on Tahoe's eastern shore, at Glenbrook, usurping a Washoe Indian seasonal home site valued for its fish and berries. The CTLFC acquired timber rights around the basin until they controlled one-fifth of basin lands. They used steamships to haul logs across the lake and utilized mills to process the lumber as it was pulled from the water. From Glenbrook a railroad hauled the lumber to the top of Spooner Summit to an 11-mile-long V flume. The lumber was then flumed down the steep mountainside to lumberyards on the valley floor below, near Carson City, Nevada. It was then loaded onto cars of the Virginia and Truckee Railroad, which Sharon owned, to be carried to the Comstock.

Another company, the Sierra Nevada Wood and Lumber Company (SNWLC), owned up to fifty-five thousand acres of Tahoe lands by 1873. Run by Walter Scott Hobart, former Nevada state controller, the SNWLC operated north of Glenbrook at a place called "Incline" because of the steep pine-laden mountainsides that towered above Tahoe's shore. The SNWLC built a mill and tramway to get lumber up the precipitous basin walls. Once on top they used the V-flume method to get their lumber to the yards on the east side of the Sierra. Incline was an area formerly valuable to the Washoes because of its abundance of numerous types of berries and its proximity to rich trout-fishing grounds. Its destruction as a resource was amplified by the disruption of two creeks draining the steep mountainside and the muddying of the formerly pristine waters along its shore.

Leland Stanford, namesake of Stanford University, onetime governor of California, and railroad king, owned an interest in another company working in the basin, the Donner Lumber and Boom Company (DLBC). As early as 1870, the DLBC built a dam at Tahoe's lone outlet, the Truckee River, valuable to northern Washoe families for its rich fishery. The company took control of the water to float lumber out of the Sierra.[9]

The Pacific Wood, Lumber, and Flume Company (PWLFC) began harvesting Tahoe lumber in 1877. One of its owners, John Mackay, became the most powerful man on the Comstock. Later in his life, Mackay battled the infamous financier Jay Gould for control of international communications systems. At Tahoe the PWLFC removed the forests situated in northern Washoe lands.[10]

The efforts of these powerful companies resulted in the dramatic deforestation of the Tahoe basin. A mining company attorney tallied six hundred million feet of lumber and two million cords of firewood harvested from the basin by 1880. He suggested, "No later visitor could conceive of the majesty and beauty fed into the maws of those voracious mills." Washoe families lost more than just scenic woodland: their mountain homes, along with the animal, plant, and fish resources available in the Tahoe basin, had been seriously compromised.[11]

At about the same time capitalists were discovering the potential for wealth in Tahoe's forests, others looked to the lake itself, where they found an abundance of Lahontan cutthroat trout. The cutthroat had evolved in the depths of Lake Lahontan, the massive Ice Age lake that covered much of what is today western Nevada. In that environment, cutthroats thrived on large schools of smaller fishes. As the Ice Age reached its end and the environment gradually warmed, Lake Lahontan's vast expanse gave way to smaller residual bodies of water like Pyramid Lake, which was connected to Lake Tahoe via the Truckee River. Cutthroat continued to live in both lakes and the river.[12]

As early as 1856, knowledge of the mountain lake's rich fisheries had spread across the region. That summer the *Mountain Democrat,* a newspaper serving the California diggings, noted a "fine fish," described as a twenty-eight-inch trout, which had come from Tahoe. During the spring of 1860, a paper on the other side of the Sierra, Virginia City's *Territorial Enterprise,* reported "many" Washoes tending to "their usual spring hunting and fishing operations" at Tahoe. Later that summer, the paper noted that "most" of the tribe was engaged in fishing at Tahoe.[13]

Washoe families were following their seasonal cycle to the shores of Tahoe during snowless months. These same papers make it clear that by the 1870s, Washoe fisheries had been dramatically transformed. The changes forced Washoes to make difficult choices. They could abandon their ancient center at Tahoe or adapt to a growing American market. Some attempted to hang on to a semblance of their seasonal cycle, sticking to remote fishing sites, while trying to avoid foreigners. But as the American population increased, avoidance proved impossible.

By 1865 Tahoe trout had become a delicacy known across the Sierra region. A newspaper from the Nevada gold-mining town of Austin reported that a "wagon load" of fresh trout from Tahoe was being offered at the "fancy price of seventy-five cents per pound." The article's author described the trout as "large" and "tempting" and enough to "cause one to regret not being a millionaire."[14]

As the mining industry grew, an increased demand spurred commercial fishers. During the 1870s up to twenty-five commercial fisheries employed large seines and trawlers on Tahoe. Hundreds of thousands of pounds of trout were being caught each year. With the emergence of the transcontinental railroad, Tahoe trout began reaching distant markets such as San Francisco, Denver, Chicago, and New York.[15]

Indians whose resource bases were steadily shrinking realized a new way to support themselves, selling fish. The market in Tahoe trout apparently attracted Paiutes as well as Washoes. Virginia City's *Territorial Enterprise* reported in June 1872 that groups of Paiute Indians were bringing gunnysacks filled with Tahoe trout to the market. Later that summer, a rival newspaper noted a Paiute "trout express" from Tahoe to Virginia City. The article described a thirty-two-mile network of runners. Each runner carried the fresh fish for about four miles before handing off to the next runner, until finally reaching Virginia City.

Historically, Paiutes may have fished the upper reaches of the Truckee River and the Truckee Meadows, but the Washoe oral tradition and archaeological evidence indicate that Tahoe itself was almost exclusively the domain of Washoes. Paiutes had in Pyramid Lake a deep, clear trout-rich fishery and therefore did not need to fish Tahoe. The article raises the question of why Paiutes would fish for Tahoe trout. Many were already bringing fish to market from Pyramid. It is possible that the article's authors did not make a distinction between Washoes and Paiutes. Paiutes had a more visible presence than Washoes in the region. But it is equally possible that, pushed from their own traditional fishing sites, Paiutes decided to sell Tahoe trout. Whatever the case, Tahoe was being heavily fished.[16]

As pressure on the lake's trout population increased, people began to worry that the "inexhaustible" supply of fish might run out. State officials took up the issue of overfishing at Tahoe as early as the fall of 1861 when the Nevada territorial legislature passed "An Act Relating to Wild Game and Fish." The act stipulated that fish could not be harvested with nets, weirs, dams, poison, "or by any deleterious substance whatsoever." Enforcement of the act was nonexistent. Three years later, in 1864, the state legislature amended the act to create a legal fishing season between April and December. In the first year, at least, the act seemed to have some influence. The *Gold Hill News* reported that since the act had gone into effect, residents of the region had "not seen a pound of the delicious trout which are usually brought over from Lake Tahoe." But by the end of April, when the season had been open for thirty days, the *Virginia Daily Union* boasted an "abundance of trout of enormous size in the market, from Lake Tahoe."[17]

Once Americans sensed the impact of overfishing on Tahoe, they quickly began looking for a place to cast the blame. While they need not have looked further than the commercial fisheries and eager American markets, the collective American animus centered on a convenient scapegoat: the Washoes. In a remarkable act of projection, newcomers began blaming people who had been the stewards of Tahoe's fisheries for thousands of years. This act of blaming Indians is part and parcel of the American colonial practice of dehumanizing and objectifying Native people. Already casting Natives as "savages" and "vagrants," it was easy for Americans to blame Indian fishers as the culprits in the declining fisheries. But there is another reason Americans found guilt with Indians. The fishing practices deemed illegal by the state did not necessarily apply to Indians. The applicability of state laws on Native people was entirely unclear. Technically, the federal government maintained exclusive jurisdiction to deal with Indian affairs, a right established by Article I, Section 8, of the U.S. Constitution, often referred to as the "Commerce Clause." This right was further buttressed by a Supreme Court ruling in 1832 that held that the State of Georgia had no legal authority on Cherokee lands. So while American fishers were forbidden from spearing spawning trout populations by legislative acts, the Washoes were not. The average American likely had no idea about federal jurisdiction and Indian rights.

In 1877 the Nevada state legislature tried to clear up the confusion. In another act aimed at protecting fish, legislators declared that Indians would not be prohibited "from taking trout in any of the streams or lakes of this State, at any time, by the same means heretofore usually used and employed by them; provided, that the same are for their own use." While confirming the Washoes' rights to fish in their accustomed ways, the legislature simultaneously stripped them of their ability to sell fish to the eager American market. This undoubtedly made life harder for those Washoes who had learned how to survive by harvesting and selling fish. By the mid-1880s newspapers in the region began publicizing the right of Washoes to fish when others could not. The *Genoa Weekly Courier* deemed the "noble red man" privileged "when it comes to catching fish." Later that same summer, the *Carson Morning Appeal* editorialized, "The Lake [sic] is about fished out, and as long as greasy Indians are allowed to spear fish in the spawning season, the supply will gradually diminish." Here again appears the American racial construct that cast Washoes as "greasy" and therefore guilty. This then is a tangible example of the intellectual component of colonization and its direct impact on Native people.[18]

In the decade that followed, the ire and prejudice began shaping actions. At the close of the nineteenth century, newspapers in the region began publishing warnings like this one from March 25, 1898: "The California Fish Commission warns the Indians that no spearing or taking of spawn trout about Lake Tahoe will be permitted this year. The Commission will maintain an efficient patrol of the streams and promptly arrest every Indian detected in violating the law." Two years later, another paper observed, "In the past [Washoes] have been driven away, but this year they will be arrested and punished." A decade later, the State of Nevada classified large fish species as "game fish," placing them once and for all under state management. It is ironic that these laws ultimately reinforced traditional Washoe systems of protecting and conserving trout populations. It would be decades before the Washoes would be able to use legal authority to establish their own similar laws in lands they controlled. Before they could codify protection protocols, they had to acquire land. Because the Washoes did not have a treaty or reserved lands until 1917, they lived in a legal limbo. Those Native communities that did have treaties could at least wield some legal pretense to protect their fishing and hunting rights. Treaties often contained provisions stating that Indians maintained their rights to hunt and fish in "usual and accustomed" places. While the concept of "usual and accustomed" would have to be litigated before the phrase had any real teeth for protecting Indian rights, the rights nevertheless existed on paper for Natives with treaties.[19]

The rise of the Comstock also stimulated the emergence of agriculture in the river valleys east of the Sierra, traditionally the winter home sites for Washoe families. By the late 1860s, a vigorous market for hay, fresh meat, and butter had developed. The earliest agriculturalists, who had arrived before the Comstock, claimed large tracts of land.

Charles Holbrook and two partners, B. G. Mast and H. F. Dangberg, claimed up to nine hundred acres in the early 1850s. They did not trouble themselves with the question of Washoe rights to the land. By this point it was just assumed that they had no rights. Therefore, the land was "free" for the claimant. By 1861 the U.S. surveyor general worried about overlapping land claims in the region. He wrote to superiors that summer, explaining, "The rapid settlement of the most desirable land is giving rise to innumerable conflicts over claims which can only be settled by a Government survey and a sale of the land according to the laws of the U.S." The surveyor general described the reason for the confusing tangle of overlapping claims. The courts of Utah, acting under Mormon law, had "been in the habit of granting to each settler in this Territory as much land as he could fence and in many instances as many thousand acres as he claimed without fencing." Expanses of rabbitbrush gave way to fenced fields of grain. By 1860 over five thousand acres in P'a·walu (central Washoe) lands (Carson Valley) were being farmed and more than ten thousand cows, horses, and sheep grazed across their lands. Farmers and ranchers would come to represent the settler colonialism that quickly gained traction in the fertile Carson Valley. By the end of the 1800s, both extractive and settler colonialism had wrought dramatic transformations across the eastern Sierra and in the Tahoe basin.[20]

Amid the "chaos of destruction," the new bureaucracy responsible for Indians in Nevada recognized the dire consequences of environmental degradation on Washoe families. Similar to what had already transpired across the Sierra in the western foothills, Washoe country was quickly transformed. While mining, logging, and fishing were steadily destroying resources, agents of the federal government recorded its impact on Washoes.

In his first report for 1861, Territorial Governor James Nye, also the acting superintendent of Indian affairs, described "spoiled" rivers along with streams polluted by heavy metals and ores due to mining operations. He chronicled countless diverted or dammed rivers and streams that were being used for mining and agricultural purposes. Nye knew that Tahoe had been the center of the Washoe world. And even though newspaper reports from the era indicate that Washoes were still fishing and living at the lake in snowless months, Nye's report made it clear that their way of life was being destroyed. The lake had been "taken possession of by the whites," who had made it "a watering place, to which large numbers from this Territory and California resort, and from which the poor Tribe are virtually excluded."[21]

The field agent under Nye's supervision, Warren Wasson, reported that same year a "rapidly diminishing" Washoe population, which he estimated around five hundred. Most anthropologists and archaeologists corroborate the Washoe oral tradition that places their precontact numbers anywhere from one thousand to fifteen hundred. Given the absence of statistical records before and directly after American arrival, it is impossible to plot the population decline. If we work from the larger of the two figures and take Wasson's estimation of five hundred at face value, two-thirds of the tribe had been eradicated; the lower estimate reveals a casualty rate of 50 percent. Without documentation, it is impossible to be exact in assessing the causes of the population decline, but widespread dispossession and resource destruction were certainly primary factors.[22]

The records of the federal government from this era, although written in the hand of various agents, often contain the filtered voices of Washoe people. As early as 1862, the reports of Wasson's successor, Jacob Lockhart, reflected the Washoe desire for protected lands, free from white incursion. In a letter to the commissioner of Indian affairs, Lockhart reported, "The wild game is being killed by the whites, the trees from which the Indians gathered nuts are being cut down, and the grass from which they gathered seeds for winter is being taken from them."[23]

Two years later, Washoes channeled their frustration through Lockhart, and on July 1, 1865, Lockhart called for two reservations. He wrote to superiors that, without other options, many Indian families continued to make their home sites on lands claimed by white owners. Consequently, whites complained to Lockhart about Indian "trespassers" and "squatters."

Lockhart reported that Washoes did not recognize the right of the newcomers to enclose and privatize their ancient lands. In 1865 Lockhart asked for reservation land in traditional year-round home areas for the Washoes. He suggested two reservations of 360 acres each along the base of the eastern Sierra. But the cogs of the large bureaucracy moved too slowly.[24]

In midsummer 1865, a new superintendent, Hubbard G. Parker, assumed control of Nevada Indian affairs. A former mine superintendent and delegate to Nevada's state constitutional convention, Parker became a major force for the dispossession and forced assimilation of Nevada Natives. His personal business interests and those of his white contemporaries often motivated his policies. The Washoe community now faced the impossible task of working with a man who misrepresented them and often deliberately misconstrued the facts.[25]

Shortly after his appointment, Parker demonstrated his use of intellectual colonization in the form of racial categorizations similar to many of his contemporaries. He identified Washoes as "a small remnant of a moving idle tribe of some five hundred" and suggested members were "naturally lazy and averse to labor or work of any kind." Moreover, he argued that because most of the land "between the rivers and lakes and the base of the mountains" had already been sold to Euro-American ranchers, there were no lands left "of value either to the white or red man." If by chance some land could be found, it would be "very expensive." Parker judged Lockhart's earlier request for land "unadvisable and inexpedient." In his dismissal of the Washoes and their circumstances, Parker exemplified a growing federal approach to Indian affairs, which demanded that Native people completely adopt the trappings of American life. His actions also clearly demonstrate the very real consequences of racial constructs as they were applied in northern Nevada. Reading between the lines of his report, one can discern the sentiment that because Washoes were "lazy" and "idle," they were to blame for their condition. Moreover, their suffering and landless condition need not trouble Americans.[26]

Nearly a year later, in his annual report to the commissioner of Indian affairs, Parker's assessment of his wards had not changed. His report this time clearly blamed Nevada Natives themselves for their deplorable situation. According to him, Washoes possessed "much less physical and mental development than the Pi-Utes [sic]." He characterized their "savage" lifestyle as "sensual and filthy." This lifestyle explained their "annually diminishing . . . numbers," as they contracted disease "through their indulgences." Despite the hostile and bigoted tone of his report, Parker supplied a revealing glimpse into the Washoe world. In the late 1860s, they were struggling to subsist on the margins of white society. His letter recounts their efforts to learn English and, in winter, having to beg for work, supplies, or clothing. Parker explained that during the snowless season, Washoes continued to make their homes at Tahoe and that they continued to harvest seeds and pine nuts while hunting rabbits and ducks.

Parker's letter illustrates that Washoes, denied land use and with diminishing resources, continued to move with the seasons, in a precarious balance between traditions and a changing world. Parker ended his letter with the callous recommendation that, due to their "rapidly diminishing numbers," no reservation was needed. To him, their failure to assimilate meant the tribe was doomed to extinction. In fact, the Washoes were rapidly developing strategies of accommodation that ultimately facilitated their survival. Parker either did not see them adapting or chose to ignore their efforts.[27]

Theodore T. Dwight interrupted Parker's term as superintendent, replacing him in September 1866, but his tenure lasted less than a year. In March 1867, Parker again assumed the superintendency. Although in office for only seven months, Dwight left behind telling records. His account reveals terrible suffering during the winter of 1867. Although continuing to hunt, fish, and collect pine nuts, many Washoes relied on begging around towns as well to stave off starvation. Dwight described Washoe families as poor, miserable, and in need of care. He suggested they be placed on a reservation a good distance from the Paiutes and concluded it would be impossible for families "to live in the locality where adventurous miners find their way, and drive off the game." He argued that the federal government had to do something.[28] Dwight's call for a reservation, like Lockhart's, went unanswered.

Once reinstated, Parker wrote superiors, assuring them that his Indian wards were fine. Remarkably, he suggested that Nevada Indians were flourishing. He described their condition as "eminently satisfactory." He went on to state that never had Nevada Indians been "so happy, or so well provided for." "It is almost impossible for them to suffer much in any portion of this superintendency now," he explained, "since the building of the Central Pacific railroad, and the discovery of silver mines in almost every portion of the country." Borrowing the rhetoric of American progress, he argued that the transformation of Native lands provided the utmost benefit for Indians: "The more this barren desert country is settled by the whites [sic] the better it is for the Indians. Every white man who makes himself a farm on any of the strips of cultivable lands adds to the comforts of the Indians more than they could get on fifty miles square in its natural state."[29]

The superintendent suggested a discontinuation of the annual twenty-thousand-dollar appropriation for Nevada Indians. In fact, he proclaimed, "The reservations [the Paiutes] have in this superintendency are at the present time of no use or value to them whatever. It would benefit them vastly more if they were abandoned and allowed to be settled by the whites." Parker's stunning pronouncements set his personal view in sharp relief. Not only did the Washoes not need a reservation, but the existing reservations held by the Paiutes needed to be opened to white "settlement." Rather than protect the Indians in the Nevada superintendency, Parker wanted to surrender all their lands and leave them as completely bereft of resources as the Washoes. In view of every other agent's and superintendent's report, Parker's assertion that the Indians needed nothing from the government except "advice" was spurious.[30]

Fortunately for Nevada Natives, the federal government did not act on Parker's suggestions and finally replaced him once and for all on September 22, 1869. His successor, U.S. Army major Henry Douglas, represented President Grant's desire to initiate a "peace process" with Native communities. Douglas laid bare Parker's misconduct and informed superiors that "Mr. Parker himself desired to have the island in Pyramid Lake [Paiute territory] withdrawn from the reservation, so that he could procure it for the alleged purpose of raising Cashmere Goats and made use of political influence to effect that object." The officer claimed that during their first meeting, Parker described the superintendency as a "sinecure" and suggested the less Douglas did for the Indians, the better off they would be.[31]

Parker's tenure illustrates the double challenge looming over communities like the Washoes. They faced not only the loss of resources but also irresponsive, and in some instances malicious, government representatives. Nevertheless, with few other options, many continued to express themselves to federal agents. A special commission sent by the federal government to northern Arizona, Utah, Nevada, and southeastern California recorded the continual efforts of Washoe individuals to reclaim their lands. The two special commissioners, J. W. Powell and G. W. Ingalls, informed superiors: "[The Washoes] appreciate that they can no longer live by hunting, fishing, and gathering. . . . They earnestly ask that they may have lands of their own." From the Washoe perspective, the world had been turned upside down. The land and water, where all life begins and ends, had been privatized by Americans and, for their purposes, systematically destroyed. The commissioners reported, "The lands along the streams and almost every important spring has either been entered or claimed."[32]

By 1876 a new federal agent misinterpreted the Washoe refusal to leave their land as a preference to remain in "poverty and wretchedness." Consequently, he judged them deficient of "industry."[33] He did not understand their commitment to remaining in their ancestral lands. He also did not acknowledge their efforts and ingenuity in attempting to tailor traditional practices to the American market. Some acted as guides or sold game, pine nuts, and fish to a ready American market, while others worked as ranch hands, laborers, or domestic servants. And a significant number of women began to craft and sell baskets.[34]

By the end of the nineteenth century, Washoes had been forced to suspend, leave behind, or adapt their precolonial modes of subsistence. Established American prejudices caused newspapermen, certain of the Indian agents, and those who had taken the Washoes' lands to portray them as the villains, bringing destruction upon themselves. Instead, they were doing what they had to do in order to survive.

CHAPTER 5

SURVIVAL

> The food from the pine nut trees is what my people eat. It is the same as our mother's milk. Your people are destroying our trees and our food, we ask you to help us so we can live.
>
> —Epesuwa, Captain Jim, 1892

In the late 1880s, a Washoe child dreamed of bears, loons, songs, and stars. To elders steeped in the old ways, he showed all the signs. He was marked for power. Born in 1885 on the fringes of Genoa, Nevada, where his parents worked on a ranch, Henry Rupert would grow to become the most famous Washoe healer. His power continued to shape the destiny of his people even after his death. It was his association with Cave Rock, on Tahoe's eastern shore, that helped protect the sacred site from recreational climbers in the twenty-first century. At the time of his birth, it had become common for Washoe kinship groups to hire themselves out as ranch hands and domestics. Often Americans allowed families to live on the outskirts of their property while they worked as seasonal laborers.

Genoa had long been used by P'a·walu (central Washoe) groups for deer hunting. Nestled against the steep eastern Sierra in the rain's shadow, the land was also valuable because of its hot springs and sources of freshwater. By the 1880s a handful of Americans controlled the region. At some point Rupert's father, Pete Duncan, deserted the family, and his mother, Susie John, worked as a domestic servant to support her children.

Elders quickly realized that Rupert was not an ordinary child. They witnessed the signs of *wegéleyú*, or power, around him, and they watched him closely. He frequently met a bear in his dreams. Bears were especially important animals to Washoes. They possessed supernatural power that allowed them to intuit a person's intentions; some doctors could acquire this skill. In his dream, Rupert would stare directly at the bear and it would disappear, and Rupert's dream body would launch toward the moon. Despite all of the environmental degradation, the dislocation, the suffering, the uncertainty, Washoe power had not disappeared.[1]

Around the same time, on a hot summer day, an American Civil War veteran and physician, Simeon Lee, was called out to treat an elderly Washoe man who had collapsed in a dusty Carson City street. Lee believed the man was suffering from heat exhaustion. The next day he made a follow-up visit. Lee found the subject seated between two women. A young Washoe boy in attendance offered his own diagnosis for the collapse: witchcraft. He told Lee, "An enemy at Double Springs had blown poison into the sufferer although they were separated by twenty long miles." The victim was Epesuwa, Captain Jim.[2]

The lives of Rupert and Epesuwa overlapped by only a few years. One, Epesuwa, would embark on a journey across the continent to meet the "Great Father" in 1892; the other, Rupert, honed his shamanistic skills and became an innovative healer, drawing from both Washoe and Western traditions. Their stories illustrate the ways in which Washoes tried to work within and against the federal agenda of assimilation. American leaders in Washington, D.C., tried to convince Epesuwa to use the Dawes Act (1887) to claim farmlands instead of the Pine Nut Mountains. Teachers and administrators at the Carson Indian School tried to expunge Washoe traditions and healing practices from young Henry Rupert. The chapter that follows draws on their experiences to help demonstrate the delicate balance many Washoes were forced to maintain as they encountered increasing demands from federal officials to give up their customs. In the process, both men, and the Washoes collectively, built a figurative bridge between the world of their ancestors and Gilded Age America.

In retrospect, it is hard to imagine that the 1800s would end in any way other than absolute disaster for Washoes. The years before the 1890s provided little reason to believe that they would be able to remain on their lands. Lake Tahoe's environment had been devastated, the Pine Nuts were overrun, and the eastern Sierra valleys had been usurped for American ranches and farms. Throughout the last decades of the nineteenth century, the federal government had been crafting policies aimed at turning Indians into Americans. Because the government claimed jurisdiction in Indian affairs, it had always sought to apply a "one-size-fits-all" approach to dealing with hundreds of diverse Native communities.

Federal Indian policy swung like a pendulum: in some instances working to keep Indians separate from America, at other times seeking to make Americans out of them. Either way, Indian peoples' ways of life were meant to disappear.

By the time the United States reached the Pacific shore, and Washoe country, the earlier policy of Indian removal proved unworkable. There was no more land in the West where Indians could be removed to in order to be "out of the way." Federal administrators therefore invested heavily in an assimilation program. The desire to Americanize Native people relied heavily on "an imaginary evolutionary scale." Politicians, Christian reformers, altruists, and others who simply wanted Indians to disappear shared a common assumption: white American society was more "advanced" or "evolved" than indigenous communities. High-level bureaucrats measured Native "progress" by estimating the degree to which communities had adapted or shed their traditional cultures.[3]

In 1879 army captain Richard Henry Pratt established the Carlisle Indian School in Pennsylvania. His school worked to expunge Indian culture; he wanted to "kill the Indian, but save the man." Upon arrival at the school, young pupils had their hair shorn and their traditional clothes burned, and they were quickly forced to select new Christian names. Students were forbidden from speaking their Native languages and made to take classes in vocational trades like blacksmithing, typesetting, carpentry, and farming. Young girls spent most of their time learning the domestic arts, which included cooking, cleaning, and child care. Pratt became fond of "before" and "after" photos in which he featured students upon their arrival at the school juxtaposed with an image of the student after a short period of residency. The images were dramatic, featuring military uniforms, tight collars, and short hair that replaced Native youngsters' traditional appearance. Federal administrators soon noticed the school's effectiveness, and quickly boarding schools spread across the West.[4]

As the reinvigorated drive continued, the rhetoric of Indian agents and officials was often steeped in the great successes of, and the continued need for, assimilation. In 1881 the commissioner of Indian affairs, Hiram Price, described the "great object" of the federal government to be the "civilization" of American Indians, and he commended the "noble work" of those who worked to "domesticate" them. Another commissioner argued that good Christians and philanthropists needed to lift Indians from "barbarism" to the heights of "civilization." He prescribed training so that Indians would learn to "rear their families as white people do." If Americans could get Indians to "forsake their savage habits," Natives might eventually achieve the "liberty of American citizenship."[5]

In the winter of 1890, the first boarding school in Washoe country, the Carson Indian School, opened its doors just south of Carson City, Nevada. Later it came to be called the Stewart Indian School, after Nevada's first U.S. senator, William Stewart. Administrators modeled the school after Carlisle, with a strong emphasis on blue-collar training that included a strict gender divide.[6]

The policies of a distant federal government did not initially bother Henry Rupert. He spent his childhood exploring the eastern Sierra, and *wegéleyú* began finding him. One day as young Rupert trekked along a desolate trail, a strange apparition manifested. It looked like a white shadowy object. When Rupert moved, the object moved; when he stood still, so did the specter. With mounting fear, Rupert approached. It proved to be a piece of white linen snagged on a tree branch. But the linen fluttered only when Rupert moved, and he could not shake the feeling that something powerful had happened.[7]

He also continued to dream. In 1892 seven-year-old Rupert had a dream about his mother. At the time his mother was upset about the death of a relative. In the dream Rupert saw his mother walk deliberately onto dangerously thin ice. Shortly after this dream, his mother walked onto an iced-over slough, attempting to take her own life. Rupert's foresight was an important sign.[8]

Power, in the traditional Washoe world, could be a burden. It came unsought, and, although in many instances it was beneficial, because it held danger it often was unwelcome. In the absence of proper training, power could sicken and kill its recipient. Or it could manifest in harmful, sometimes evil, ways. Elder mentors looked for the signs of power early, so they could train their mentees carefully. Once acquired, power could not be shed. One of the most respected Washoe doctors in the early twentieth century, Beleliwe, explained, "You can't get rid of [power] unless you die."[9]

Rupert's signs of power caused his older brother-in-law Charlie Rube and his uncle Welewkushkush to take a special interest in him. Both were men of power, commonly referred to as "doctors." Charlie Rube was an antelope "boss," while Welewkushkush was known to be a potent shaman. Power often stayed within particular families. In the words of a Washoe elder, "Them people that [are] from a doctor family, they have dreams and get curing power." It was almost inevitable, according to another source: "If you come from a family of dreamers there ain't nothing you can do. You're trapped by it." Power brought opportunity as well as danger. Developed properly, it could help individuals like Welewkushkush cure illness. It allowed others, like Charlie Rube, to manage animal, fish, and plant populations.[10]

Welewkushkush proved to be an important guide for young Rupert. He allowed his nephew to attend his healing ceremonies. Rupert remembered his uncle performing remarkable feats. In one instance, his uncle walked barefoot across fire and came out unscathed. Another, more significant, event took place on the shore of Lake Tahoe. There a young boy, one of Welewkushkush's apprentices, had become deathly ill. The doctor said that a water being had claimed the boy's soul.

Washoe tradition holds that mysterious beings populate the waterways of the Tahoe basin and eastern Sierra. The center of their world exists in the waters around Cave Rock on Tahoe's eastern shore. Cave Rock, one of the most sacred sites, marks a meeting place between the worlds of humans and water beings. A well-known Washoe story recounts the events that followed when a fisherman unwittingly caught one of these beings. Thinking it an unusual fish, the fisherman sent it to an aquarium in San Francisco. When the water being finally broke free, it caused the great earthquake of 1906.[11]

Convinced that one of these beings had taken the boy's soul, Welewkushkush walked into the lake while shaking a rattle. Witnesses claim he was completely submerged for ten minutes. Upon returning from the depths, he walked around the boy's body four times and instructed the boy's mother to shout her son's name four times. When the boy awakened, his nose started to bleed, a sign that power was at work. The doctor instructed the boy to face the lake and shake his rattle. Gradually, the boy began behaving as if awakened from a dream; he was cured. Welewkushkush had negotiated with the water beings for the boy's soul.[12]

Rupert's training would be interrupted in 1894 when government authorities forced him to attend the Carson Indian School. The young, budding shaman found the military-like school stifling. He was not alone. Many Washoes recalled their experiences or the stories of their great-aunts, great-uncles, grandparents, and relatives who attended the boarding school. Frank Rivers, a former student, spoke of the day federal officials hauled him to school. "They just came right into our camp and rounded up us kids and took us to school." Rivers explained. "Neither he nor the other children nor the parents could understand what was happening, for none of them spoke any English."

Elder Winona James remembered as a child hiding from federal officials as they searched for pupils. James's grandmother did not want her to go. When James finally entered the school, she remembered it as a "very dramatic experience." Once the students were at the school, administrators maintained complete control over their wards. Students had no say in when they could leave to visit their parents. And parents had no control over when their children would be allowed to come home. James recalled being forced from bed early in the morning to "drill before breakfast just like the army." If her family wanted to have her visit, they had to sign her out. She lived at Stewart throughout the year, including summers and vacations.[13]

Worried parents often waited for weeks or months before receiving news about their children at the school. In one instance, a concerned mother wrote to the school's superintendent, inquiring about her son. She claimed that her previous letter had been returned to her, stamped from the "dead letter office." She wrote: "Does this mean that my son is dead?" Two weeks later, she received the response: "I regret to state that Pedro Cordova died at this school."

In another telling exchange, Susie Corbett, a student at the school, wrote to ask if she could return home for the summer to see her mother and sisters. She closed her letter with a heartfelt request: "Please let me go." In a short response the superintendent told Susie it would be best for her to remain in school for the summer, but maybe she could go home the following year.[14]

Rupert, like many others, tried to escape and ran away from the school. He was quickly corralled and returned to the school. He wasted no time in making a second attempt. His return this time came with a violent whipping from a school official. But that did not stop him from trying again. Eventually, Rupert stopped working to escape. Lessons and regiment could not drive the *wegéleyú* from him, though. During his fourth year at the school, he had the dream that set in motion his shamanic development. Late in his life Rupert explained his dream. "I was sleeping in the school dormitory. I had a dream. I saw a buck in the west. It was a horned buck. It looked east. A voice said to me: 'Don't kill my babies anymore.' I woke up, and it was raining outside, and I had a nosebleed in bed." Rupert interpreted the buck, always a powerful symbol, and rain as signifiers that he would develop the ability to influence the weather. The eastward-looking buck warned Rupert that he could use his power for good or bad. He also learned from the dream that his primary source of power would be water.

Later, one widely reported incident involving water led to his acquisition of a nickname. While out hunting, Rupert wandered into a dry wash. A flash flood suddenly threatened to sweep him away. But as the water neared, it parted and harmlessly passed him by. Some people in the region began calling him "Moses," and current-day Moses Street in Carson City, Nevada, is named after him.[15]

If administrators at the Carson Indian School knew about Rupert's dream and his growing power, they would have actively worked to stamp out his "Indian medicine." Shamans posed a direct threat to the federal agenda of assimilation. A special court of Indian offenses in Nevada outlawed the practice of "so called 'Medicine M[en]' or Indian doctor[s]." Rule 9C for the court specified that shamanic work could earn imprisonment "for a period not less than 10 days, or until" the doctor provided evidence of their "intent to forever abandon the unlawful practice." But Rupert did not abandon his practice. His power grew. By the middle of the twentieth century, both Native and non-Native patients from across the Sierra Nevada sought his healing. And his legacy would play a significant role in helping to protect the Washoes' sacred site at Cave Rock in the twenty-first century.[16]

Amid the "success" of the boarding schools and the popular chorus of cries calling for Indian adaptation, in 1887 Congress passed the Dawes, or General Allotment, Act. Mirroring the Homestead Act of 1862, it proposed to carve reservations into individual properties. By the government creating distinct parcels of land, the long-standing communal, economic, and social bases of indigenous communities would, theoretically, be broken. Male heads of households received 160 acres (a quarter section), single individuals (including women) received 80 acres, while orphaned members under eighteen received 40 acres.

The act stipulated that any leftover land, after allotments had been made, could be purchased from the community and resold. Some of the profit from land sales would be put toward Indian education. These funds lured Catholic and Protestant missionaries onto Indian land to build missionary schools that steeped the Indians in the economic and cultural doctrines of America.[17] Section 4 of the act addressed the situation of landless peoples like the Washoes. It stated that those Indian communities that had no land could use Section 4 of the act to claim federal lands not otherwise appropriated. Administrators intended for the landless tribes to claim irrigable farmlands where they might learn to be farmers and small landholders. Given the dire circumstances facing Washoes, along with the zealous desire of the federal government to assimilate them, it seems unlikely that they had any chance of protecting culturally significant nonirrigable lands. But that is exactly what they would do, following Epesuwa's journey.[18]

In 1892, the same year that Rupert dreamed about his mother, another Washoe man of power was at work. This man's power was different. Epesuwa was known to whites as Captain Jim. He was kind, generous, and modest. These traits, along with his love and concern for the Washoe people, led many to identify him as a leader. Prior to Euro-American colonization, local Washoe communities recognized leaders as those with the most experience and seniority within a specific domain. Different individuals led in distinct capacities. Each kinship group had leaders for different functions. There would be those, like Charlie Rube, called animal bosses, who maintained a close connection with a specific species of animal and directed communal activities regarding the hunting of that animal. Antelope charmers or bosses, for example, could, through ritual practice, communicate with antelope and convince them to give up their lives. There would also be leaders among herbalists, curers, shamans, and warriors. Even though there might be one elder whose counsel was held above most others, leadership was generally spread out through many individuals among the different kinship groups.

Charlie Rube claimed that he had "heard of no chiefs 'of [the] whole tribe' before white man's time." But as non-Natives moved into Washoe lands, they continually sought a "headman" to negotiate with. After colonization the first recognized "leader" had been Lenúka, also called by whites "Captain Jim," but not to be confused with Epesuwa. According to Rube, "The whites had singled him out and called him 'captain.' He would speak some English and thus the whites would come to him." Rube went on to say that many Washoes believed Lenúka abused his authority. Rube's father claimed that Lenúka gave Washoe lands to whites for twenty dollars a month. This purported practice eventually led him to be "witched and killed by a shaman named Wagotom." Clearly, this initial "leader" did not maintain, and perhaps never had, a mandate from the entire community.

Conversely, Rube described Epesuwa as someone who maintained the trust and support of many Washoe families. He was a "big time captain." Rube remembered him as having "a better way of thinking than other people." He was "capable and level headed. People looked up to him [and] respected his judgment." By the time Epesuwa emerged as a "leader," Washoe conceptions of leadership had begun to change.[19]

Epesuwa decided to circumvent field agents and take Washoes' claims straight to Washington, D.C. Early in 1892, he met with tribal members to discuss the continuing destruction of their lands. Smaller meetings had been taking place sporadically over the previous year. Key Washoe individuals involved in these gatherings included Henry Rupert's father, Pete Duncan; Si-sa Minkey; Washoe Johnny (Peace Maker); and Captain Joe.[20]

The group of Washoe representatives, meeting in 1891 and 1892, contracted the services of a lawyer, James Torison of Carson City, who helped them write a formal petition to be delivered to Washington, D.C. The coalition raised $180 to sponsor a trip to Washington. This was not enough for the entire delegation to travel east, and they decided to send Epesuwa with an interpreter, Dick Bender.[21]

On April 15, 1892, the two men set out to visit the nation's capital. Like many leaders who tried to meet the "Great Father," Epesuwa and Bender encountered a dizzying maze of bureaucrats and assistants to officials. They successfully met with Nevada's congressional delegates, and Washoe tradition holds that at some point during their thirteen-day stay, Captain Jim also met with President Benjamin Harrison. In the Washoe version, upon meeting the president, Epesuwa extended a handful of pine nut flour and said, "My brother this food from the pine nut trees is what my people eat. . . . [I]t is the same as our mother's milk when it is made into soup. . . . [Y]our people are destroying our trees and our food. . . . [W]e ask you to help us so we can live."[22]

Whether Epesuwa delivered those words to President Harrison or not, they reflect strong cultural values. The comparison of pine nut flour to mother's milk reveals how deeply they felt about the delicate protein-rich nuts, along with the groves, weather patterns, and landscape that nurtured them. The T'agim Gumsabay?, or first pine nut festival, was an annual expression of the Washoes' deep connection to the pine nut trees and their fruit. Epesuwa's plea illuminates the desperate conditions facing Washoe families. Equally, his words reflect the determination of Washoes to protect and reclaim lands of critical importance to their ancestors, the Pine Nut Range.

If Epesuwa did talk with Benjamin Harrison, it is unlikely that the president was a sympathetic listener. Harrison ran one of the most notoriously corrupt administrations of the nineteenth century. He viewed the Indian Service as a vehicle for gaining political support. He placed cronies and hacks in Indian agencies across the West. His self-serving political maneuvers contributed significantly to the Wounded Knee Massacre of 1890.[23]

The historical record does clearly indicate that Captain Jim and Bender met Nevada senator William Stewart and Judge Horace F. Bartine, Nevada's lone delegate in the House of Representatives. Stewart and Bartine then introduced the Washoe spokesmen to a congressional delegation. Stewart was a particularly powerful figure in Washington. He had served in the Senate from 1864 to 1875 and had been reelected again in 1887. He had been a personal friend of President Abraham Lincoln, who tried unsuccessfully to get him to accept a position on the Supreme Court. Stewart was involved in the writing of the Fifteenth Amendment to the Constitution, in the form that was finally passed, and played an important part in the passage of the National Mining Laws of 1866 and 1872.[24]

Senator Stewart, familiar with northern Nevada and the Pine Nut Lands from years of mining there, tried to persuade Captain Jim and Bender to apply for farmland, not pine nut groves. He suggested they ask for agricultural parcels in the Humboldt Valley, outside the tribe's traditional territory.[25]

Despite Stewart's attempts to persuade them otherwise, the Washoe delegation left Washington with assurances that they would get allotments in the Pine Nut Range. Representative Bartine wrote a letter addressed "To the Washoes." In the letter he stated, "The Commissioner [of Indian Affairs] acknowledges that their cause is a just one, and that the U.S. government should help them in their distress." Bartine also informed them that $1,000 of emergency funds would be dispersed immediately for the "feeble and infirm." He said he planned to work with Stewart and Nevada agents to "procure legislation for their permanent relief."[26]

In 1893, a year after Captain Jim's trip to Washington, special allotting agent Michael Piggot arrived in Carson City and began receiving groups of Washoes. Even when the government decided to allocate land, responsibility for procurement fell on tribal members. They had to get to Carson City, and Piggot expected them to be able to identify and describe the boundaries of the land they wanted. If they did not speak English, they had to bring their own interpreter. The Washoes met each requirement. Remarkably, Epesuwa, Dick Bender, and the Washoes had successfully used the assimilative Dawes Act to protect their T'a·gim ʔaša.[27]

The Washoe experience with the Dawes Act was not entirely unique. Other small western tribes and individuals found creative ways to preserve culturally significant lands and traditional practices within the assimilative paradigm established by the federal government. For example, small bands of Pomo Indians in Northern California began leveraging the tools of capitalism to return to the lands of their ancestors that had been appropriated during and after the gold rush.

Because the federal government never ratified treaties made with California Indians, many continued to be "homeless" well into the 1900s. Just a couple of years before Epesuwa's trip to the nation's capital, a group of Pomos pooled their money so that they could purchase more than fifty acres of land near the town of Ukiah, California. The practice of buying land communally and then pursuing legal action to protect the land as community trusts served as the basis for the creation of several California rancherias. Those Pomos who started this demonstrated a creativity and adaptability similar to Washoes who claimed land under the Dawes Act.[28]

Washoes never intended to build year-round homes in the Pine

Nuts. In 1903 W. E. Casson, special allotting agent, and James K. Allen, superintendent of the Carson Indian School, reported that fact to the government. Moreover, they pointed out, the allotments were not helping to assimilate the Washoe people. Casson and Allen requested more land for the Washoes.[29]

Directives coming from the commissioner of Indian affairs, Robert Valentine, prescribed a continuation of the assimilative federal agenda. Valentine informed agents and superintendents that Indians should not be allowed to hold unused allotment lands. He suggested nonirrigable allotments be disposed of and imagined that "habits of thrift and industry" would follow. Valentine's directive promoted a process by which individual Indians could start living without "departmental control" and become American. It would be more than a decade before the Washoes would receive lands on which to build homes. Although a small number of community members eventually parted with their parcels, most never relinquished the original allotments.[30]

Records from the early twentieth century provide a window into the years between the acquisition of allotments and the purchase of the Washoe colonies in 1917. Washoes learned quickly that allotment boundaries created by a distant bureaucracy would not be respected.

In the spring of 1905 Hangalelti (southern Washoe) community members traveled from their homes near Woodfords Canyon, California, to the office of the superintendent, Calvin H. Asbury, in Carson City, Nevada. The group lodged an official complaint about trespassers on their allotted lands. One non-Native man in particular, they explained, regularly cut timber on their property, "claiming that it was his right in payment for water" that Washoe families used. The man, who goes unnamed in the documents, owned land upriver from the allotments. Superintendent Asbury would be a long-tenured agent in the Indian Service who had a sometimes turbulent relationship with the Washoes. Later in his career, he was adamant in attempting to outlaw Indian religions, including the Crow Tobacco Society and the western Peyote church. One well-known anthropologist described him as a "nefarious zealot for destroying Indian religions." Asbury noted that he would have suggested the families take the matter up in court, but he doubted they "would get justice." The superintendent concluded a letter to the commissioner of Indian affairs by stating that he did not have "time to go into the details" of the situation, and consequently he took no action.[31]

Five years later, in 1910, representatives from Hangalelti country again informed Asbury about trespassing. In the years since the first report, the newcomer had enclosed valuable portions of Washoe land, while he continued to regularly harvest timber that belonged to the allotment holders. Asbury explained to the Washoe individuals that in boundary disputes on allotted lands, normal procedure dictated that the allottee pay for a resurvey. He admitted to superiors that he had been apprised of the situation a number of years earlier, but explained it had not been "practicable" for him to investigate. The complaints coming from southern Washoe families, and the lack of response by federal agents, represent a discernible pattern of relations across Washoe country.[32]

In a similar case, a P'a·walu (central Washoe) couple, Spotted and Anna George, expressed their concerns regarding mining damage on their allotted lands. Upon investigation, Asbury noticed that near their allotments one mine had produced considerable wealth. Many non-Washoe miners continued to work the Georges' and neighboring allotments, often finding "good indications" and extracting valuable ore. Superintendent Asbury suggested the Georges "relinquish" their allotments for nothing in return. The agent charged with representing Washoe interests chose to promote the federal assimilative agenda instead of pursuing justice for the Georges. It is likely that there were more exchanges like this one that did not make it into the written record.[33]

While Asbury investigated the Georges' land, he also tracked down the heirs of a deceased allottee, Gemima Maxwell. He provided an affidavit of heirship for her family and then requested relinquishment papers. Asbury described Maxwell's land as mineral rich but claimed the land held "absolutely no value" for Washoe families.[34] Again, Asbury saw no value in mineral-rich lands for Washoe allottees; instead, he believed Maxwell's heirs would benefit more from simply having no land so that they would be completely dependent on American business owners and ranchers. This pattern of behavior makes it absolutely clear that Washoe families had to work extremely hard to protect their lands and to promote their own interests.

Two months after Asbury's request for relinquishments, J. H. Dortch, chief clerk for the Bureau of Indian Affairs (BIA), informed him that relinquishments could not be made without first assigning new lands. Asbury wrote to the commissioner of Indian affairs five days later to explain his request. He argued that no good land could be had for Washoe families and wondered why the bureau wanted him to replace "worthless" land with more "worthless" land. Asbury explained that he had sent in the relinquishments mainly as an "experiment."[35]

While working for relinquishments, Asbury also advised the commissioner that purchasing a reservation for the Washoe "would be a distinct step backward." The creation of a reservation, in Asbury's view, would postpone, if not preclude, the emergence of Washoe self-sufficiency and adaptation. Instead, Asbury advocated small individually owned homes near white ranches where Washoe families could work. Once in their own homes, Washoe families could send their children to public schools, and within the course of a generation or two the Washoes may cease to be "Washoe" entirely.[36]

In 1910 a Washoe man from Welmelti (northern Washoe country), Richard E. Barrington, wrote to Asbury, informing him of his decision not to take up residence on his allotment. He explained that many northern Washoes did not want their allotment lands because they could not make year-round homes there. Instead, they wanted to find land "better fitted for farming." Barrington's letter reveals a Washoe contingent anxious to become farmers and demonstrates the efforts of individuals to re-create themselves in order to survive. Barrington did not mention leaving Washoe country, but he was learning to live on it in a new way. In the years to come, Barrington purchased a lumber mill, amassed a small fortune, testified before the Indian Claims Commission on behalf of the Washoes, and became a respected elder.[37]

A year later Dick Bender, who had accompanied Epesuwa to Washington in 1892, paid to have his allotment resurveyed. Bender's survey turned up evidence of boundary tampering. Most Washoe landholders did not know the exact location of their allotment, and they generally calculated boundaries by landmarks like springs, mountains, trees, or rocky outcroppings. If boundary stakes had been placed during the allotting process, unscrupulous newcomers could move them with impunity.

Bender's surveyor discovered that the original allotment boundaries "had been moved a distance of some thirty rods" so that, conveniently, a strip of good timberlands fell just outside Bender's land. When questioned by the surveyor, Bender's non-Native neighbor claimed the boundaries had been that way when he purchased the land. Asbury determined to write the offending party and warn him of his trespass but told Bender the boundary could not be reestablished without the authority of the surveyor general's office.[38]

Another Washoe man in P'a·walu country, Harry Fillmore, expressed discontent with his allotment. In the summer of 1915 he wrote Asbury, asking if he could trade his allotment for farmland. Fillmore indicated that a Euro-American rancher wanted to make a trade.[39] Asbury informed Fillmore that he could not trade, "owing to the fact that the title is held in trust by the Government and it can only be disposed of by the Department."[40]

Many Nevadans began rallying to the Washoe cause. As early as December 1909, James Finch, secretary to the Nevada governor, had written Nevada senator Francis Newlands on behalf of the Washoes. He reported regular visits by Epesuwa to the governor's office, where he lobbied for better treatment of Washoes. Epesuwa explained to the governor that many had taken to working odd jobs as laborers for whites, and some families "faced starvation." Even in old age, Epesuwa wanted to serve his community. In January 1908, despite infirmities, he began preparing for a second trip to the nation's capital. He claimed that he wanted to seek repayment for guns he claimed Washoe families had loaned Americans during a battle with the Northern Paiutes in 1860. Apparently, many who borrowed the guns died in the initial clash with Numaga, and the weapons were never returned. Epesuwa regularly appealed to Calvin H. Asbury, the new superintendent of the Carson

Indian School, who tried to persuade him not to go. Asbury suggested that the money it would cost for the trip would "keep him [Epesuwa] very comfortable the rest of his life."[41]

The Washoe leader insisted, "He must go." The superintendent informed superiors that the younger Washoe generation would not support a trip. In Asbury's view, the new generation did not "listen to the old man"; they understood they had to "get out [to] earn a $1.00 or 2.00 a day by working on a ranch, instead of sitting around and talking about their fish." Asbury predicted that the younger generation would soon "select a new leader from the young men, who can read and write and understand the new ways." Asbury was referring to the young Washoe students who had been enrolled at the Carson Indian School for the past decade. There is no record of Epesuwa undertaking a second journey. The governor's secretary James Finch urged the federal government to do something, emphasizing what was rapidly becoming a prevalent theme, due in large part to Epesuwa's efforts, that the Washoes had not taken up arms against whites and actually helped them in the confrontation with the Paiutes in 1860. He stressed the fact that the Paiutes enjoyed "two large, fertile reservations," while Washoes held no productive farmland. Finch wondered why such a case of "rank injustice" had not been corrected sooner.[42]

Two years later, in 1911, Nevada congressman E. E. Roberts described the Washoes to Robert Valentine, the commissioner of Indian affairs, as "one of the most worthy Indian Tribes in the United States." Roberts requested immediate action on their behalf.[43]

The saga of Washoe allotments makes it clear that there would be no quick or easy remedy for years of mismanagement, exploitation, dislocation, poverty, and injustice. The episode also illustrates the growing ability of Washoes to express their concerns and frustrations. Many began asking for irrigable land. Many of the younger generation, and in particular graduates of the Carson Indian School, embraced the idea that they could live on their traditional lands in a new way, with farms and ranches. Some of those who had worked for American farmers and ranchers longed for the opportunity to work their own piece of land. Most understood by the early 1900s that there would be no return to a precolonial past. The question became how to move forward. But most important, the history of the pine nut allotments, federal assimilation, and the growth of Henry Rupert proves that despite the federal government's best efforts, Washoes would not collectively abandon their lands or their heritage.

CHAPTER 6
WASHOE COLONIES

> My grandfather used to say in the years to come things are going to change. It isn't going to be like this. You have to learn to get out and live among white people. You have to know their ways.
>
> —Belma Jones, Washoe elder, 1992

Washoe families faced vexing challenges in the early twentieth century. They also encountered new opportunities. Their leaders sought government assistance to facilitate their survival. Federal administrators continued to look for solutions built around assimilation. Like all Native peoples in the rapidly changing American West, the degree of exposure to challenges, opportunities, and federal assimilation practices depended on numerous variables.

Some, like Louisa Keyser, Datsolalee, found entrance into the nascent American Arts and Crafts movement. Keyser and many of her Washoe contemporaries began to supplement their families' incomes by creating curio baskets for an eager tourist market. Discussed later in this chapter, the story of Keyser provides a vivid example of adaptation and cultural continuity. Other Washoes, like Dick Bender and Captain Pete (discussed below), continued to try to work through official federal channels to protect their allotments and to try to gain more land. They had varying degrees of success. By 1917 the cumulative efforts of many individuals led to federal appropriations for the purchase of lands that would become the Washoe colonies. Prior to the creation of colonies, the federal government decided that Washoe allotments could be leased to generate some income from lands that were not farmable.

With respect to the larger question of Washoe survival, federal agents believed a possible solution could be found in the large swath of lands that was marked for irrigation in northern Nevada after 1902. The Carson and Truckee River watersheds became the site for the first great experiment in the federal government's western water-reclamation program. What better solution to the Washoe subsistence problem than exchanging the pine nut allotments for small plots of newly irrigable acres? The effort to remake western lands through massive federally funded irrigation works provides an excellent example of American colonization. The process began with one fundamental supposition: water in the West needed to be improved. Implicit in this idea is the belief that Americans could do better than the first occupants of arid western lands. Washoes and other indigenous peoples of the West would have to move aside while Gilded Age technologies and investments worked to create what historian Donald Worster has labeled a "hydraulic society."[1]

The federal government had been studying the issue of watering the arid West for decades. The first official to systematically map waterways with a plan for the irrigated future was the one-armed Civil War veteran John Wesley Powell. In 1869 he charted the Colorado River from Green River, Wyoming, to the Grand Wash Cliffs, near the Utah and Nevada border. His 1878 *Report on the Lands of the Arid Region of the United States* argued that the dry desert basins of the West could be remade only through massive technological development, but Powell was also a realist. In 1893 he informed those gathered for the Second International Irrigation Congress in Southern California that there would not be enough water to irrigate the West the way investors and boosters might imagine. His considered opinion would not stop developers from trying. The federal government would provide the money, plans, and engineers for the massive irrigation works; they would build the infrastructure, and they would control it.[2]

The National Reclamation Act of 1902 called for a monetary fund supplied by the sale of western public domain lands to be dedicated to irrigation work. Three weeks following the act's passage, the secretary of the interior established the Reclamation Service, renamed the Bureau of Reclamation in 1923. Francis Newlands, a congressman, and later senator from Nevada, played a significant role in getting the act passed. And he wanted the first project to be in his congressional district, of northern Nevada.[3]

The Carson River draws its headwaters from high in the eastern Sierra. The east and west forks converge southeast of Genoa, Nevada. Once joined, the river winds steadily to the north and east across fertile valleys and then alkaline flats, before reaching its terminus in the Carson Sink. For thousands of years, marshlands around the sink area provided homes for small bands of Northern Paiutes. In this mostly arid region, Paiute families depended heavily on the resources provided by the Carson drainage. Much like their Washoe neighbors, they participated in a seasonal cycle, linking their pine nut lands in the Stillwater Range with the broader sink lands. This region, especially the Lahontan Valley, southeast of the Carson Sink, was colonized during the mineral rushes in the second half of the nineteenth century. Powell had identified the Lahontan Valley as a potential site for an irrigation project, and there Carson and Truckee River waters were eventually joined to form a storage reservoir with the potential to irrigate more than 200,000 acres.[4]

In September 1903 work began on the Truckee-Carson project, later called the "Newlands Project," for the politician who promoted it, rather than for Powell, who envisioned it. Engineers diverted Truckee River waters into the Derby Canal east of Reno, Nevada, thereby turning it south to join the Carson. The completion of the Lahontan Dam in 1915 created the reservoir to hold the rivers' mixed waters. The dam cost well over $1 million, and the reservoir can hold almost 300,000 acre-feet of water. By the late twentieth century, the man-made lake was irrigating close to 140,000 acres of land.[5]

As part of the irrigation project, the federal government had appropriated 232,000 acres in Churchill County, ostensibly for the creation and sale of small family farms. Farmers could use the "reclaimed" waters of the Carson and Truckee, and the arid lands of northern

Nevada would be remade. It seemed as if this project could potentially include irrigable plots for Washoe families, and in 1904 the commissioner of Indian affairs suggested just that idea.⁶ It made perfect sense from the federal perspective. The offices of reclamation and Indian affairs both existed within the Department of the Interior; theoretically, the land transfer could have been streamlined with minimum paperwork.⁷

While the plan appealed to government officials, Washoes never seriously considered the land swap. The Lahontan Valley and Churchill County had always been Paiute lands. Seven years later, in 1911, when the second assistant commissioner of Indian affairs, C. F. Hauke, offered the same solution, Indian agent Calvin H. Asbury responded by noting the sentiment of an outspoken P'a·walu: "Spotted George is not willing to take land, and use it, among the Paiutes under the Truckee-Carson project near Fallon, Nevada, and in this he is [representative of all the Washoes]."⁸

During the spring of 1912, Asbury set out to tour Washoe lands. After his trip he reported finding 275 Washoe individuals who worked on ranches but had no homes. Of the 275, Asbury suggested that only 22 needed government rations. He believed that those he termed homeless "would not be benefited by receiving help from the Government." He went so far as to state that "little actual suffering" was taking place. He noted that a petition had been made to the Nevada state legislature for Washoe land appropriations, and he hoped small plots of tillable land would help "properly civilize" Washoe families.⁹

The sum of Asbury's correspondence in the early twentieth century reveals an agent who largely failed to consider the complexities or ramifications involved in the Washoe case. He consistently emphasized the need for Indians to abandon their traditions and embrace American practices, which is exactly what most of his direct supervisors wanted to hear. The suggestion that "little actual suffering" took place represented either a basic misunderstanding of the situation or callous disregard. By the end of the following year, a physician in the region would report that sick Washoe individuals without means were being left to die.

When Asbury suggested more land, he did so with the hope that Washoes would become "proper" Americans. It is a testament to Washoe resiliency that they did not completely surrender an ancestral heritage that compelled them to remain on their lands while the federal government worked to assimilate them. Of course, they had to change to survive; they entered the American wage economy, switched to a new currency, and adopted new clothing, all while learning a new language and new customs and trying to fit into a new culture. Amid all of that change, some found ways to adapt distinctly pre-American practices. By doing so, they contributed to the local and regional economy. In the case of the Washoe basket weavers, they fundamentally shaped the market in Indian wares that stretched from Tahoe to San Francisco and south to Southern California.

Louisa Keyser, also known as Datsolalee, one of the most prolific basket weavers in North America, illustrates this point. Her work directly fueled the local Indian arts market and eventually spread well beyond the eastern Sierra, attracting the interest of wealthy collectors from around the United States. The steel magnate Gotlieb Adam Steiner, from Pennsylvania, purchased a basket considered to be Keyser's masterpiece, named "Beacon Lights," in 1914 for $2,000. The purchase made the news in both Carson City's and San Francisco's newspapers. The *San Francisco Examiner* on April 4, 1914, described the transaction as "the highest price ever paid for a Nevada basket." Two years later, Steiner purchased two more of Keyser's baskets. While reaching a broad collecting audience, Louisa's design innovations simultaneously inspired new generations of weavers across the American West.[10]

Keyser's generally accepted Washoe name is Dabuda. Born sometime around 1844 or 1845 among the Hangaleti, her experiences as a girl and young woman must have been similar to those of many of her contemporaries. She learned to weave by the instruction of older female relatives. During her early life she undoubtedly produced baskets for everyday uses that included food storage, food serving, seed winnowing, and fish traps. However, after the mineral discoveries of 1858 and the succeeding destruction of the area's ecosystems, traditional uses for the baskets decreased. Living in the southern lands near what is today Woodfords, California, it is possible that Dabuda's family worked as domestic hands among various mining camps. In 1888 she married a Washoe man named Charlie Keyser and became Louisa Keyser, the name she preferred until her death in 1915.[11]

By 1895 Louisa had come to the attention of her future patron Abram Cohn. The son of Prussian immigrants, Cohn and his family moved to Carson City, Nevada, in the 1880s. His father opened an emporium on Carson's main street, which Abe managed and eventually took over, renaming it "Cohn's Emporium." While Cohn was interested in Indian art and its ever-growing value among American collectors, it was really his wife, Amy, who took an active role in promoting and marketing the work of Keyser.[12]

Amy Cohn's interest led Abe to dedicate Emporium space to the wares being created by Native artists, mostly women. Louisa quickly became the most important. The timing could not have been better. During the early 1900s, Americans became interested in the "primitive arts" as a component of the Arts and Crafts movement of the late 1800s.

Partially in response to the growing industrialization of American cities, the movement cut across architectural styles, literature, and art in an attempt to recapture and channel what had seemingly been lost by modern society. It generated reverence for a romanticized past, fostering appreciation for a simpler time. Successful middle-class and wealthy American families could demonstrate their material success by featuring folk or Native arts in their homes. It was also during this period that enterprising white women, like Amy Cohn, could find leverage in the public arena by becoming experts and patrons of American Indian art. The historian Margaret Jacobs describes how this allowed these women to "exert a new source of cultural authority and to shape a new vision of womanhood." Louisa found a new way to support her family and ultimately survive through her work for the Cohns, while Amy found opportunity to enter the traditionally male realm of sales and commerce. Together they drove the market in Indian wares in the Tahoe region for a decade, drawing the attention of a national audience.[13]

Around the same time that Keyser became known to the Cohns, Louisa became acquainted with Dr. Simeon Lemuel Lee, a Civil War veteran who had established a medical practice in Washoe territory in 1870. Dr. Lee collected baskets from across the West and kept a detailed inventory. His records reveal the genius of Washoe weavers and their growing ability to create wares for an American market. Some have speculated that Keyser's *nom d'art*, Datsolalee, derived from "Dr. Lee." The *D, S, L,* and *L* from his name, Dr. Simeon Lemuel Lee, became *Datsolalee*. It is possibly true but impossible to prove. *Datsolalee* is also close to the Washoe word that translates as "wide hips," another possible source for her public name. However Keyser came by this name, Amy began to use it with vigor on all of Louisa's pieces.

Once it became clear how talented Keyser was, the Cohns offered her patronage that included a small house next to their own mansion, along with food and health costs for life as long as she promised to weave exclusively for the Emporium. This relationship could be described as exploitative, and it certainly was, but it also afforded Keyser an opportunity to make money and dedicate her energy exclusively to the production of her wares. With this time and support, Keyser created one of the most expansive and impressive basket collections in the world. Widely acknowledged by collectors and scholars alike as the work of true genius, her productions pushed Washoe basketry into a new realm, one that existed at the confluence of tradition and assimilation.

For her baskets Keyser selected all of her own materials. This required an intimate knowledge of plants, growing conditions, and harvesting techniques. She was just as meticulous in her harvesting and preparations as she was in her weaving. One of the advantages of weaving for the Emporium was the exposure Louisa had to baskets coming from neighboring peoples. She was particularly influenced by creations coming from Pomo Indian weavers near the California coast. The Pomo gift basket directly inspired Louisa's creation of a style that would come to be known as the degikup. She adopted the general shape of the Pomo gift basket, with a small flat bottom that grows increasingly larger into a sphere-like shape before culminating in an opening roughly the same size as the small bottom. Keyser began using distinctive designs and some traditional motifs in red and black situated on a white or light background. Observers have noted that as Keyser's baskets age, they "assume a harmonious blending of each hue; the white becomes richly golden, the black shines like polished ebony and the red deepens into a blood ruby tint."[14]

In 1900 Amy brought Louisa to Tahoe City to weave publicly in an attempt to gain more attention. Her work gained significant positive attention, and the next fall she was invited to show at both the Nevada and the California State Fairs. By 1903 Amy and Abe decided to open a small curio shop at Lake Tahoe during the summers, which they named the Bicose. The Bicose functioned until the year Amy died, 1919. Louisa became a well-known fixture in the popular culture of the Tahoe and eastern Sierra region. Amy advertised her work purposefully to appeal to the Arts and Crafts crowd. Toward that end, Amy fabricated a past for Datsolalee, calling her a chief's daughter who had been born in 1835. These two twists on Louisa's biography would appeal to collectors because the role of a chief's daughter elevated her status and cultural capital. The earlier birth date made Datsolalee part of a precolonial past, therefore lending more authenticity to her creations.

With each basket Amy also included an authenticated certificate that included the length of time taken to produce, the basket's age, significant design features, and often explanations of the symbols. Marvin Codhas, the anthropologist most familiar with Keyser's work, has convincingly determined that Amy fabricated most of the descriptions. She would often ascribe meaning to symbols on the baskets that was not accurate. She wanted to make Louisa's work "appear exceptional yet traditional," while also making her "seem as colorful as possible." Amy clearly wanted Keyser to appear "traditional." The fact that she was witnessing a historic transformation in which Keyser and others were adapting traditional practices to help them survive was likely lost on her.[15]

Keyser, certainly the most famous of the Washoe weavers, was not the only one creating magnificent works during this period. Many others, most of whom worked without a patron, also employed their unique skills to generate income for their families while expressing themselves artistically. Among these weavers were Lena Frank Dick,

Maggie Mayo James, and Sarah Jim Mayo. Dr. Lee's basket ledger contained a specimen that he labeled "the gem of the Washoes." A woman he called "Ceese," and whom he identified as Keyser's cousin, had made it. Lee insisted that Ceese's work was as magnificent as her cousin's. He explained that Ceese was "to dot-so-la-lee [sic] what Rafael was to Michael Angelo [sic]. She may not be superior to the former but in no way is she inferior." Lee purchased "the gem of the Washoe" from Cohn for five twenty-dollar gold pieces. "Ceese" is almost certainly Scees Bryant Possock (1858–1918), who was actually Keyser's sister-in-law. Abe Cohn sold many of Possock's baskets, and, similar to Lee, he believed she was one of the best Washoe weavers living during that time.[16] The Washoes strategically adapted; they learned how to function within Gilded Age America to protect their own interests, but it was difficult and they were not always successful. As they fought to survive, the suffering continued.

While Asbury was overlooking dire Washoe situations, a shoe-store owner in Gardnerville, a small town in the Carson Valley, proved more sympathetic. In May 1912 Oley O. Haugner wrote to Asbury on behalf of needy Washoes. Haugner had been working in an unofficial capacity as a distributor of government rations for the Washoes from his store. The spring of 1912 would be difficult, and he told inquiring Washoes that he had only "very limited" funds. Haugner's letter calls into question Asbury's contention of Washoes' well-being, since in previous months many Washoes had come in search of aid.

But now Haugner felt compelled to write about one man in particular, Captain Pete, whom he described as a "good, peaceful, old gentleman." Captain Pete claimed he had been elected to the "chieftainship of the Washoe Indians at Gardnerville" in June 1911. He was well educated, able to read and write English. He consistently argued for the welfare and betterment of his people.[17] Haugner had known Captain Pete for thirty years and said that in the early days when there was "Indian trouble," Captain Pete mediated between parties, and in the words of Haugner he "all ways [sic] done what was right [toward Americans]." Haugner reported that Captain Pete had been in to see him and asked if he "could get [a] little help until he could go up to the lake" for the summer. Captain Pete told Haugner that he was "very hard up," for he had to support a blind wife and two grandchildren.

Captain Pete's assertion that he needed help only until he could get to the lake reveals a survival strategy practiced by many families: they continued to engage in an altered form of their traditional seasonal cycle. Tahoe remained a center. But each year brought further challenges. By 1912 Washoe families faced stringent restrictions. Captain Pete asked Haugner to tell Asbury that whites continually stopped him "from hunting and fishing." Moreover, in what was becoming a common complaint, he said that ranchers continued to "run their sheep over" what land he controlled. Destruction of the Tahoe forests for capital purposes along with overgrazing livestock, owned by newly arrived ranchers, demonstrate that both extractive and settler forms of colonialism were taking a terrible toll on Washoe families by the early 1900s.[18]

Because Captain Pete had been advocating Washoes' concerns, Asbury knew him well and did not share the high opinion of Haugner. A month earlier, in May 1911, the superintendent had written him a terse letter. He reminded Captain Pete that the Washoe people had chosen to take the Pine Nuts instead of farmland. Asbury believed Washoe difficulties represented a problem of their own making. He judged them harshly for electing "to take the worthless land in the Pine Nut Mountains." Asbury held Captain Pete and Washoe elders responsible for influencing younger Washoe individuals in that decision. Asbury concluded by outlining the future policies of the Indian office in limiting its contribution "to the support of any man or family who are in position and able to earn their own way." He advised Washoe individuals that they could not depend on the government for help.[19]

Asbury's pronouncement would not have been news for Washoe families. A litany of letters regarding Washoe destitution attests to the government's repeated failures. On December 11, 1913, Captain Pete and another Washoe elder, sixty-five-year-old Bill Fillmore, visited Haugner. They informed him that the Dangberg family was running sheep on their Pine Nut land every summer, without offering any compensation. Captain Pete had been sick all summer and had no prospect for making a living during the winter. Further compounding the situation, the 1913 pine nut harvest had been dismal, and many families had no food stored. Haugner stated, "It looks very tuff [sic] now."[20] Asbury responded the next day that Captain Pete could pick up three pounds of lard monthly and six pounds of beef weekly for his own use. He advised that the distributor could not increase the rations.[21]

Asbury wrote another letter on the thirteenth to Haugner, explaining his reluctance to grant rations for Captain Pete. He believed it would set a negative precedent and that others would begin calling on the government for supplies. On a more personal note, Asbury described Captain Pete as "naturally lazy" and a "loafer" who "sponged off the other members of the Tribe for his support." He argued that if Captain Pete could hold a job, he might be capable of maintaining his family. With regard to Bill Fillmore, Asbury, who had been reassigned from superintendent to special agent, wanted more details before he would grant any support. Until he received the necessary facts, he could not give "the matter further consideration."[22]

Prior to Euro-American arrival, Washoe families had been able to support themselves; the ethic of generosity bound kinship networks together. The infirm, elderly, and handicapped received support from their community. Colonization disrupted familial support networks, while rendering much of the land unusable; consequently, many began going hungry, particularly those most susceptible.

Hunger and homelessness contributed to increasing cases of Washoe illness. On December 2 a resident of Woodfords, California, Mrs. Merrill, wrote to Asbury, alerting him to a skin illness affecting many Washoe children. The schoolteacher in the district reported a widespread outbreak of a rash, which often led to "larger sores." Mrs. Merrill claimed the epidemic extended beyond the school, as she heard of victims who did not attend school.[23] A week after Merrill's letter, Asbury visited the home of a Washoe woman, Molly Pete, where he observed a boy with the skin disease. Asbury consulted with the visiting physician for the Carson Indian School, Dr. E. T. Krebs, and diagnosed the boy's condition as "impetigo." The agent outlined a treatment program and ordered all afflicted families receive the same.[24]

One week after writing about the outbreak, Mrs. Merrill alerted

Asbury to an orphaned Washoe boy, Leman Miller, who needed clothes and shoes for the winter. Asbury collected clothes for Miller at the Carson Indian School and sent them to Merrill. Unfortunately, the shoes did not fit. Merrill asked if she could exchange them for the right size and closed her letter by informing Asbury that the same evening he visited Molly Pete's home (December 8), one child had died, and it looked as if two more would follow. Mrs. Merrill claimed Washoe families wanted a doctor to visit as soon as possible. In a dismissive response, Asbury suggested the shoes for Miller be given to another child, noting an exchange would "not be convenient" even if he could find the right size. With regard to the child's death and the skin pathogen, Asbury believed the medicine he sent would begin to help, but only if taken "faithfully and according to directions." Asbury claimed to be "familiar with the difficulty of getting Indians to use treatment carefully" and suggested a doctor could do no more than advise people to use their "medicine." On December 13 Dr. Krebs compiled a list of Washoe maladies and identified close to one dozen individuals in "need of medical or surgical services." Krebs revealed the depth of federal neglect when he observed that the most critical among the Washoes had "no means" and consequently were "left to die unattended."[25]

Prior to colonization, Washoe healers effectively cured many health problems. The eastern Sierra environment provided an abundance of medicinal herbs that curers employed with considerable success. Now, many traditional medicinal plants were lost to white development. Moreover, the diseases arising after colonization had not been encountered before, and Washoe doctors did not have experience dealing with them. Krebs pointed out that ailments such as cancer, pneumonia, pleurisy, bronchitis, trachoma, ulcers, dysentery, and pulmonary tuberculosis had become common. A few days prior to writing, Krebs examined a woman who died in "her wickieup [sic] probably from pneumonia or exposure to cold." Krebs's revelations regarding Washoe suffering contradict Asbury's pronouncements. Asbury, the person best positioned to help Washoes, insisted on a strident approach, many times, as in the cases of Bill Fillmore, Leman Miller, and the sick children in the Hangalelti community, with very little personal contact.[26]

Health care was not the only problem confronting Washoes. In the summer of 1913, the issue of Washoe allotments became more complicated. Before Washoes claimed their allotments in 1893, white ranchers grazed their livestock across the Pine Nut Range freely. Following the issuance of allotments, no one considered the subject of grazing. As a result, the Pine Nuts continued to be used, as one federal investigator put it, "under the free help yourself system, first there, first served." As Captain Pete's complaint and the investigator's report evidenced, there was "no control, no guiding hand." Stockmen did whatever they wanted without regard for legal Washoe interests. Unrestricted grazing led to severe vegetation depletion and soil erosion. Illegal overgrazing, mining, lumbering, erosion, and the general disregard for Washoe rights contributed to the mounting Indian frustration and confusion. The persistent efforts of Washoe individuals induced federal agents to search for a quick solution. Asbury wondered if perhaps lease arrangements could be made to generate some income for Washoe families.[27]

The question for the bureaucrats dealing with the Washoes was how Natives would become Americans if they did not reside on and work their land as small farmers. Early on, after passage of the original Dawes Act (1887), problems with allotments had spurred congressional action.

In February 1891, the Dawes Act had been amended to provide for the leasing of allotted land, with the federal government still acting as trustee. Subsequent amendments pertaining to leases approved in 1894, 1897, 1899, and 1900 permitted lands to be leased when the secretary of the interior, under the advice of a field agent, believed it to be in the best interest of the Indians. Old age, disability, or insufficient resources of individuals might justify leasing; in addition, if allottees could not reside on and improve their plots, then the lands might be leased. As time passed, the Washoe allotments appeared to be ideally suited for leasing.[28]

In the summer of 1913, Asbury asked the new commissioner of Indian affairs, Cato Sells, for permission to lease Washoe allotments in toto. He reported widespread grazing across the allotments by "sheep men" owning land in the vicinity. The agent wanted "to make some arrangement" to generate income for the Washoes in return for grazing privileges.[29] After first stating the now familiar refrain that a serious mistake had been made by allotting lands not suited for farming, Sells concurred that an agreement could be brokered between the stockmen and allotment holders so that a reasonable fee could be collected for grazing privileges.[30]

With the commissioner's permission, Asbury began drafting a notice to be posted in the towns of Carson City, Minden, Gardnerville, Genoa, Sheridan, Centerville, Markleeville, Holbrook, Topaz, and Wellington. The notice stated: "The Alloted [sic] Washoe Indian Land situate[d] in the Pine Nut Mountain Range is subject to a leasing privilege for the following uses: grazing of stock, mining and prospecting. Firewood timber may also be purchased under contract." Somewhat after the fact, Asbury also informed residents that any persons using Indian land without permission were guilty of trespass.[31]

The notices quickly attracted attention. On November 26, 1913, Mr. and Mrs. Merrill wrote to Asbury to inquire about leasing Washoe land. The couple had attempted to deal directly with allottees but could not find them, and they noted, "It seems all the Indian land holders are near Carson on a rabbit hunt." Like so many other documents dealing with the Washoes, the Merrills' letter tells more than one story. As late as 1913, when the couple inquired about the land, many Washoe families continued to participate in communal rabbit drives. And because of this, lease negotiations were left for federal agents to conduct without the presence of the allottees.[32]

In December 1913 another interested resident, L. M. Jacobson of Gardnerville, received a letter from Asbury, informing him that he was too late; a deal had been struck between the Pine Nut Stock Growers Association and the federal government on behalf of the Washoes. Asbury formalized the contract between the Washoe allottees and the association on January 1, 1914. The lease allowed the association to graze animals across the Pine Nut allotments for five years, for $1,012.95. Asbury suggested that Jacobson might still be able to join the association and therefore benefit from the lease agreement.[33]

Clearly, leasing the allotments would not provide support for Washoe families to survive independently: the per capita distribution of lease money after the first year amounted to anywhere from $1.80 to $2.40 per person, depending on the amount of acres they held. Collecting payment for the leased lands was difficult. Allottees had to answer a number of questions and hope that their answers matched the federal records. If they did so, their thumbprints were taken and a small check was issued.[34]

Twenty-four years after Washoe allotments had been made, a petition written by Dick Bender highlighted Washoe frustration: "We Washoe Indians ought to have our full rights on our Pinenut land." Bender was illuminating the confusing nature of federal policy. On the one hand, promoters of assimilation and the Dawes Act wanted to cultivate self-sufficiency and capitalistic impulses. On the other hand, the mechanisms of control built into the act mired Indian communities in governmental paternalism; Indian allotment holders did not really own or control their land.[35]

The fifth provision of the Dawes Act required that patents for allotments be kept in trust by the federal government for a twenty-five-year waiting period. Following the waiting period, titles could be granted to the Indian recipients in fee simple, that is, without restriction. As evinced by Bender's statement, it is unlikely that the allotting agent Michael Piggot, or subsequent federal representatives, explained that to Washoe allottees. The fifth provision ostensibly sought to protect Indian lands from eager capitalists who might try to take advantage of Indian property holders. However, it created more problems than it prevented. As years passed, owners and their heirs found they could not trade or sell their land because they did not hold actual title.

Washoe individuals continued to meet and discuss plans for protecting themselves and their land. In 1914 a group of more than twenty individuals sent a petition to the U.S. Congress along with a curio basket to President Woodrow Wilson. The basket, crafted by Sarah Jim Mayo, wife of Captain Pete Mayo and the youngest daughter of Lenúka, the first Captain Jim, took two years to make and portrayed the act of Lenúka securing arms for the whites in their struggle against the

Paiutes in 1860. The basket Sarah created included the woven English phrase

> Nevada and California
> Sarah, I am his daughter
> Captain James, first chief of the Washoe tribe
> This basket is a special curio, 1913.

Unfortunately, no one knows where the basket is today or if it still exists.[36] The petition, which the basket accompanied, called for assistance in procuring family homes with "ground to cultivate." Its authors pointed to the irony that tribes "who were enemies of the whites" were "treated with far greater consideration" than the Washoes, who had befriended them.

Petitioners also complained about their inability to hunt and fish without first obtaining government permits. They wrote, "Being a poor people there are many of us who cannot pay these fines and in consequence must often suffer for want of fresh meat and fish." The petitioners went on: "After many meetings and conferences with our tribesman from all over the State of Nevada, held here in Carson this past winter, and now coming to a close, it was decided that we as a committee should take this method of making an offering to your honorable body, and ask for the better conditions that our race might be perpetuated." The concluding paragraph of the petition referred all future responses to "Captain Pete, Chief of the Washoe Tribe." The petition contained the names of twenty-three Washoes, although fifteen names had only an X next to them. The majority of the petitioners came from P'a·walu (central Washoe) lands. A census done three years later, in 1917, found many petitioners living in Genoa and on H. F. Dangberg ranch lands.[37]

Seven months after the petition had been sent, Captain Pete visited Asbury and asked him to write to Washington, D.C., to inquire about the basket and the petition. Asbury chided Captain Pete on his effort to go over his head. He said that evidently, "[Captain Pete] could handle this matter better than it was being handled; and that if he still thought so, [Asbury] did not care to interfere in the matter." Captain Pete persuaded Asbury to change his mind and write the commissioner on his behalf. But when he did, the agent emphasized his own good work at getting Washoes to assimilate, while casting Pete as a malcontent and ne'er-do-well. Asbury claimed the petition, prepared by some of their "friends," represented "but very few of the Washoe Indians." He then described Captain Pete as "very jealous of his title and honor as chief of the Washoes." Asbury concluded by stating, "I write this letter and submit a copy of the communication (petition), which I received through a friend, who happened to have access to it and without the knowledge of the Indians."[38]

One month after Asbury wrote to the commissioner regarding the petition and the basket, the assistant commissioner of Indian affairs, E. B. Meritt, wrote a letter addressed to Captain Pete et al. He included a copy of a letter from President Wilson to Nevada senator Key Pittman in which the president expressed thanks for the basket. But the letter and basket did not produce the results the petitioners had desired. Wilson acknowledged their "courtesy" and assured the Washoes of his appreciation but said nothing about land or aid. Near the end of his communiqué, Meritt expressed what appears to have been the central point motivating him to write. He reminded Captain Pete that Asbury and other federal officials in Carson City should be consulted in all matters. He assured Pete that Asbury and others had the Washoes' "interests at heart." He concluded, "It would be more advisable for you to conduct matters in which you are interested through the proper officials of the Indian Service." Captain Pete, and other Washoes, after long years of association with the federal government, knew better, and their persistent efforts and the arrival of a new agent would eventually result in further land acquisitions. The lost basket can serve as a metaphor for the federal treatment of Washoes during the early 1900s, but thanks to the persistence of individuals and the community as a whole, things were about to change.[39]

In 1915 Nevada senator Key Pittman proposed land for the Washoes and other "homeless" Nevada Indians. A Democrat, Pittman began his first senatorial term in 1912. Eventually reelected five times, he served as the chairman of the Foreign Relations Committee during the crucial years of World War I.[40] An adamant supporter of President Wilson, Pittman served as a member of the Senate Committee on Indian Affairs during the Sixty-Fourth Congress. While serving on this committee in 1916, Pittman proposed a bill for $100,000 to establish homes for Nevada Indians. Secretary of the Interior Franklin K. Lane supported Pittman's proposal but suggested the amount be substantially less. Domestic budget reductions were prevalent as the United States prepared to enter World War I. Lane thought $15,000 would be enough to set in motion a program aimed at Indian self-reliance. Pittman acquiesced without argument, and 1916 became a landmark year for the Washoes.[41]

Section 13 of the Indian Appropriation Act of 1916 contained $15,000 for the "purpose of procuring home and farm sites, with adequate water rights, and providing agricultural equipment and instruction and other necessary supplies for the nonreservation Indians in the State of Nevada." Section 13 also appropriated an additional $15,000 specifically earmarked for the "purchase of land and water rights for the Washoe Tribe of Indians, the title to which is to be held in the United States for the benefit of said Indians."[42]

To oversee these expenditures, the government appointed the special supervisor Lorenzo Dow Creel. A West Virginia native and former college professor, Creel had begun his government career with the Census Office in 1900. Two years later, he became an agent for the Crow Nation in Montana. In 1907 he assumed the duties of superintendent for the Indian school in Wadsworth, Nevada. Creel then moved to Florida in 1910 to work with the Seminoles.[43]

Once reassigned to Nevada in 1916, Creel received orders on November 16 to meet with the special agent Asbury and Colonel L. A. Dorrington, special agent in charge of the Reno Agency. The three formulated a plan for using the new congressional appropriations. As Creel later recalled, "The peculiar conditions prevailing in Nevada demanded careful study. Land with water rights might be obtained but $30,000 would not go far." Federal agents did not consult tribal members in these initial meetings. They decided to pursue land with water rights, but where that was not possible they would look for land near ranches, conveniently located for Washoe laborers. Thus armed with a plan, Creel set out to find property for the homeless Nevada Indians, including the Washoes.[44]

Creel, Dorrington, and Asbury wanted to provide land for Native families so they could become self-sufficient. The commissioner of Indian affairs, Sells, believed the government had an obligation to protect Indian land. Implicit in Sells's belief was the notion that Indians should become self-sufficient and independent. The Washoe case, similar to many across the West, reveals the contradictory nature of federal policy, which often created a no-win situation. While federal officials promoted self-sufficiency through the acquisition of farming parcels, large portions of Indians' lands were being leased or sold with no plan to replace them. The men assigned to purchase land for the Washoes sought arable land that could be carved into individual settlements, thus hastening the assimilation process. Whether that would happen remained to be seen.[45]

Creel spent the winter of 1916 traveling throughout the Carson Valley. He visited Washoe labor camps situated on various ranches. In a report to the commissioner in March 1917, Creel described how difficult it would be to get good land. After his initial study, Creel wrote that he had "gained enough knowledge of the geographical distribution of the camps in the valley and their relation to the various ranches and the attitude of the whites in regard to the Indians to realize that we were up against a very serious condition in the attempt to purchase land for the Indians of this valley." Creel did not specifically say what made the situation so difficult, but no doubt white ranchers did not want to "compromise" their land base or water rights. Furthermore, the large ranch owners would have been reluctant to see Washoe laborers settle somewhere other than the outskirts of their lands, as they would lose their primary source of labor.[46]

While visiting the principal ranches, Creel conducted a census. He calculated about 260 Washoes living and working on white ranches, the largest number, 72, residing on Dangberg lands. The founder of the Dangberg ranching empire, H. F. Dangberg, had immigrated to the Carson Valley in 1853, from a province in Westphalia, Germany. He made his first land claim in 1856 on the east fork of the Carson River. The generous land policy put in place by the original settlers, the Latter-day Saints, called "the Mormon Law," had been overhauled by a committee of citizens in 1853. The new law was still generous. It allowed single men to claim 320 acres, while married men could acquire up to 640 acres. The claimants had to produce $100 worth of "improvements" within sixty days to gain legal title.[47]

Dangberg's younger brother Hennrich August and his wife, Frederika, joined him in 1858. Together the brothers built one of the largest and most successful ranching businesses in the Carson Valley. The Dangberg enterprise would not have succeeded without Washoe labor. Furthermore, the Dangbergs depended on leasing Pine Nut allotments to graze their stock, therefore doubling their dependency on Washoes and clearly proving the importance of Washoes in the early economy of northern Nevada.[48]

H. F. Dangberg died in 1904. His son Henry Fred, known as Fred, became the managing partner of the recently incorporated H. F. Dangberg Land and Livestock Company. Growing up in one of northern Nevada's most powerful families, Fred Dangberg Jr. enjoyed a high standard of living. Biographers describe him as a hard worker whose actions continue to influence northern Nevada. He helped design and build the town of Minden, Nevada; he served as a Nevada state assemblyman and held two separate terms as a state senator; he sat on numerous boards; and he directed the Federal Land Bank.

Fred Jr. had a taste for the good life. When he traveled, "everything was first class. He would stay in the finest hotels and dine in the best restaurants." He gained a nonresident membership position in the elite Bohemian Club of San Francisco. Still in existence, the club's list of former members includes newspaper magnate William Randolph Hearst and Richard Nixon.[49]

Hoping to purchase a suitable site for the Washoe "colony," Creel approached Fred Jr. Creel referred to potential Washoe lands as "colonies" because they would be strategically located so that residents could work in nearby American communities. It is remarkable that in just seventy-five years, Washoes had gone from encountering small groups of straggling foreign explorers, then small communities of American settler and extractive colonialists, to becoming "colonists" themselves by 1917. Washoes had become foreigners in their own lands. Dangberg expressed his family's desire to build houses in which the Washoes could live as long as they continued to work for the family. Creel viewed the proposal with a critical eye. He reported that Dangberg wanted to place Washoe laborers on a tract where he could "control them." Creel pointed out that Dangberg would permit them to reside there, "as their work and conduct was satisfactory, but would oblige them to vacate such houses as they would build as soon as their services were unsatisfactory." Dangberg's proposal amounted to twentieth-century feudalism, with "employees" holding homes in exchange for labor until their inability or unwillingness to work led to their eviction.[50]

Creel stated that Dangberg's manner "nettled" him as well. After subsequent meetings, Creel decided Dangberg did not have the best interests of Washoes in mind, labeling the rancher "insincere." Nevertheless, he "smoothed over the matter as diplomatically as possible." He realized that not dealing with the Dangbergs would be a problem due to the large number of Washoes living on their lands. Moreover, he recognized that the Dangbergs were well connected throughout northern Nevada; the family was used to getting its way.[51]

The longer Creel dealt with Dangberg, the more frustrated he became. He complained that the family owned or controlled almost all the land and water in the area suitable for Washoe homes. Dangberg, in Creel's view, took an immense amount of pride in the development of Minden, which Creel acknowledged to be "far ahead" of other Nevada towns. The federal agent wondered why Dangberg allowed a "squalid" Washoe "village" adjacent to Minden to detract from an "otherwise beautiful town." He believed that had the Dangbergs wanted to, "by almost a word" they could have provided nice homes or "cottages" for Washoes. At one point, Dangberg offered to trade 80 acres of land for "full control" of all Washoe allotments. Creel labeled the suggestion an "insult." But he did not want to give up. He suggested Colonel Dorrington attempt to "awaken the conscience" of the Dangbergs.[52]

A study of the Douglas County *Book of Deeds* for 1917 reveals Dangberg's willingness to practically give away lands to other parties. During the fall and winter of 1917, the Dangberg Land and Livestock Company sold at least four parcels. On November 27 the company sold

190 acres with water rights to H. Lange for a total of ten dollars. On the same day the Dangbergs sold 836 acres to William Houssman for ten dollars. The deals likely included provisions that did not make it into the deed books, which would explain Dangberg's willingness to sell, but it is clear that when he wanted to, Dangberg would part with lands and water.

The November sales raise the question of why he would not sell to the federal government for the benefit of Washoe families. Part of his reluctance certainly had to do with controlling the Washoes' labor. But Dangberg may also have harbored a personal grudge against the federal government. As early as 1871, the Union Mill and Mining Company, in which future U.S. senator Francis Newlands's father-in-law was the controlling owner, battled H. F. Dangberg and other ranchers in the Carson Valley over Carson River water rights. The ranchers ultimately won the case, but the bitter struggle between Senator Newlands and the Dangbergs continued for decades. In the early twentieth century, the government appropriated water, formerly controlled by the Dangberg family, for the Newlands Project, authored by Newlands. The project allowed irrigation of arid lands in other Nevada counties and later used other rivers to develop agriculture throughout the West.[53]

Creel's letters, while chronicling his struggle to acquire good land, also provided more evidence that many tribal members had combined their traditional ways with wage labor in the American economy. Locating themselves on farms and ranches, many Washoes provided the labor for the profitable businesses to develop. A Washoe elder in the late twentieth century reported, "The Indians were the only laborers [ranchers] had." She went on to describe Washoe laborers as "just like slaves. . . . I think that's what they were." When Creel began inquiring about land, ranch owners felt threatened; they did not want to see any changes in the status quo that had, for many years, afforded them cheap labor.[54]

Creel eventually decided it would be best to ask the Washoe people's advice on such an important matter. He hired an interpreter named Benny James, whom he described as "a very intelligent mixed blood Washoe." James, who came from southern Washoe country, was a forty-nine-year-old leader who had gained renown as a hunting guide at Lake Tahoe. Even with James serving as interpreter, many Washoes chose not to speak to Creel because they associated nothing but bad things with representatives from the government. Those who chose to speak told the agent that no federal official had ever taken the time to ask their opinions. Others expressed fear that Creel "was setting a trap for them." It would take action and deeds to change Washoes' minds, not promises like those broken in the past.[55]

Between trips to the various Washoe camps, Creel visited with other ranch owners, asking them if they would sell any parcels of land. Like the Dangbergs, who found the valley a cattleman's paradise, they proved reluctant to help. Fear over compromising their water rights became a common theme. Ranchers feared "trouble by reason of the Indians' use of the water in an indiscriminate and unregulated manner." This represented a particularly ironic sentiment. The Washoes had lived in the Carson River valley for thousands of years. They dammed and diverted streams when necessary, but there is no evidence that the integrity of the rivers or springs was ever compromised. The land use perpetuated by miners, ranchers, businesses, and the federal government created the water shortage. Newcomers had been worrying about water since first coming to Nevada. In May 1854, a meeting of citizens had passed resolutions providing that no household should be deprived of water and that "when two or more lived on the same stream they should share water according to the number of acres cultivated, each using for alternate days when it is scarce." To the ranchers in the early twentieth century, it was the Washoes who did not know how to conserve resources. The ranchers' projection of their own fears onto the Natives represents a psychology of conquest grounded in twisted perception. Fears of water disputes also could have been a convenient excuse for those who held discriminatory views of Washoes. Whatever the cause, most American ranching families refused to help.[56]

Creel had all but given up his search for centrally located land in the Carson Valley when he met rancher William F. Dressler. Dressler told Creel, "I am anxious to do something for these Indians and I will give you 40 acres of as good land as I have." His offer, however, did not include water rights. Still, Creel accepted immediately and had a deed drawn up and signed. Creel reported, "This land is a deep sandy, clayey loam, intermixed with a few boulders.... We now have a tract of land where the Washoes can at least make a winter camp on their own land."[57] The land sold by Dressler was close to, but not directly on, the Carson River. When Creel and Dressler had surveyed the land, they found a 40-acre tract next to the river, but the owner refused to give up that property. Dressler sold what became the Dresslerville Colony to the United States for ten dollars in gold.[58]

Having concluded his dealings in the Carson Valley, Creel began his return trip to Reno. As he waited at the Minden train station, Dangberg followed him onto the train and "accosted" him. Dangberg led Creel to the empty smoking compartment for more privacy. Still not comfortable, Dangberg again led Creel off the train and out of earshot from passersby. In hushed tones Dangberg stated that he would not consider setting aside home plots for Washoe families. He made a slightly new offer, however, to sell 80 acres of land, at several hundred dollars per acre, if perpetual grazing rights in the Pine Nuts were included.[59]

It is likely that Dangberg had found out about Dressler's donation and wanted to head off the deal or at least provide an alternative closer to his own property. The census conducted by Creel clearly demonstrated that Dangberg relied heavily on Washoe labor. The Dangbergs had a lot to lose if Dressler provided land for the Indians away from the Dangberg ranch. But even with much at stake, Dangberg made demands that the government agent could not meet. It is probable that Dangberg's byzantine maneuvering reflected a realization that this was his last opportunity to try to get money from the federal agent. His biographers reveal a factor that may help explain his behavior: he had a propensity for gambling and drinking. A room on the second floor of the Minden Inn was known for "marathon games" hosted by Fred Jr. Moreover, his gambling had been leading to serious losses since 1912. At the time of his meetings with Creel, he was involved in "a complicated shell game" using company funds to cover his losses, and shortly thereafter the family removed him as manager of the estate.[60]

While refusing the Dangberg offer and securing the Dresslerville land, Creel also purchased land for the Washoes in Reno and Carson City. These lands were easier to acquire, since they did not have the agricultural potential of those in the Carson Valley. Creel bought 156 acres in Carson City near the Carson Indian School for $3,500. In Reno he purchased another 20 acres that would be used by both Washoe and Paiute tribal members. This tract lay on the border between Reno and Sparks, south of the Truckee River. The land, priced at $300 an acre, came with water rights. The deed was acquired in April 1917, and the site subsequently became known as the Reno-Sparks Indian Colony.[61]

After the properties had been acquired, Creel wrote that more needed to be done for Nevada Natives. "When we consider the fact that the homeless Indians of Nevada have received no aid or consideration from the Government aside from this appropriation . . . I believe you will agree with me that the department owes them a debt which should be repaid."[62]

Creel had sought to partially rectify the wrongs inflicted upon the Washoes. His success was limited by the financial parameters set forth by Congress and the uncooperative attitudes of northern Nevada landowners. Using the means available to him, Creel had secured a minute fraction of the Washoes' traditional holdings. It gave them a toehold. Their challenge would be to gain economic viability while living in impoverished circumstances. The task was all the more difficult as they sought to make their way while maintaining elements of their cultural heritage.

CHAPTER 7

PREJUDICE AND PERSISTENCE

> I am the descendant of the Indians who welcomed the first white men who came into this Carson Valley. I sure appreciate the New Deal. Today it seems the Government is coming to realize [it is] about time to talk true.
>
> —Willie Smokey, vice chairman, Washoe Tribe, 1940

The same month the agent Creel made the purchase for the Reno-Sparks Indian Colony, Douglas County commissioners in Minden, Nevada, were dealing with Indian affairs in their own way. On April 5, 1917, the board passed by unanimous vote Ordinance no. 6. Section 1 of the ordinance required all Indians to "leave and be out of the town limits of the towns of Gardnerville and Minden by the hour of 6:30 o'clock P.M., of each and every day." Section 2 listed the punishments for those who might violate the ordinance: a fine up to twenty-five dollars or imprisonment, "not to exceed ten days," or both. And Section 3 made it "the duty of all peace officers of Douglas County, to enforce the provisions of this ordinance."[1]

The county used a high-pitched siren or whistle to signal the approaching hour when Indians had to be out of town. Washoe elder John Dressler recalled, "All of our people that came to town would have to leave at six o'clock when the siren went off on top of the telephone building." Bernice Auchoberry remembered, "When the whistle blew you had to be on your way home." Her father was arrested for violating the ordinance.[2]

In the hyperpatriotic atmosphere leading up to and during World War I, residents of Douglas County viewed Washoes' ethnic, cultural, and social differences as threatening. One year after passage of Ordinance no. 6, in 1918, the Douglas County Council of Defense ordered all Washoes to carry work cards. In terms similar to the post–Civil War Jim Crow laws of the South, the cards stated, "All Indian ranch hands in Douglas County are expected to be employed during the coming haying season. Any Indian who will not work will be presecuted [sic] as a vagrant." White ranch hands did not have to carry work cards. This is a pivotal moment in the process of delegitimizing Washoe people as the rightful first inhabitants of the region. By failing to acknowledge the Washoes' ancestral rights, the growing Euro-American community was simultaneously devaluing their history. This process has only recently begun to slowly turn around, thanks in large part to the tireless efforts of Washoe community members who have worked to remind the larger community that they were there first and that their ancestors had been there for thousands of years.[3]

Amid the swell of patriotism and prejudice, Washoes' first concern never strayed far from physical survival. The methods chosen by many illustrate their determination to cobble together an economic existence that allowed for a continuation of the traditional seasonal cycle, albeit with different modes of existence.

In September 1924 Captain Pete received a contract for $100 to clear eight acres of land on Tahoe's western shore. After one week of long hours, Pete had nearly completed the work. William Johnson, the owner of the land, ordered Pete and his crew to stop and tried to settle for $3 a day, or $26.15. Captain Pete went to the superintendent of the Reno Indian Agency to report the breach of contract. The superintendent ordered Johnson to honor the original agreement and pay the outstanding $73.85. Johnson's attempted breach of contract illustrates a continued lack of respect many newcomers exhibited toward Washoes. This episode also illuminates the growing trend of Washoe families working within the American capitalist system, learning and attempting to claim their rights. Their acceptance of and adaptation to capitalism were tempered by their desire to do so while maintaining a lifestyle in accordance with their old seasonal cycle.

Families sought summer work near their ancestral lake and returned to ranches close to the pine nuts in the fall. Building their lives around seasonal work, while not conducive to advancing capitalistic "careers," nevertheless helped them construct a bridge between the world of their ancestors and twentieth-century America. The circumstances were forced on them, but their choice to respond in a way that maintained tradition demonstrates both necessity and cultural resiliency. The circumstances were far from ideal. In choosing to maintain a livelihood of their making in the eastern Sierra, many continued to suffer the effects of economic hardship.[4]

One Washoe elder, Belma Jones, who was born in 1912, recalled as a child spending "every summer" at Lake Tahoe. In early spring her father set out to fish various runs on his way to the lake. Spring trout catches and subsequent feasts became extensions of precolonial ceremonies, marking the season when things are reborn. Jones remembered the celebrations fondly and said that families participated "whenever [they] could."

With the mining and logging industries in steep decline, Lake Tahoe had become a seasonal destination for tourists; resorts emerged to serve the growing number of summer visitors. With the Comstock's ore depleted and the Tahoe basin mostly clear-cut, title to the cutover lands could be acquired cheap, often just by paying back taxes. Entrepreneurs began taking advantage of the inexpensive land. Resorts on lakeshore property sprang up along with second-growth forests. Owned and operated by non-Washoes, these early resorts provided employment opportunities that allowed Washoe families to return to Tahoe during the summer. Although forbidden to trespass in some areas claimed by Americans, Washoes made camps as close to their traditional lake homes as possible. The Jones family, because they were Hangaleltiʔ (southerners), summered on the south shore, near a place Americans called "Bijou," meaning "gem" or "jewel" in French. Bijou had been an important Washoe summer site, marked by a large number of grinding stones, revealing the numbers of families that had summer homes there. It had also served as a trailhead for a major pathway leading to the Carson Valley. During the height of the Comstock era, it became a way station, with a railway pier built out into the water to allow trains to dump timber so barges could haul it to sawmills on the east shore. At Bijou Jones's mother worked as a laundress, while her father tended cattle. Her uncles and other male relatives also often found work by supplying firewood to resorts.[5]

Children, according to Jones, enjoyed the freedom to hike, swim, and play games. Families picked wild strawberries, which they mixed with fresh cream when they could afford it. "We just had a good time because there were other families there," she said. "So that's what we did during the summers, we just had a wonderful time." In the fall the Jones family returned to the Carson Valley. Jones's recollections reveal aspects of the generation of Washoes born after the devastating first wave of colonization. Her grandparents and parents did not burden her excessively with the pain and sorrow of their lost way of life, instead perpetuating as much of it as they were able.[6]

Another Washoe elder, Winona James, born in 1903, also remembered annual trips to Tahoe. Her family left Carson Valley near the first of June and returned at the beginning of September. Her family "made that [trip] every year." Like Jones, James remembered her grandfather going to the streams and lake to fish, while "Grandma made baskets and sold them." James explained that as autumn drew near, her family "had to get ready to get pine nuts," and by September 1 they would be returning to the Carson Valley.[7]

The grandson of Frederick Dressler, the American who had sold the land for Washoe homes in the Carson Valley in 1917, also recounted the seasonal nature of Washoe work. During the fall months, he recalled, the Washoes who worked for his family left for the Pine Nuts, where they stayed for about a month. They took horse-drawn wagons and loaded them with nuts, some of which they sold at market. According to Dressler, American ranching families missed their Washoe help during the fall, but they had become accustomed to the seasonal rounds. Bernice Auchoberry, born in 1914, explained, "We always went out every fall, every September, and we'd go out and gather nuts. We'd get enough for the winter."[8]

Washoes' adaptation to American society provides a microcosmic example of what was happening across the American West as Indian communities struggled to survive. Native people and their traditions were changing, not disappearing.

In the words of a Lakota elder from South Dakota, Olney Runs After, whose Cheyenne River community had "survived the programs designed to kill it," "We Indians will be Indians all our lives, we never will be white men. We can talk and work and go to school like the white people but we're still Indians."[9]

In Nevada during the early 1920s, Indian agent Lorenzo Creel believed the Washoes had adapted to the colonized world. In his view, the Washoes had shown promising initiative by fencing their lands and building a serviceable well. Still, the relationship between the Washoes and the federal government perplexed many observers. The Nevada Superintendency lacked the necessary funds to assist its charges or to care for the indigent. Agent Creel claimed he did not have "a cent" to aid the recently established Nevada colonies; he believed the success of the Washoe colony was "assured without any further government aid," but he noted that funds would be helpful.

In 1922 Creel announced the works of Baptist missionaries, who had been in the area a number of years. Creel mentioned that an "active and energetic superintendent" headed the group. The missionaries bought five acres adjacent to the Washoe colony and built a community center, including a classroom. They did not limit their work in Nevada to the Washoes; they took up work among the Paiutes and Shoshones in distant sites as well: Battle Mountain, Elko, and Winnemucca. In October 1922 the Baptists opened a school specifically for Washoe children. Creel viewed their school as more efficient than the federal boarding school. He predicted that it would usher in a "new era in the life of the heretofore much neglected Washoe Indian." The missionaries maintained a presence in the Washoe community, advocating for the tribe. They had little success in assisting the Washoes in their economic struggles, but their spiritual efforts gained converts, and the Baptist religion remained one of the prevalent Christian religions among tribal members throughout the twentieth century.[10]

In May 1922 the superintendent for the Reno Indian Agency, James E. Jenkins, questioned and pressured Creel about the Washoe land-purchase appropriations. Creel attempted to placate the skeptical Jenkins with assurances of Washoe success. Throughout Creel's time as special agent in Washoe country, he maintained an even-keeled temperament. Even when Dangberg pushed a hard bargain, Creel seems to have kept his cool. Therefore, one particular letter to Jenkins exposes the level of his frustration with Jenkins's prying. In previous correspondence Jenkins had asked him to either finish the original plans for Dresslerville by turning it into a workable farm and ranch or "dispose of all property." The thought of liquidating the property struck Creel as nothing less than a "calamity." Creel reminded him that aside from a very few destitute elders, not one Washoe individual received "a penny" from what he termed the "great government of the U.S." Creel emphasized the fact that the Washoes had survived "through their own efforts."

For Jenkins, the assimilation of Washoes was not taking place fast enough. Jenkins had a long history of service in Indian affairs. He had been a special agent assigned to the Red Cloud Agency on Pine Ridge in 1900, and three years later he supervised the removal of the Cupeño Indians in Southern California. He brought with him to the Reno Superintendency a strong desire to stamp out Indian culture. He believed that Indians would "never become civilized as long as they" continued to "follow old customs harmful to their advancement." He tried to end the Washoe girls' puberty ceremony. He deemed Washoe treks into their sacred Pine Nut Lands for harvesting disruptive to their children's development. He tried to outlaw traditional hand games along with the practices of Washoe shamans. Jenkins's assault on Washoe traditions provides evidence that these practices continued; they were not abandoning their traditions as they adapted to the American market. But it also proves that those who wanted to continue Washoe customs would face significant obstacles. Agents like Jenkins represented the intellectual component of colonization that when activated became physical. His assumption was that Washoe traditions were bad. They kept Washoes from becoming fully American. The need to turn them into full Americans demonstrates a belief on his part that being Washoe, or Washoe American, was not good enough. Whether altruistic or evilly intentioned, Jenkins served an American colonial agenda that wanted to see Washoe people disappear.[11]

Meanwhile, poverty and sickness plagued Washoes throughout the 1920s. The land purchase of 1917 had not been a panacea, and the Citizenship Act of 1924, which made citizens of all American Indians, further complicated their relationship with federal officials. The shoe-store owner Oley O. Haugner continued to remind federal officials of their duty to Washoes. Responding to Haugner in December 1924, Jenkins acknowledged that ranching profits in northern Nevada had been down and that a "large number of able-bodied Washoes" could not find work. In what Jenkins saw as a monumental turn of events, he claimed that the Citizenship Act had absolved the federal government from the bulk of their responsibilities to the Washoes. To illustrate this point, Jenkins explained how he had to pay sixty dollars of his own money because during a flu epidemic twelve Washoe children had been treated at five dollars a visit—fees the General Accounting Office would not pay. Jenkins instructed Washoe individuals and concerned neighbors to petition counties or Nevada state officials for aid. Five years earlier, the ever-changing and confusing federal agenda had prompted the governor of Nevada to demand an explanation regarding the "exact relations existing between the tribe and the Indian Service." Governor Emmet Boyle, at that time, emphasized his interest in assisting the tribe, "partly as a sentimental recognition of valuable services rendered by the Washoes in the early days of this state, and partly because of the apparently superior character of the members of this tribe." Now his concern would be echoed, as confusion over the new act would be widespread. In the end, the providing clause of the act, which guaranteed continued federal protection of Indian property and legal rights, was used to maintain assistance to the tribes, including what little help Washoes were being afforded.[12]

With regard to the assimilation of Native children, despite all the frustration and confusion in Nevada, the federal school at Carson continued its work. The approach to integrating Indians into American society had always contained a gender-specific component: boys received agricultural training or practical skills such as blacksmithing, while girls attended courses in the arts of American domesticity. The nature of education had been articulated clearly by the commissioner of Indian affairs John Oberly as early as 1888, one year after passage of the Dawes Act. He envisioned campuses where buildings could be converted into mock homes where Indian girls could learn how to "cook, to wash, to make and mend clothes, to sweep, to make beds—in short, [girls] could be instructed in all things that are taught to white girls in homes of civilized communities."[13]

Instead of building "homes" on school grounds, Carson Indian School administrators began an "outing" program, sending pupils to white homes. Initially, they sent students to live with nearby Nevada families. Influential non-Native families often wrote to the school's superintendent, asking for live-in Indian help. Their letters expose the quid pro quo nature of the developing outing program, which in its earliest stages included both males and females.

As early as 1911, one inquirer, Mr. Flanigan, wrote to the superintendent C. H. Asbury, asking for a "good steady Indian boy" who could care for livestock and "milk a cow." In a response to another inquiry, Asbury explained that "more experienced girls" required more than $12.50 per month, but informed a Mr. Atherton that he could secure a "bright young girl" for that price, although $16 a month would secure one of the "better girls."[14] In April 1914 Jesse B. Mortsolf, the new superintendent of Carson Indian School, wrote to the commissioner of Indian affairs, describing the nature of outing work. Mortsolf expressed disappointment with the treatment Stewart pupils had received from families in Nevada and justified the need to send girls to California, where they would enter the "best" homes and encounter "elevating influences." In 1913 twenty-five girls went to California, mostly Oakland and Berkeley, accompanied by a Carson matron. Although Mortsolf found that after 1913 many of the girls did not want to return to California, the Berkeley and Oakland programs continued.[15]

Although girls had been sent to the Bay Area for several years, the Berkeley "outing" center, overseen by the "outing matron," was officially established in 1916. By 1925 the number of girls working in California had risen to one hundred; some of these girls lived there year-round and attended public schools. In 1926 Frederick Snyder, now superintendent at Carson, offered a frank appraisal of the outing practice, informing the commissioner that parents of Carson pupils strongly opposed the practice of sending their children to California. He suggested that only "tact and persuasion" had allowed the outing program to continue. As evidence the superintendent sent along a letter from one pupil's guardian, asking why her cousin Aggie Gilbert was not at Carson, "where she should be." She reminded the superintendent of Aggie's young age and could see no reason Aggie would be so far from home.[16]

Both Belma Jones and Winona James attended the Carson Indian School, and their divergent experiences represent the complex reality of children trying to link the worlds of their families and twentieth-century America. Jones recalled Stewart as a place she could escape Euro-American prejudice against Indians. At school "we were all Indians so we didn't go through that prejudice." Jones remembered being sent to Berkeley, and she had heard from other girls that "some of the [host] families were terrible they were like slave drivers." But Jones never encountered a family like that, and she generally liked school; she eventually transferred to the boarding school at Riverside, California, and completed high school.[17]

Winona James, on the other hand, did not like the American school. Her grandmother did not want her to go, and she hid from those who searched Washoe country for Indian pupils. James's sister and brother went to Stewart before her; eventually, her sister entered the outing program and lived with a family in California. When James finally entered Stewart, she did not like it at all. Instead of sending her back for a second year, James's grandparents kept her in hiding.[18]

The overall effects of the vigorous era of forced assimilation, best characterized by the Dawes Act and schools like Stewart, received national attention in 1928 when the Brookings Institution published a report, *The Problem of Indian Administration*. Also known as the "Meriam Report," after the main author, Lewis Meriam, the comprehensive document offered a scathing indictment of federal Indian policy up to 1928. It adjudged allotment a "dismal failure." In the view of the authors, the act succeeded only in further alienating Indians from the American system. And they roundly condemned the educational philosophy that removed Indian children from their homes.

Indians did not need a report to tell them that federal policies had failed. From 1887 to 1934, Indian landholdings would shrink by more than ninety million acres. Although the Hoover administration commissioned the report, by the time the recommendations reached the Indian Affairs Office, it was too late. Soon a nationwide depression gripped the United States, and Hoover lost his reelection bid to Franklin Roosevelt.[19]

Roosevelt appointed Harold Ickes as secretary of the interior in 1932, and Ickes made John Collier the commissioner of Indian affairs. In the early 1920s, Collier had assisted Pueblo Indians in creating the All-Pueblo Council that, among other actions, blocked a U.S. Senate bill that would have assigned water and land jurisdiction to state courts that typically favored white claims over Indian rights. Collier also collaborated with other wealthy Americans sympathetic to Indian causes and formed the American Indian Defense Association. As the executive secretary for AIDA, Collier traveled between the nation's capital and reservations in efforts to help protect Indian lands. As Indian commissioner, Collier would work to help preserve Indian cultures, while simultaneously asking them to adopt new governments, modeled on the American constitutional system. Well intended, he nevertheless continued a paternalistic and at times heavy-handed federal policy, which alienated many in Indian country. Nevertheless, he hired or advanced the careers of Indians within the Bureau of Indian Affairs and, taking advantage of the building inertia toward social welfare generated by FDR's New Deal policies, began directing money toward Indian land-development projects. In 1934 Collier, along with a skilled set of advisors, drew up a sweeping bill aimed at overhauling federal Indian administration, the Indian Reorganization Act.[20]

The bill as originally conceptualized called for the creation of tribal governments. It also addressed the need for federal employment of qualified Indians. The proposed bill further recommended that schools begin developing an Indian-centered curriculum and suggested unsold surplus allotment lands be restored to community ownership. The bill embodied Collier's vision of a wholesale reorganization of the Indian Bureau. In his view, it would work to undo "a century of mismanagement and mistaken policies" that squandered Indian resources and, in many cases, left them completely dependent on the federal government.[21]

Although Congress reduced the bill, the key provisions survived: allotment ended, surplus lands were consolidated, tribes gained the authority to issue and review leases, and communities could set up constitutional governments. An important stipulation of the act required each tribe to hold a referendum on the IRA.[22]

Acknowledgment of Indian agency and adaptability during the early twentieth century provides a context for understanding why many communities accepted Collier's IRA. In the Washoe case, calling to mind their attempts to bridge the distance between tradition and twentieth-century America helps with that explanation.[23]

On the first of November 1934, the superintendent of the Carson Indian School, Alida Bowler, wrote to Collier, inquiring about the process of the IRA referendum among Nevada Indians who did not live on a major reservation. Bowler, a personal friend of Collier's and a member of the American Indian Defense Association, worried that she would have to organize and conduct separate elections across all the "forlorn Indian colonies in Nevada." She expressed particular skepticism regarding her ability to "get all of the scattered Washoes to vote."[24]

Collier's assistant commissioner, William Zimmerman Jr., responded to Bowler, emphasizing that all those who lived on colony lands were entitled to vote. He implicitly suggested that Bowler would need to organize an election for each colony. Zimmerman told Bowler to emphasize Section 1 of the act, which prohibited further land allotments, a bane to many tribes. This demonstrates both Collier's desire for local superintendents and agents to make a hard sell of the IRA and the bureau's unfamiliarity with the Washoes, who had no reason to dislike the allotting process—which had helped them gain their sacred Pine Nut Lands. In the end, Zimmerman asked Bowler to focus most of her attention on large reservations like the Paiutes' Pyramid Lake.[25]

In February 1935 communities across Nevada met separately to discuss the process and prospects for self-government contained in the IRA. Nearly all Washoe adults at Dresslerville attended the conference. John Holst, the supervisor in charge, came away from the meeting believing that most looked favorably on the IRA. The Reno colony provided a distinct challenge due to the presence of both Paiute and Washoe families. Holst described the Reno conference as anything but "harmonious." Many at Reno doubted that a council could be formed that might represent the interests of both groups. The meeting ended with a discussion of dividing the council equally between the two, and Holst optimistically hoped for "more cooperation between the tribal groups."[26]

June 10, 1935, found 100 or so Washoes gathered at the Dresslerville colony in good spirits. Colony residents and nonresidents had voted on whether to accept the IRA. Many had participated the night before in an all-night dance and had taken part in sporting events, including a small rodeo, throughout the day. As dusk began to fall and barbecues burned, Bowler gathered everyone together to announce the results of the referendum. The people cheered as the announcement revealed that those Washoes who had voted approved the IRA by a vote of 104 to 1. They would now become the federally recognized Washoe Tribe.

In a letter to the commissioner, Collier, written the day after the referendum, Bowler triumphantly reported, "All of their principal men and women were delighted with the results and felt proud of the showing they had made." Bowler described a level of enthusiasm among the Washoes that motivated her not to exclude anyone who wanted to vote on the "new deal." One elder, close to seventy years old, walked a distance of thirty miles to vote. The woman led Bowler to understand that she was descended from one of the "old chiefs," and the superintendent noted that the unnamed woman had a deep love for the Carson Valley, describing it as the "place where she belongs." Clearly, this elder believed a vote for the IRA would help the Washoes remain in their homeland.[27]

The vote in favor of the IRA is controversial today. Some see the vote as an act against Washoe traditions and point out that only a small number of Washoes actually voted. Others believe it was the best of limited choices available to them. But at the time, tribal leaders thought it was a necessary and valuable step forward. In the preceding half century, it had taken herculean efforts by leaders and community members to get their voices heard and their concerns addressed. The decision of those who voted to accept the IRA represents a desire to control their own destiny and protect their remaining landholdings.

When juxtaposed with communities who gained reservations in the nineteenth century, it becomes clear that there can be no "one-size-fits-all" analysis of the IRA. Large Plains communities such as the Crows, who gained a reservation in the early 1800s, had had more time to set up a formal body of leadership to represent their interests in the federal and state arenas. By the time Collier proposed the IRA, the Crows had already become comfortable with their new form of government and did not want to see yet another change imposed by outsiders. The Crows ultimately rejected Collier's act. Their refusal can be used as a counterbalance for understanding Washoe acceptance. Unlike the Crows, the Washoes had much to gain by accepting the IRA, most important a tribal government with regular access to federal officials.[28]

On January 24, 1936, the secretary of the interior approved the Washoe Constitution, which stipulated that four council members would be elected to represent Washoes living on the colony, while three members would serve for "scattered," or off-colony, members. Hank Pete was among those elected to represent noncolony Washoe. At one of the first Washoe Tribal Council meetings in 1936, Ray Fillmore gained the first chairmanship position, Willie Smokey became vice chairman, and Roma James was selected secretary-treasurer. The council spent much of their first year organizing and outlining the duties of the new government.[29]

But questions remained about how the new council would function and how much power they would actually have. These questions would slowly be answered over the decades that followed, but almost immediately a sticky legal question emerged. Were the Washoe colonies actually "Indian country" in the legal sense of the word? Were they like the neighboring Pyramid Lake reservation to the north or something else?

A court case brought the question into focus, and a Supreme Court ruling decided the issue.

In the mid-1930s three Washoe individuals used their automobiles to transport liquor onto the Reno-Sparks Indian Colony. Federal officials filed suits in order to confiscate the automobiles used to transport the alcohol. They argued for forfeiture of the cars because it was illegal under federal law to traffic intoxicants in "Indian country." The case that followed orbited around the question of whether the colony constituted "Indian country" in a legal sense of the phrase.

In 1936 the federal district court in Nevada dismissed the suits, ruling the colony was not "Indian country" and therefore not subject to federal law. Federal officials appealed the case, and the Ninth Circuit Court of Appeals upheld the district court ruling.

The case went before the U.S. Supreme Court, and on January 3, 1938, the High Court ruled that the colony was in fact "Indian country." The justices reasoned that the Reno colony had been "validly set apart for the use of the Indians." Furthermore, the Indians had a long-standing relationship with the federal government, and therefore "it is not reasonably possible to draw any distinction between this Indian 'colony' and 'Indian country.'" The two previous rulings were overturned, and no question remained that the Washoe colonies from that point forward would be no different from other federally recognized reservations. While the courts wrestled with the legal complexities of the Washoe colonies, the infant Washoe Tribal Council had challenges of their own.

In the spring of 1937, the council turned its attention to critical and often divisive community issues. Among their concerns were ongoing health problems, alcohol abuse, land development, money management, and the maintenance of Pine Nut allotments. Another topic that garnered interest inside and outside the tribal lands quickly took up a large portion of the council's time. On April 5, 1937, Hank Pete addressed the council with regard to "Indian herb medicine," peyote (*Lophophora williamsii*). Pete described peyote as a "dangerous" herb that could prove "very injurious." He suggested the council take action to prevent the spread of peyote among the Washoes. The vice chairman,

Smokey, responded by describing peyote as "harmless" and reminded the council of religious freedoms guaranteed by the U.S. Constitution. He hoped Washoes would not become divided over the issue. He would be disappointed.[30]

The battle over peyote had begun with its earliest introduction among Washoes. The first known peyote meeting in Washoe country had taken place in 1932 under the guidance of Raymond Lone Bear (Ralph Kochampanaskin), a Ute man married to a Washoe woman, who had learned the Peyote Way while living for many years on the plains. The new faith lost its following in large part due to Lone Bear's struggle with alcohol, which landed him in jail more than once. Discredited, Lone Bear stopped holding meetings. For a brief period, it looked as if the Peyote religion would disappear from Washoe lands. Then in the fall of 1936, a southern Washoe man, Ben Lancaster, returned home after twenty years in the East. Lancaster had been introduced to peyote by Comanche friends in 1921 while working as a ranch hand in Oklahoma.[31]

From time immemorial, the use of peyote in religious ceremonies had been common in parts of the Americas, notably Mexico and South America. The low-lying cactus plant grows abundantly in northern Mexico and in a small section of Texas. The tops of the peyote cactus, referred to as "buttons," contain alkaloids, including mescaline, which when taken orally can induce altered states of consciousness. Ironically, modern transportation facilitated the spread of the ancient practice. In the late nineteenth century, the emergence of interconnected rail lines in the West allowed for peyote to move farther among North American Indian communities. By 1881 two railways passing through Laredo, Texas, provided for the regular distribution of peyote. The rail line heading north out of Laredo led directly to Indian Territory, or what would become Oklahoma, a burgeoning nexus of communication for Native communities across the West.[32]

The ritual use of peyote, as it emerged in North America, centered on all-night prayer meetings in which participants ingested peyote for the purpose of cleansing and healing. Practitioners then and now believe that peyote provides a link between adherents and a Supreme

Being. Many followers of the Peyote Way describe all-night rituals as extremely difficult. The bitter taste and nauseating affects of the herb, often accompanied by depression or periods of isolated introspection, can create anxiety.[33]

In addition to the physical reaction to the plant, psychological stress may have been caused because Washoe followers of the Peyote Way were struggling against tradition and Christian missionaries. As a peyote movement developed in Washoe country, adherents began questioning and eventually dismissing the shamanistic concept of power. Instead of a neutral universal force, for them, all power existed within the sacred herb. Practitioners became instruments of peyote's will in the words of one peyotist: "We don't talk about power like them old doctors do. We just say the medicine. The medicine is greater than any of them other things because it was here before any of them."[34]

A significant variation in the ritual occurring among the Washoes involved the role of women. Many communities forbade women from attending or participating in the sacrament, but the Washoes reserved "places of honor" for female participants. Eventually, the ritual developed so that the road chief, or ceremonial leader, could be assisted by his wife or another female relative. She would be in charge of bringing water to participants at midnight and breakfast in the morning, both of which she had to pray over, "for it to hold up the life of the people."[35]

Another variation with the Washoe Peyote Way had to do with songs. Plains communities usually adhered to a regimen of four songs per session, the opening, midnight, morning, and closing. Among the Washoes, because the practice was so new, individuals could sing any song they knew. One follower commented, "A song just ain't to play with. It's for a reason. It comes out of the mind. If you got good thoughts that song comes out of your body clear and strong. . . . [I]t's like praying . . . like the cedar smoke. . . . All the songs we sing in this church here is good."[36]

Members of the fledgling Peyote Church followed strict tenets that often included adherence to some traditional cultural values combined with the avoidance of alcohol. Many Washoe peyotists made it a point to demonstrate that since their adoption of the Peyote Way, they abstained from drinking in order to "just live quiet and do what we think is right.... We want to be strong in mind and body like them old Indians a long time ago."[37]

The emergence of the Peyote Church in North America represents a phenomenon scholars refer to as "pan-Indianism," a movement linking distant individuals from diverse cultures. One Washoe practitioner expressed it as follows: "Every minute, someplace in the world, there is some members holding meetings. That keeps the connection going.... If we do it right ... if we sing and pray good and keep our ideas on the medicine, it connects us with all them other Indians singing and praying all them other places."[38]

While peyote linked disparate communities across great distances, it had the opposite effect among the Washoes. Divisions quickly emerged because the new form of worship challenged traditional forms of religion and leadership roles. Simultaneously, a number of Washoes had embraced a form of Christianity taught by the Baptist school and the Carson Indian School. The growing divide surfaces repeatedly in tribal council minutes and agency correspondence from the 1930s. The same year Ben Lancaster had returned to Washoe country, the superintendent Bowler wrote to E. A. Farrow, the superintendent of the Paiute Indian Agency in Cedar City, Utah, asking for information on peyote. She complained that in her estimation, Lancaster "cloaked [all] his activities with religious rituals."[39]

Farrow responded by expressing sorrow that peyote had made it to the Washoes, although he had expected it would, given the rapid spread he witnessed at his agency. He sent Bowler an informational pamphlet on the "drug" and offered some personal observations. Most grievous from his perspective: "A" students became "apathetic," "uninterested," and unable to work. But Farrow reminded Bowler that the constitutional freedoms granted religious worship in the United States applied to the Peyote Church. He compared peyote to the use of wine in Christian services, noting that problems occurred from the amounts used. "The use of wine in the sacrament is not in large quantities. If the same limitations were placed on Peyote, no objections could be made." In acknowledging receipt of Farrow's letter, Bowler agreed that as a closely moderated religious sacrament, peyote posed no threat. But she sensed among the Washoes a practice that resembled more a "profitable 'racket' than a religious movement."[40]

Bowler's suspicions may have increased when she discovered that in the years before his return, Lancaster had taken the name Chief Grey Horse and traveled across the United States selling "Chief Grey Horse's Indian Herbs—a Natural Laxative." Edgar Siskin, a Yale anthropologist who studied peyote use among the Washoes, came to believe after numerous interviews that the desire for personal gain reached an "exaggerated emphasis with Lancaster." Omer Stewart, also an anthropologist, supposed Lancaster exploited his followers, although he refused to label Lancaster "irreligious or insincere."[41]

In April 1937 a group of twelve Washoes sent Bowler a petition, which began, "We the undersigned do not want Peyote meetings held around here, or among our people." The petition stated that the "grandfathers and grandmothers" believed the use of peyote to be a "bad habit." The petitioners further stated that if the meetings continued, Washoe families would become enemies. Bowler's research on the herb and its ritual use allowed her to assure the petitioners that peyote was not habit forming. She explained that no federal law prohibiting the use of peyote existed. Moreover, she told them that many Native communities across the country practiced the peyote faith, some of whom belonged to Christian churches, thus making it difficult to forbid its use.[42]

Though Bowler could do nothing aside from encouraging the petitioners, they would not have to wait long for Lancaster's movement to be disrupted. Initial Washoe adherents found in peyote a potential cure for illness, an ally in the battle against intoxicating liquors, and a chance to define an Indian-centered religion, but soon alleged sexual indiscretions raised suspicions about Lancaster. Reports led Bowler to believe that Lancaster might have been "spiking" his followers' sacrament. Although there is no record of the results, in August 1938 Bowler wrote to Washington, D.C., asking for a chemical analysis of "some powder" taken from Lancaster.[43]

Tribal chairman Ray Fillmore offered this account of Lancaster: "In the second year Ben started fooling around at the meetings. He told people to have a good time, to get acquainted, to be sociable. Ben himself went in for it. He had many wives—young girls. . . . That's why most of the people in Dresslerville didn't want Ben to hold meetings there." By 1938 the form of peyotism introduced by Lancaster had largely disappeared. According to Stewart, only one family continued his version of the practice.[44]

Despite the controversy surrounding Lancaster, a contingent chose to continue building and shaping the new religion. The anthropologist who has worked the most with the Washoes, Warren d'Azevedo, describes a cohesion among those who sought to continue. They saw their religion as the best solution to poverty and difficult living conditions. In their faith they sought to reestablish the "positive values" of their pre-American past. Practitioners viewed this as a "collective endeavor, a helping of one another and a unity with nature." In the words of one post-Lancaster practitioner, "Maybe the Peyote is trying to show me, the people should not be afraid of old Indian ways. Maybe the medicine changes all that and turns it into good. Everything depends on keeping straight with the medicine."[45]

The prolonged battle over peyote, while difficult and contentious to those involved at the time, can be viewed with the benefit of hindsight as the birth of twentieth-century Washoe governance. The new government was not perfect, and some Washoes would never accept a government so different from tradition. But it is once again a testament to the strength of Washoe people that they rolled up their sleeves and went to work. Plagued by the difficulties emerging from the peyote faith, as juxtaposed with the weakening of shamanistic practices and the burgeoning strength of the Christian religion as well as the acute effects of poverty and ongoing efforts to maintain traditional culture, the people struggled to move forward. While some would continue to look with skepticism, if not hostility, toward this new colonial government, tribal leaders at the time strongly believed the IRA had dramatically furthered their political interests.

Christmas Eve 1938 found Washoe Tribal chairman Ray Fillmore in an optimistic mood as he wrote to the commissioner of Indian affairs, John Collier. His letter began by stating that the IRA "has given back to us the right to help and plan our own affairs." He and the community had much to be happy about. In particular, they could celebrate the recent acquisition of more than 600 acres of irrigable farmland. The land had been purchased on behalf of the Washoes by the federal government in accordance with Section 5 of the Indian Reorganization Act. The community gained title to the two properties the following spring, in March 1938. The first purchase, the Heidtman property, consisted of 404 acres, and the second, the Faletti Ranch, contained 200 acres. Situated next to Dresslerville on the east fork of the Carson River, the ranches had already been made productive by the previous owners, and, more important, they came with much-needed water rights. After gaining the land, the Washoe took a $10,000 loan from the $10 million revolving credit fund established by Section 10 of the IRA.

The credit plan approved by the federal government for the Washoes appropriated $3,594 for livestock and $3,177 for equipment. The remaining balance allowed them to purchase seed, feed, labor, power machinery, and miscellaneous items. During the late nineteenth and early twentieth centuries, many community members had adapted to the wage economy by selling their labor (often in accordance with their ancient seasonal cycle). Now, in the third decade of the twentieth century, Washoes were poised to adapt in a different fashion. Armed with a new government, land, and access to money, many Washoes set out to become agriculturalists. With the farm's first year of production, Fillmore believed his community had gone from "merely existing" to "making a living."

It gave Fillmore a sense of pride to demonstrate to "white friends" that given the same opportunities as non-Native agriculturalists, they could keep up. He cataloged the 1938 harvest: 320 tons of alfalfa, almost 50 tons of barley, 15 tons of oats, and close to 60 tons of potatoes. Along with the corporate tribal enterprise, many Washoe families had begun their own personal gardens.[46]

In a 1938 report titled "Rehabilitation of Landless Indians," an agent documented for the record twenty-two "unusually fine" Washoe family gardens, which he valued at $500. He also estimated the value of diverse crops and livestock maintained by the tribal enterprise (alfalfa, barley, oats, potatoes, peaches, pears, wool, lambs, cream, and hogs) at $6,600. The agent also noted the construction of twelve new concrete and tile homes on tribal lands as well as three root cellars. In conclusion, the agent echoed Fillmore's optimism and informed the commissioner that the Washoes possessed $1,500 for their first loan repayment.[47]

During the fourth annual Intertribal Conference of Nevada, held in late August 1939, Nevada Indians met for discussions and to make a report for President Roosevelt. The Washoes and five separately chartered Indian communities (Fort McDermitt Paiutes and Shoshones, Pyramid Lake Paiutes, Yerington Paiutes, Walker River Paiutes, and Te-moak Western Shoshones) collaborated on a "Brief Statement Concerning Indian Reorganization Act Credit Revolving Fund Operations in Nevada." The committee stated that Nevada Indians had earnestly taken advantage of the opportunities made available by the IRA. They believed the land could be made more productive, although this could not be done "with bare and empty hands." The committee members realized that all the necessary equipment would have to be obtained and thus began talking about credit plans to acquire additional necessary goods.

In 1938 the six tribes had approved credit plans, and the federal government dispersed a total of $118,000 worth of loans. The Te-moaks received the most, $45,000, and Walker River the second most, $22,000. The $10,000 taken by the Washoes represented the second-smallest loan. The Intertribal Council of 1939 noted the "commendable attitude" displayed by each of the tribes toward repayment of the loans. Compared with "credit operations among white agricultural operators the Nevada Indians have a right to be proud of the record made during these first years. For the most part borrowers have willingly met payments due, not only of interest, but of capital." The Washoe payment of $2,000 at the end of 1938 represented 100 percent of the payment due.

President Roosevelt responded with a brief letter, saying he read the Intertribal Council's report "with interest." He expressed gratification in discovering that the revolving credit funds had helped Nevada communities and said tribal members should "be proud" of their record. Roosevelt concluded on the hopeful note that Nevada Indians would "keep up their splendid repayment record."[48]

The year 1939 proved to be nothing like the bumper year experienced by Carson Valley agriculturalists in 1938. Late in 1938 floods damaged crops, and then a hard freeze in mid-June seriously impaired all grain crops; barley fields were nearly complete losses. The Washoes would not be able to meet their loan repayment for 1939, and they followed the Intertribal Council's suggestion that they seek an extension. The next year, at the fifth Intertribal Nevada Conference, despite all of the recent problems, Washoe Tribal Council vice chairman Willie Smokey unequivocally labeled the IRA a "benefit for the Washoe." He addressed himself to "not only the Indians but to the others" as well. He expressed appreciation for the IRA, which he claimed allowed him to speak "[for his] people for the first time." He went on, "I am the descendant of the Indians who welcomed the first white men who came into this Carson Valley. I sure appreciate the new deal. Today it seems the Government is coming to realize [it is] about time to talk true."[49]

On the political front, the Washoe Tribal Council had been exploring the benefits and limitations of their new governing structure. In Washington, D.C., Congress took up Bill 1752, which sought an exemption of Nevada tribes from the provisions of the IRA. After a September 1941 council meeting, the chairman, Ray Fillmore, wrote to the Senate Committee on Indian Affairs and described the proposed legislation as an attempt to take away the tribe's "only instrument to strive toward progress and democracy." He briefly listed some of the positive developments made under the IRA, including improved housing and acquisition of farming land. Fillmore plaintively concluded, "Please don't let the bill pass."

Commissioner Collier forwarded Fillmore's letter to Senator Elmer Thomas of Oklahoma, chair of the Senate Committee on Indian Affairs, a staunch Collier opponent. At the same time, Collier responded to Fillmore, thanking him and expressing confidence the bill would not pass. If it did, he had assurance from President Roosevelt that the executive veto power would be exercised. In the end, the bill did not pass, but it presaged a movement that would begin after Roosevelt's death. Led in part by Senator Thomas, a powerful group would attempt to undo the IRA. The infant Washoe nation would face difficult questions about its legal identity.[50]

FIGURE 2. Deʔek Wadapuš, "Cave Rock." One of the Washoes' most sacred sites, Cave Rock towers three hundred feet above Tahoe's eastern shore. The Washoes won a historic legal battle to protect this site from sport rock climbing in the 1990s and early 2000s. Courtesy of Darrel Cruz, director, Tribal Historic Preservation Office.

FIGURE 3. Simee Dimeh Summit on Highway 395. This road sign features the Washoe phrase meaning "Double Water." Many passersby likely do not know the phrase comes from the Washoe language or that the thousands of acres of piñon pine forests adjacent to the sign were vigorously defended by Washoes in the late 1800s. Courtesy of Carole Michelsen.

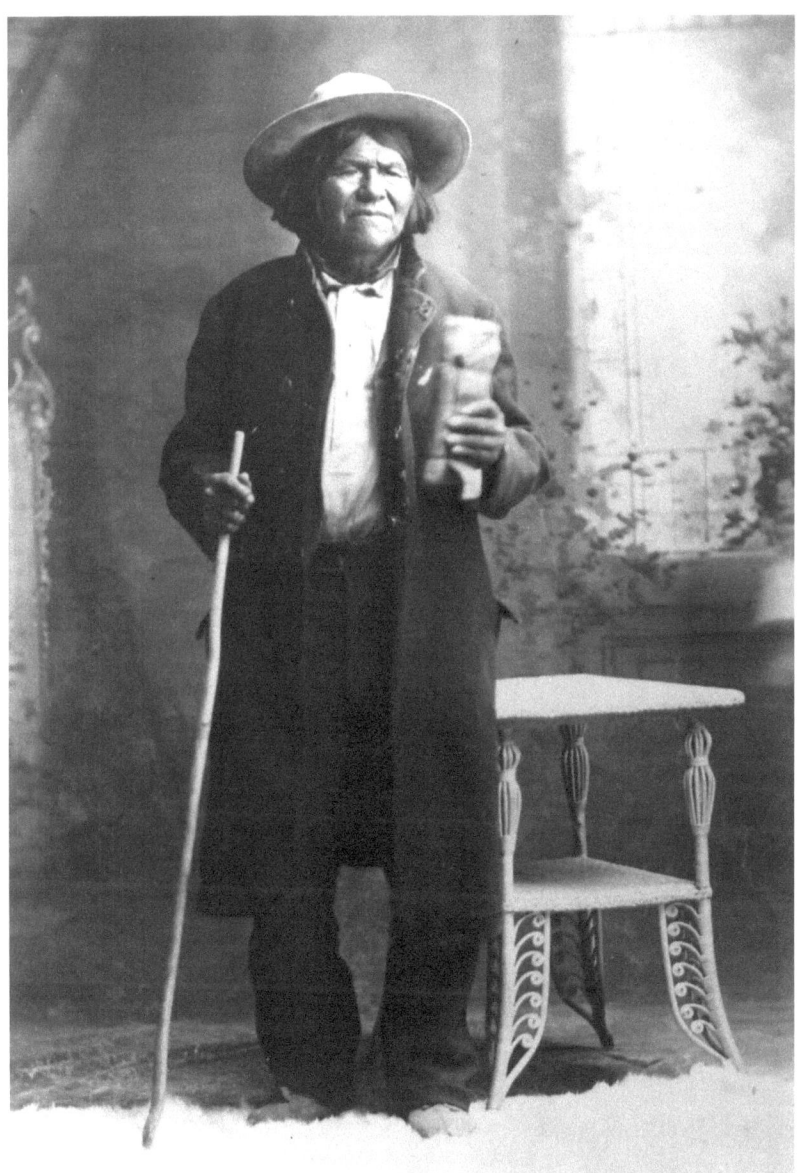

FIGURE 4. Epesuwa, Gumalanga, or "Captain Jim." Portrait taken in the late 1800s or early 1900s. In his left hand Epesuwa carries a bundle of documents, including a letter of reference from the governor of Nevada. Epesuwa made the long journey to Washington, D.C., in 1892 to defend the Washoe piñon pine groves. Courtesy of the Nevada Historical Society.

FIGURE 5. Manta Smokey, working on the Dangberg Ranch, ca. 1915–30. The Dangbergs depended on Washoe labor to build a ranching empire on the Carson River in the late nineteenth and early twentieth centuries. Washoes, in turn, adapted their traditional seasonal cycle to include new forms of wage labor, which still allowed many of them to travel seasonally between Lake Tahoe and the Carson Valley. Courtesy of Special Collections, University of Nevada, Reno Libraries.

FIGURE 6. Four generations of Washoes in the Carson Valley. Unidentified Washoe women stand with baby in a traditional Washoe cradleboard. Possibly taken at the Dressler or Dangberg Ranch, ca. 1920–30. Courtesy of Special Collections, University of Nevada, Reno Libraries.

FIGURE 7. Henry Dressler and his wife, Molly, with their children on the Dressler Ranch. Many Washoe families worked for the Dressler family, and in 1917 Frederick Dressler sold land that would become the Dresslerville Colony to the federal government. Courtesy of Special Collections, University of Nevada, Reno Libraries.

FIGURE 8. Datsolalee, or Louisa Keyser. Keyser was a masterful weaver. She is credited with creating the degikup style of basketry. Her work is featured in public and private collections around the world today, including the Smithsonian's National Museum of the American Indian. Abe Cohn and his wife, Amy, dedicated a significant amount of their time and Emporium space to the promotion of Indian baskets. Courtesy of the Nevada Historical Society.

FIGURE 9. Maggie James, one of the great Washoe weavers of the early twentieth century, with several of her works. This postcard—a photograph taken at Lake Tahoe—from ca. 1920 helps prove that Americans were interested in Washoe weavers. Courtesy of Special Collections, University of Nevada, Reno Libraries.

FIGURE 10. Charlie Rube, antelope boss and Henry Rupert's brother-in-law. He was an important mentor for young Rupert. Rube was also a critical source of information for Omer Stewart, the anthropologist and expert witness in the Washoe Claims Commission case. Courtesy of Special Collections, University of Nevada, Reno Libraries.

FIGURE 11. Continuing traditions: Ethan Wyatt placing a willow trap for fall fish runs, 2013. Courtesy of Canyon Florey © Women of the Mountain.

CHAPTER 8

CARRYING IT

> We have got this thing started, and we have got to carry it.
>
> —Johnnie Frank, Washoe Tribal chairman, 1943

At a tribal council meeting on November 4, 1943, the vice chairman, Willie Smokey, acknowledged that the federal government had taken control of the Washoe ranches and decided to run them until the end of World War II. He pointed out, "The council has little to say on the operation," and worried, "If I give my ideas, I would be criticized." The newly elected tribal chairman, Johnnie Frank, replied, "Don't get downhearted on this. We have got this thing started, and we have got to carry it." He further urged, "Don't be like a sick horse, because once a horse lays down sick, it doesn't get up."[1]

As the 1940s unfolded, the tribal council struggled with the balance between autonomy and federal oversight. While choosing to be immersed in running the Washoe ranches, federal officials gave the responsibility for the leasing of the Pine Nut allotments to the council. In the past, the federal government had negotiated the leasing arrangements for allotment owners. The case of leasing the pine nuts provides a distinct example of emerging Washoe governing practices and the challenges involved in trying to build consensus among community members.

The tribal council first sought community input before setting a monetary value for the Pine Nut Land and negotiating lease prices. This was a fairly traditional approach, to search out community input and make a decision based on individual responses. That practice had served Washoes well in the generations before colonization. The spread-out nature of their kinship groups meant that consensus had to be achieved between only a relatively small group sharing for the most part a distinctly Washoe worldview. Consensus building in the twentieth century proved far more difficult. The effects of prolonged colonization further factionalized the community. A pitched battle over leasing the Pine Nuts ensued, epitomizing the new era of Washoe governance.

After receiving community input, the council issued a first draft of their lease plan. A small faction immediately scuttled it. The council believed the protesting faction had been influenced by the principal leaseholders from the Pinenut Stock Growers Association. The PSGA had held the lease on Washoe allotments since 1914 and apparently liked the terms repeatedly offered by federal officials. The association did not want the newly empowered tribal council to start raising prices. Also, the question remained of whether decisions made by the council would be upheld. Chairman Frank reminded council members that the federal superintendent, and ultimately the secretary of the interior, maintained oversight power on everything they did.

Council member Henry Rupert, now in middle age and reaching the height of his shamanistic power, stated frankly, "The council has no authority." He then expressed a sentiment likely shared by many involved with the project: "I am just sick and tired of that pine nut business." At the next council meeting, Rupert again broached the subject: "I don't like to face those stockmen because I faced them twice, and they are a hard bunch." The vice chairman, Smokey, concurred: "I never had any luck by meeting with them." The Washoes' experience with the stockmen illustrates the difficulty they continued to face when dealing with American businessmen. It is likely that old prejudices influenced the negotiations. Members of the PSGA remembered the recent past when Washoes were itinerant laborers beholden to American ranching families.[2]

The previous lease agreement between the PSGA and the Washoes was set to expire on December 31, 1943. The council advertised around the Carson Valley to attract new lease offers. The council eventually offered a five-year lease to L. P. Allard beginning on January 1, 1943. It seemed as if the council had resolved part of their problem by going around the PSGA. But Allard failed to make bond, allowing the PSGA to secure a ten-year lease.

The problem of administering the Pine Nuts persisted throughout the 1940s. Since the first agreement in 1914, the leasing of the Pine Nuts had never generated enough revenue for Washoe families. By November 1943, the tribal council reported, "Very little income is realized by the individual allotment holders." Further, the council argued, "The problem is rapidly growing much more difficult to handle to the extent that in some instances the divisions now are so small that the common denominator runs into the eighth millionth, resulting in no returns whatsoever to the individuals." The council expressed a "strong desire" to come up with a plan where all of the Pine Nuts would become the collective property of the tribe and in April 1949 even passed a resolution regarding the idea, but they were never able to implement it.[3]

Throughout the years of World War II, the Washoe Tribal Council presented a supportive front to federal officials. Early in the war, the council made a suggestion that the Washoe community collect scrap iron and junk it to purchase bonds for the "Indian boys in the army service." The superintendent of the Carson Indian Agency claimed, "As far as this group of Indians is concerned, their attitude toward the War is not one of complacency."[4]

In the years following the war, just as the Washoe Tribal Council worked to streamline itself, the pendulum of federal Indian policy swung again. The dawning Cold War era ushered in a new governing ethos steeped in a deep suspicion of anything remotely "un-American." Native communities would be caught in the crosshairs of a vigorous drive for homogeneity.

In a complete break from John Collier's IRA and New Deal Indian policy, the government now sought to terminate the relationship between itself and Indian communities. In essence, the new federal policy of "termination" sought an amelioration of Indian self-rule and the disappearance of tribes as political entities. In retrospect, the

Collier years constituted merely a brief interlude in the incessant federal goal of assimilating American Indians.

Years of FDR's New Deal had galvanized opponents of big government, and Collier's tenure as commissioner generated equal fervor among those opposed to his Indian policies. Now, with Roosevelt and Collier gone and a shifting sentiment among voting Americans, Congress took action.

The first piece of termination legislation, the Indian Claims Commission (ICC) Act, seems an unlikely mechanism for dissolving the federal-Indian trust status. Years before, Collier had proposed a court of claims in which Native communities could present their long-held grievances and finally have "their day in court." Indian leaders across the United States looked favorably upon the idea, but when Collier stepped down, others, with a perspective very different from Collier's, favored such a court for their own purposes.

By the time the Indian Claims Commission Act reached Truman's desk, it had been shaped to function as a "final accounting" for Native claims. Congress passed the bill in 1946, and upon signing it Truman remarked, "With *the final settlement* of all outstanding claims which this measure insures, Indians can take their place without special handicaps or special advantages in the economic life of our nation and share fully in its progress."[5] The act gave the commission five years to hear all cases and created two distinct phases: the title phase and the value phase. During the title phase, Indian communities would have to prove that they had exclusively occupied their land from "time immemorial." If a tribe made it past the title phase, it would next begin the value phase. Commissioners could grant one-time-only monetary awards; no land would be returned.

Many tribal leaders, including Washoes, initially supported the act. Their enthusiasm quickly waned. Truman failed to appoint a Native representative to the commission. Instead, he selected three political allies. Eventually, as the caseload increased, two more judges were added. The complex issues under consideration forced continual extensions of the original charter, and instead of concluding its business after five years, it functioned until 1978, thirty-one years.[6]

The year after the Claims Commission Act, 1947, the Senate Civil Service Committee subpoenaed William Zimmerman, acting commissioner of Indian affairs, to present Congress with a list of communities potentially ready for a termination of their trust status. The Zimmerman plan drew three broad categories according to their level of preparedness. The first group, those most prepared for termination, included the Iroquois, Flathead, Klamath, and Menominee. When Congress finally passed termination legislation in the 1950s, they terminated tribes from Zimmerman's first group.[7]

While the Washoes were not in Zimmerman's first category, the specter of termination nevertheless reached them. During the Pine Nut meetings of the early 1940s, Washoe Tribal Council members heard vague mention of a government desire to "turn over their own affairs to them." But without a regular community income and developed infrastructure, the Washoes would not be subject to a specific termination bill.

Two years after Zimmerman's testimony, in 1949, President Truman initiated an investigatory commission to examine the organization of the executive branch. Chaired by former president Herbert Hoover, the commission quickly drew attention to the Bureau of Indian Affairs. They added fuel to the termination fire by declaring tribal culture virtually destroyed. The commission recommended that the "handful" of remaining Indians should have their politically autonomous status dissolved. The commission advised the federal government to hand over social services for Indians to states and incorporate Native Americans as taxpaying citizens.[8]

Accepting the commission's recommendation, Truman appointed Dillon Myer as commissioner of Indian affairs in 1950. During World War II, Myer had served as the director of the War Relocation Authority, overseeing the internment of Japanese Americans. A longtime critic of Collier's policies, he encouraged the development of an Indian relocation program, started by the BIA in 1948. The project initially sought to relocate Navajos to Denver, Los Angeles, and Salt Lake City. The bureau set up relocation offices in those cities to help assist families who moved. In 1950 Myer extended the program to include more than just the Navajos. By 1960 the bureau had set up ten additional relocation offices, in Chicago, St. Louis, Oakland, San Francisco, San Jose, Dallas, Oklahoma City, Tulsa, Phoenix, and Albuquerque.

The bureau began advertising relocation on reservations, utilizing posters, films, and guest speakers. Small grants to cover travel costs and a few weeks of living expenses were offered for those willing to move. Theoretically, relocation centers would help with job placement, housing, and medical care, although many who relocated recalled moving into impoverished areas with virtually no guidance. By 1960 nearly thirty-three thousand Indians had moved to urban areas.[9]

When Dwight Eisenhower gained the White House in 1952, proponents of the termination agenda reached full stride. In August 1953 Congress passed two measures aimed at eliminating the unique Indian relationship with the federal government. The first, House Concurrent Resolution 108, stated that Congress would pursue a policy to make Indians "subject to the same law and entitled to the same privileges and responsibilities as are applicable to other citizens of the United States." Congress intended for "Indians within the territorial limits of the United States [to] assume their full responsibilities as American Citizens." To casual observers, the legislation appeared just and favorably disposed toward Indian rights. But Indians were not and are not just like other Americans. Their distinct histories and complex relationship with the U.S. government dictate a special relationship, brought into relief by the termination legislation. That same year, Congress passed Public Law 280, which gave civil and criminal jurisdiction over Indian affairs to five test states: California, Minnesota, Oregon, Nebraska, and Wisconsin. Alaska, upon statehood, became the sixth "mandatory" test state. A provision of P.L. 280 held that nonmandatory states could choose to acquire jurisdiction in Indian country. Nevada would do just that in 1955.

Indian communities had long governed their own local legal affairs. The only outside investigations came from the federal government. Even then the government had cause to act only in specific criminal investigation where a "major" crime had been committed. Assigning civil and criminal jurisdiction to the states threatened to undermine local Indian authority and, at the very least, make administering tribal affairs more difficult.[10]

In the spring of 1948, far from Washington, and mostly unaware that the Claims Commission Act was part of a new assault on tribalism, the Washoe Tribal Council prepared to move forward with their claims for the Indian Claims Commission. They contracted the services of legal counsel George F. Wright, who agreed to represent them on a contingency basis: his pay would be between 5 and 10 percent of the final award. Wright explained in a letter to tribal council member Hank Pete his intention to hire a well-established law firm in Washington, D.C., to help with the case. Wright seemed to be a good choice for the Washoes. He was raised in rural Nevada but also had urban experience. He grew up on a ranch in Ruby Valley, Nevada, and had graduated from high school in Elko, Nevada. After graduating from the University of Nevada, Reno, he attended law school at the University of Michigan. Upon passing the bar, Wright practiced in San Francisco for nine years before returning to Elko.[11]

On April 21, 1948, Ralph Gelvin, superintendent of the Carson Indian Agency, attended the Washoe Tribal Council meeting, and while they waited for Wright to arrive he explained the provisions of the ICC.[12] From the start, questions emerged over whether California Washoes and Nevada Washoes would file together. It also appeared the Washoes were split over hiring Wright. Hank Pete wrote Wright after the meeting and claimed that the majority of Washoes in the Carson Valley favored hiring him and that he would do all he could to secure Wright's appointment. He believed in the end they would formalize a contract with the attorney. Pete also expressed an idea that "it didn't make any difference if the California [Washoes] agreed with us or not."

Just over a week after Pete sent his letter of support to Wright, the lawyer sent a proposed contractual agreement and a map illustrating the approximate boundaries of the lands to be claimed under the ICC Act. Two months later, Pete wrote Wright, confirming that the California Washoes did not want to consolidate their claim with Nevada communities. According to Pete, "They had their own claim which they considered better than the Nevada claim." Pete reported that in a meeting, he tried to persuade the California contingency that they should pursue their claim as one tribe, but he "didn't get a very good reply." He concluded that Wright would have to figure out whether the California and Nevada groups should file a joint claim.[13]

At the tribal council meeting on July 20, 1948, Pete introduced a motion, seconded by Tom Sallee, to select George F. Wright as a Washoe Tribal attorney, for a period of ten years. The motion passed. Council members and an interested community now eagerly anticipated legal restitution and compensation for lands seized illegally over the past century. The case had begun.

Five months after the council passed the resolution hiring Wright, H. M. Knutson, the acting superintendent for the Carson Indian Agency, sent him a letter, officially giving him permission to handle Washoe claims. The contract had been approved by the Department of the Interior.[14] The five-month delay between the council's approval of Wright and the Department of the Interior's official consent was a harbinger of checks and impediments to come. In fact, many of the Washoes who initiated the work would not live to see the settlement, as their claim would not be resolved until 1975.[15]

The snail's pace, and Wright's failure to provide regular updates, did not sit well with members of the council. At the beginning of May 1949, ten months after Wright had been hired, Pete and fellow council member Ronald James visited the Reno law firm of Carville and Carville. They asked the lawyers about the status of their claims case. Edward P. Carville was the governor of Nevada from 1939 to 1945; it is likely that Pete and James believed he might have some information for them because of his former position. Former governor Carville wrote to Wright, explaining, "We could not advise them and would not attempt to in view of the fact that you are representing them." Carville recommended Wright give the Washoe community an update.[16]

Two weeks later, on May 16, Wright sent a letter to Pete with disappointing news. Wright had only that day sent contracts to lawyers in Washington, D.C., who would help prosecute the Washoe case. Wright hired C. T. Busha Jr. and John Lewis Smith Jr. He explained to Pete that the Department of the Interior would have to approve the contracts of the D.C. attorneys before the "research and negotiations for settlement could begin." He expected the contract would be approved in the "near future." The same day, Wright sent a letter to Busha, explaining he had been "rather busy with numerous matters." His letter to Busha reveals how little had been done since his hiring. Wright now thought they should determine an approximate amount of monetary aid or "compensation" the federal government had given the Washoes over the past century. Wright did not know exactly how much land the Washoes had but assumed they received allotments before 1900. Wright foresaw a problem determining the exact lands originally held by the tribe. He suggested once the contracts were approved that Busha consult early maps of Nevada filed with the Department of the Interior.[17]

The "near future" predicted by Wright turned out to be more than three months. On August 23 Wright wrote the Washoe Tribal Council, informing them that the Department of the Interior had approved the contracts of association with Busha and Smith, whom he described as "very able attorneys" with "excellent reputations." For Wright, it was finally time to act. Two weeks earlier, Busha had prodded him, saying, "This is the time before the Texas and California boys get all the money." Busha's sentiment captures the frenzy-like atmosphere that engulfed many legal practices during the height of the ICC proceedings. Wright now asked for some of the Washoes to give him detailed information about their traditional landholdings. He laid out seven questions. The last question asked for the names and addresses of the "real old time Indians" for depositions regarding original territorial boundaries. The same day, Wright wrote to Busha, concurring that they should "commence right away" on the claim. He again suggested that Busha and Lewis find out exactly what the federal government had previously given the Washoes.[18]

By 1950 Wright was being assailed from all sides. On January 7, Carnegie Smokey, secretary of the council, wrote to Wright, informing him that he had been asked by the council to inquire about progress. Smokey described circulating rumors among the Washoes saying the case had been dropped. Many community members had been asking anxiously about the claim. Smokey also informed Wright that his primary contact, Hank Pete, had not been reelected and was no longer on the tribal council. Smokey concluded by requesting that Wright forward all relevant information regarding the status of their claim.[19]

Busha continued to give voice to his own impatience. On January 31 he wrote Wright, asking why he had not heard from him recently and requesting that Wright contact him soon. One week later, E. Reeseman Fryer, the superintendent for the Carson Indian Agency, wrote to Wright on behalf of the Washoes to learn about the progress, or lack thereof, regarding their claims. He complained, "The tribe is totally in the dark, and as a consequence, is suffering the frustration of ignorance in connection with their claims." Fryer believed an explanatory letter from Wright addressed to the tribe would help quell the unrest.

On June 5 Wright received a letter from the commissioner of Indian affairs, Dillon S. Myer, requesting a prompt response regarding the status of the Washoe case. He reminded Wright that Section 12 of the ICC Act stipulated claims would be heard for a period of five years only. Myer advised Wright that the period was set to expire at midnight on August 12, 1951.[20]

By July 5, Busha had become desperate. He sent Wright a newspaper clipping with the glaring headline "$10,000 Awarded to Every Ute for Seized Land." The total settlement for the Utes amounted to almost $32 million. Busha suggested that the "enclosed clipping will show that we are losing time." He believed the Washoes "ought to be in as good a position as the Colorado Utes." By the fall of 1950, Busha's desperation gave way to condemnation: "We are disappointed in not hearing from you," he said, pointing out, "Mr. Smith's reputation and mine are at stake with the Indian Bureau."[21]

It is not hard to imagine that by 1951, many Washoes had ceased believing they would ever get their day in court. Three years had already passed without progress. The tribal council began making inquiries with the Claims Commission. In early February 1951, Busha informed Wright that he and Smith had been summoned by the chief of claims to answer concerns expressed by tribal chairman Tom Sallee. Busha and Smith pointed to Wright, informing the chief commissioner that they were waiting for information from him. Busha concluded by stating that he did not wish to appear "negligent" and asked Wright to advise him as soon as possible. Wright's longhand scrawl at the bottom of the letter indicates his desire to respond quickly: "Will forward all information right away after the meeting with the Washoe Indians on Feb. 19, 1951." Wright intended the meeting to be an information-gathering session.

On February 6, Wright responded formally to Busha, asking him for the information he had requested two years before. Busha and Smith had not yet sent him maps or amounts for potential offsets to be claimed by the federal government. Wright also informed Busha that Northern Paiute and Washoe land claims had significant overlap. Lawyers for the Paiutes had been taking depositions in Nevada to help prove their claim. Wright suggested Busha and Smith contact the attorneys for the Paiutes and "effect a compromise" to save time. He also announced that the Claims Commission had ruled the California Washoes and Nevada Washoes had to file a joint claim.[22]

Many Washoes showed up for the meeting at Stewart, Nevada, on February 19. Hank Pete and Tom Sallee offered testimony, which depicted a deteriorating Washoe lifestyle since the early Euro-American immigration period. Pete, at the age of sixty-nine, could speak from experience about the late 1800s. He informed Wright that fish and game had been "plentiful" prior to the American arrival. He described traditional hunting and fishing methods. Sallee also provided information. He described the methods the Washoe used to ensure maintenance of healthy fish populations. Fishers did not overfish a particular area and "tried to let the female fish go by." Wright gathered the information, supplying the Washoes with little news about the status of the case.[23]

While the ICC case was taking up the lion's share of the council's attention, another topic that would be the subject of lengthy litigation into the twenty-first century cropped up in April 1951. The council approved a petition that called for the creation of a public park on the eastern shore of Lake Tahoe at a place the Washoes called "De?ek Wadapuš"; to whites, it had become "Cave Rock." The park would serve as a "monument to the Indian people of the state of Nevada, and properly mark said park to point out the significance of its dedication."

The council had no way of knowing that more than fifty years later, a monumental struggle to gain recognition and protection for Cave Rock would lead to a nearly twenty-year dispute, finally resolved in the Ninth Circuit Court of Appeals.[24]

On July 3 that same year, Burton A. Ladd, the superintendent for the Carson Indian Agency, wrote to Wright on behalf of the Washoes. He reminded Wright of the August 12 deadline and informed him that the tribal council needed a status update. Meanwhile, in Washington, D.C., Busha and Smith moved to get relevant information to Wright. A week after Wright sent his latest request for maps and offsets, Smith sent six separate maps. In an accompanying letter, he described an inquiry about the offsets. He was told by the secretary of the Indian Affairs Senate Committee, Albert A. Grorud, to wait because the government, as part of their defense, would provide a detailed accounting of money spent on behalf of the Washoes. Smith concluded by stating that the Paiute case had already begun in January and suggested he was still trying to work out a compromise concerning the territorial dispute.

With less than two months until the deadline, Busha sent one last letter. He intimated that their collective legal team was "being criticized" around Washington for not filing their petition. Finally, Busha received a letter from Wright, dated July 8, in which the Washoe claim was laid out. Wright calculated a total of 6,318,080 acres traditionally under Washoe control. He estimated the value of each acre at $1.25, thus totaling $7,897,600. He also calculated a 6 percent interest per annum beginning in 1863, creating an interest total of $41,599,208. Wright claimed an additional $10,000,000 for loss of game and fish, tacking on 6 percent interest per annum beginning in 1900 (although he guessed he may have to adjust the interest date to 1910 because fishing in Tahoe remained relatively good until then), totaling $30,000,000. The grand total came to $89,496,808. Wright concluded by acknowledging he had been slow to complete his work because he had been on vacation. He asked Busha and Smith to go ahead with the petition before the August deadline.[25]

One month after Wright's enumeration, on August 9, 1951, Smith and Busha filed Docket no. 288, *The Washoe Tribe of the States of*

Nevada and California, Plaintiff v. The United States, Defendant. The claim described the loss of fishing, hunting, and timber resources. It estimated that the mineral rushes of the nineteenth century led to the extraction of billions of dollars' worth of precious metals. Yet the claim asked for less than half the amount Wright had calculated. The petition stated that "from time immemorial," the Washoe had been in control of 9,872 square miles, or 6,318,080 acres, of land. The community maintained uninterrupted occupancy of these lands until the beginning in 1848, when "without the plaintiff's consent" the United States took possession of all lands with no compensation.

Next, Busha and Smith addressed lands that had been purchased or set aside for the Washoes. In conclusion, they itemized the amount under consideration, which they had adjusted from Wright's initial suggestion. They asked for $7,811,985.84 for lands "wrongfully taken" (including interest), $10,000,000 for disturbance of fishing and hunting rights, and $25,000,000 for timber and mineral resources "wrongfully removed." The amount totaled $42,811,985.84. It had been three years since the tribal council hired Wright. Finally, their claims had been presented to the federal government.

Busha and Smith had not reached a compromise with the attorneys for the Paiutes. When Smith served the federal government, the assistant attorney general informed him the Northern Paiutes had "claimed quite a bit of the Lake Tahoe area."[26]

Not long after the petition was filed, Busha passed away. Several months after his death, Wright wrote Smith, laying out a research agenda for substantiating the Washoe case. He suggested Smith consult the congressional reports of John C. Frémont's western exploration and find Agent Lockhart's report from 1865 recommending reservations for the Washoe. Wright also passed along important information regarding claims that overlapped. He had correspondence from Jay H. Hoag, an attorney involved with the Paiute case. Hoag represented many communities and had already tried the Pawnee case, among others. Hoag said that in cases where tribes claimed the same land, the commission turned down all claims on the basis that no one owned the land.

In a telephone conversation, Hoag and Wright each acknowledged the potential difficulty surrounding an eastern border of the Washoe claim. Wright and the Washoes claimed the border fell just east of Sparks, Nevada, but the Northern Paiutes believed their western boundary extended well into the Sierra foothills, west of Reno and Carson City, Nevada. Hoag passed along a further tip: he recommended the Washoes hire appraisers to estimate values of the land as it was when the government took it in 1848.[27]

On June 4, 1953, Smith sent Wright potentially devastating news. He explained that the government had served the combined counsel (Wright, Smith, and Busha) with a motion to consolidate the Washoe case with sixteen other claims coming out of California. In the worst-case scenario, the consolidation might have caused the commission to dismiss all Washoe action. Less dire, but nevertheless troubling, a consolidated case would mean splitting the monetary award among all other litigants. The commission decreed on November 19, 1953, that the Washoe Docket would be combined. Wright, and Smith objected and the commission agreed to hear evidence as to why they should not be included. Over the subsequent years, it would be up to the Washoe attorneys to prove exclusive occupancy and distinct title to the lands being claimed.[28]

By 1955 the federal government had prepared its response to the specific Washoe petition. The first line of defense, which proved to be their standard practice, was to claim that the Washoes were "not a tribe, band or other identifiable group of American Indians." The government made the same argument earlier with Southern Paiute claims. In the Southern Paiute case, it argued that Great Basin communities were too culturally alike to be identifiable as a unique tribal entity. Next, the defendants challenged Washoe title to the land and claimed their occupancy did not constitute "a property interest under the Constitution of the United States." The response went on for six pages, challenging every element of the original petition. Finally, the government concluded by asking for the plaintiff's petition to be dismissed.[29] The claims court did not dismiss the Washoe petition, and in July 1955 the case went before the commissioners in San Francisco.

The Washoes were not idle, waiting for their claims to be addressed.

They had enough experience with the federal government to realize they could not count on anything. They set to work maintaining community lands, refining tribal governance, and keeping a sharp eye on the ever-oscillating federal agenda. In the winter of 1952, the tribal council had reaffirmed the community's commitment to agriculture, planning in the spring to change the ranch fields to diverse grain crops and potatoes. They also decided to continue nurturing parent stock in cattle, sheep, and hogs to "enable a continuing operation."[30]

Only three years later, hampered by a couple of bad harvests, a tightening market, and frustration with strict federal oversight and less than capable non-Washoe foremen, enthusiasm for the ranching project had waned. In 1955 the council decided to abandon the work and lease the tribal ranch lands. During a spring meeting, the council resolved to sell all livestock, farm machinery, and crops. They chose to allow a lease to use the lands for one growing season, after which they would offer a five-year lease to the highest bidder.

In June 1955 Wright began the next chapter in what had become the ICC saga, informing community members that the tribe would have to hire an anthropologist to help them establish their territorial claim. Wright explained that disputes over their boundaries necessitated the aid of an expert, Dr. Omer Stewart. Upon being introduced, Stewart gave them new information, telling the assembly that they would have a tough battle because the Claims Commission did not want to award a large sum of money to a small community. Wright informed them that the case was set to begin in the middle of July.

At the same time, in the summer of 1955, having liquidated its agricultural holdings, the council took up the pressing issue of termination. At a special meeting, Alida C. Bowler, former superintendent of the Carson Indian Agency, now working for the National Association on Indian Affairs, described the contours of termination legislation to the council. She told them the federal government wanted to "go out of the Indian service." Bowler stressed that no matter what happened, the council should maintain control of tribal property. She also advised them to begin watching very closely federal legislation by sending a delegate to Washington, D.C. In the event of termination, the Washoes would need to be familiar with Nevada state law. The council made plans to research and document applicable decrees.[31]

A month later at a special meeting called by Delaney Kizer, the vice chairman, Ronald James, the council secretary, read the provisions of Public Law 280. A long discussion ensued, followed by a unanimous vote against the law. The Washoes, in common with tribes across the United States, could see no good reason to terminate their relationship with the federal government to come under state jurisdiction.

Unfortunately for the tribe, there was a subsection of the law whereby a state could opt to claim jurisdiction without tribal approval. In this instance, Nevada did so, leading to twenty years of conflicted governance. Finally, in 1974 the State of Nevada retroceded their jurisdictional claims over Washoe country back to the tribe.[32]

Amid the chaos of termination and the ICC case, throughout the mid-1950s the tribal council continued dealing with day-to-day issues, including several alcohol-related incidents, which caused Kizer to warn that children "were being influenced"; disturbances by unruly teens after dance parties at the community center; and, in January 1956, flooding that left silt deposits covering some forty acres of croplands and destroyed five miles of fencing. In mid-February 1956, the council passed a resolution to join the National Congress of American Indians, which had been formed in November 1944 by representatives from more than fifty Native communities. The organization was playing an active role in fighting termination legislation, which undoubtedly provided a key reason for the Washoes to join.

The ICC hearing to determine Washoe territorial rights had stretched through September 1955. On July 7 Wright called anthropologist Stewart, who had earned his doctorate at the University of California, Berkeley, under the guidance of Alfred Kroeber and Robert Lowie. Stewart at the time was a professor at the University of Colorado. He had also trained with Julian Steward at the University of Utah. In a matchup between teacher and student, Steward served as an expert witness for the defense team. The two professors' last names are so similar, it is easy to get confused. *Stewart* was on the Washoes' side; *Steward* served on the federal government's side.

Stewart explained to the court that he first worked with the Washoes in 1936 while a graduate student at Berkeley. His principal contacts within the community included Dick Bender and Charlie Rube. From his fieldwork and reading of scholarly literature, Stewart confidently asserted that the Washoes had indeed lived in their eastern Sierra home as a distinct community for several thousand years. Stewart referenced the archaeological work of the well-known Berkeley archaeologist Robert Heizer, claiming that prior to Euro-Americans' arrival, there had been no significant change "or break in the archeological record after roughly the time of Christ, that is, 2000 years ago."[33]

The Washoe team provided the court with detailed depositions from Washoe elders, including one from Richard Barrington, born May 22, 1880. Barrington grew up in Washoe lands and in 1890 began attending the Carson Indian School. For a brief interlude, Barrington attended the Carlisle Indian School in Pennsylvania (1898–1900) before graduating from Carson in 1901. In 1902 he returned to Welmelti (northern Washoe) country (near Loyalton, California) and began working in the lumber business. Beginning in 1917 he worked for the Bureau of Indian Affairs in Nevada and New Mexico. He ultimately returned to the land of his birth and in 1945 built a lumber mill in Quincy, California. Nearly a decade after he gave his testimony in 1964, the University of Nevada, Reno, awarded Barrington with an honorary degree as an outstanding and distinguished Nevadan. Wright described him as "humble but competent," brave, and just.

In his deposition Barrington recounted the tremendous amount of resources originally utilized by the Washoes; he listed foods, herbs (both medicinal and edible), game, birds, fish, and bodies of water. He also described the seasonal cycle beginning in March, when families could catch spawning cutthroat trout making their way up the Truckee River. Since he came from Welmelti country, Barrington's deposition focused largely on the northern country, but he remembered fall on the lower Truckee River, where fish could be easily had. He recalled the painful days when non-Washoes overfished Lake Tahoe and introduced the mackinaw, which destroyed native fish populations. Also during the Comstock era, lumber mills deposited so much debris and sawdust in the upper Truckee that the cutthroat population declined dramatically. Barrington's deposition concluded by noting that when he was a child, the game population had been so drastically reduced that Washoe hunters had a hard time.[34]

During the hearings Wright challenged the commission's decision to consolidate their case with California claims. His argument was helped by the tribal council, which had passed resolutions refusing to acknowledge the rights of litigants in California cases to collect on behalf of the Washoes. The lawyers for the California groups did not object to Wright's pleading, nor did the court.

Toward the end of the case, the government called as their expert witness Julian Steward, professor of anthropology at the University of Illinois. Because of their previous mentor-disciple relationship, it first seemed Steward's testimony might undermine Stewart's. Steward tried to argue that the Washoes had no political organization or understanding of landownership, but under cross-examination he confessed he had never conducted fieldwork with the Washoes. He had to admit a relative unfamiliarity with them, especially in comparison to his former student Stewart. In a letter regarding the case, Wright described Steward's testimony as "very much open to attack." Wright was able "to get him to admit that he just did not know what use or lack of use the Washoes made of the territory."[35]

When the title phase of the Washoe claim was completed, anxious community members could do nothing but wait for the commissioners to decide on their case. Deliberations dragged on for another two years. Finally, on January 20, 1958, the Claims Commission ruled in favor of the Washoes. Having convinced the commission that they had lived in their eastern Sierra home since "time immemorial," they would be allowed to enter the award phase. Their case would not be folded into a larger suit, including other California tribes, which would have certainly diluted Washoes' claims.[36]

Between 1947 and 1978, the commission dismissed 204 dockets, but the Washoe case survived, and lawyers prepared for the next stage. For the difficult award phase, Wright first met and negotiated an agreement with lawyers for the California claims. They set definitive boundaries to avoid overlapping claims.[37]

Next the legal team prepared to present valuation for Washoe lands, and the lawyers turned to the community for help. Nicholas Allen, an attorney based in Washington, D.C., who had replaced Busha, sought the input of Washoe community members. The response of the councilman Earl James revealed a Washoe perspective that valued the land and ecosystem before a cash award. In the view of James and other Washoes, these lands "were our home" and provided everything needed to survive. Putting monetary value on their home would be difficult to do. But the commission was not in the business of giving back lands; it would have to be money.

James noted the exorbitant price of lands selling around Lake Tahoe and concluded on an ironic note, saying the "white man's ingenuity and foresight" had led to a severe depletion of fish and game, along with the disappearance or reduction of lakes. He reminded Allen that the longer the settlement took, the more the federal government would claim in back charges. "We do not want the U.S. Government to be spending our money for us." When it came to setting actual prices for the land, James and other community members could only guess. They recognized that billions of dollars had been extracted in the form of timber and mineral resources, but to them the land was invaluable.[38]

On September 21, 1960, Arthur V. Watkins, the newly appointed chief claims commissioner and former senator from Utah, held a conference with all members of the bar representing Indian communities. Watkins had been the spearhead of the federal government's disastrous termination policy of the mid-1950s. In his new role as chief claims commissioner, he addressed the need to "step up" the claims process. He imagined with the number of dockets pending that the Claims Commission would not finish for at least another ten years. The results so far had been disheartening. Only 128 of 596 dockets had been completed, and of those a mere 28 had been awarded compensation; the remaining 100 had been denied. The commission's findings up to 1960 obliged the Washoe legal team to be precise in requesting a monetary value.

Four days after the conference Earl James wrote to Wright, expressing the frustration felt by many in the community. He reminded the attorney, "This matter has been pending for twelve years, [and] most of us are becoming aged." The fact that many Washoe elders could no longer work spurred James's hope for an early settlement. Despite the wishes of Washoes and the efforts of Watkins, the process would not go quickly. The next step required hiring appraisers. On October 18, the Washoes hired Noble T. Murray, who specialized in appraising agricultural lands.[39]

By 1961 a primary concern among the Washoes centered on claims to their ancestral lake. Rumors had been circulating among the community that Wright intended to leave Lake Tahoe out of the valuation. Community members began asking legal representatives, other than Wright and his team, about whether the lake could be claimed. In the spring of 1961, Earl James again wrote to Allen and in no uncertain terms stated, "Lake Tahoe is indeed the center of our lands." He wanted to know why Wright might leave it out. James reminded Allen, "Our tribe has always fished it for as long as we have been told by our ancestors that they themselves knew of their forefathers." James described family burial grounds at the lake and wondered, "Why isn't the lake ours?" He concluded by stating that if Wright left Tahoe out, the Washoes would no longer want him as their counsel. The thought of their sacred lake not being included in their ancestral lands would symbolically sever the ancient relationship between Washoes and the center of their world.[40]

But the claims court did not recognize or give value for water itself, even if it was considered sacred. In a document titled "Rules for Appraisal of Indian Lands," the commission stated, "Water as a commodity is never given any value, nor is the land under the water given any value. . . . It is actually immaterial whether the water acreage is deemed 'excluded' or 'included.'" This rule, perhaps never clearly explained to Washoes, effectively dismissed their claims to the center of their world and continues to confuse community members to the present day.[41]

While the appraisals dragged on, the Washoe government continued to address the day-to-day needs of their community. A tribal resolution from early in 1961 provides a window into the larger concerns of the council. At the behest of the secretary of the interior, the tribal council submitted recommendations to his special task force. The council listed ten action items that ranged from the improvement of water and sewage systems at Dresslerville to the overhauling of federal Indian administration. The council revealed their continuing frustration with Washington politics. They pointedly called for the position of commissioner of Indian affairs to "be taken out of politics so that American Indians will no longer be victims of administrative shifts." This suggestion proves that the council had become savvy regarding political maneuverings and the constantly oscillating federal agenda.[42]

By 1962 almost all the activity surrounding the Washoe case centered on land appraisals. The tribe hired the firm of Shenon and Full, mining engineers and geologists out of Salt Lake City, to determine the value of mineral deposits taken from their territory. For the valuation of timber resources, the Washoes contracted with timber management expert Myron Wall Jr. Last, Noble Murray would appraise the farm and ranch lands. Of the utmost concern for Wright and Allen was the question of fair market value. Wright suggested they use land-sale records from the early 1860s when they could find them. With regard to mineral lands, the value could not simply be set to the amount and price of ore extracted. Instead, all market factors and conditions had to be applied, including fluctuating markets (supply and demand), accessibility, mining cost, milling, and transportation. By February 1963 Wright felt he had the case in good shape; he would use Richard Barrington and Leslie Jake, the tribal chair, as witnesses, along with all appraisers.[43]

On February 26, 1963, Wright informed the tribal council that the Claims Commission would be hearing the valuation phase of their case at the end of April. On March 12, the council reported that the news had renewed their hope. Fred Richards, council secretary, observed, "[The elders] have been buoyed up, keeping them from sinking into eternal despondency." He noted that a feeling of "unity and oneness" now linked Nevada and California Washoes together. Richards warned Wright to expect a long-distance phone call or two from Washoe country. "The tribesmen feel that it is not only good but needful that we talk together and invoke the blessings of the Great Spirit upon us and our cause."[44]

The trial began in late April 1963 and stretched through May. Wright presented a solid case, and Barrington's testimony made a good impression—showing the human side of the Washoe claim. Barrington's knowledge of Washoe lands and traditional practices impressed listeners. Wright later wrote that the court found him to be "very enlightening and impressive." Wright believed the testimony given by Leslie Jake was important as well.[45]

In October 1963 Barrington wrote to Wright to let him know he had been discussing the case with the tribe. He told community members not to "expect too much as the government always gives as little as possible in Indian cases, but always dishes out billions for foreign aid." Barrington proved to be an astute student of the government.[46]

The Washoe team had sued for $16,100,000, down considerably from Busha and Smith's initial estimate of almost $43 million and Wright's $89 million. The U.S. government claimed the Washoes should be allowed only $2,476,000, allowing no compensation for the loss of hunting and fishing resources. The commissioners weighed both estimates and announced their ruling, by coincidence, on Nevada Day, October 31, 1969. Their award valued Washoe mineral lands at $2,666,500. For removal of the minerals, the commission granted $1,125,000. In determining the value of fish, they referred to an earlier ruling in the Tlingit and Haida Indians of *Alaska v. United States* (1968), which found fish to be *ferae naturae*, "capable of ownership only by possession and control. . . . A fishing area subject to Indian use can never be possessed." The commission allowed that the value of lands adjacent to fishing areas would be "enhanced," and they took the value of fisheries into consideration when they ruled the total compensation for meadowland and sagebrush land to be $719,850. For timberlands, the commission gave $450,000, plus another $10,000 for the removal of lumber. Finally, the commission awarded $719,850 for farming and grazing lands along with $82,000 for town sites. It calculated total compensation for the Washoes to be $5,053,350.[47]

But the Washoes had to wait another six years to receive even that payment, aptly labeled by anthropologist Warren d'Azevedo "a token figure." Awarded moneys were not dispersed until 1975. In 1973

Congress passed Public Law 93–135, "The Indian Judgment Funds Distribution Act," which provided the governing principles for payment. Many hurdles had to be cleared to gain the money. The act stipulated that the secretary of the interior had to present Congress with a specific plan for how the money would be spent. The act required the secretary to provide consultants to help the tribes plan for the dispersal.

The tribal council worked hard to put in place a plan that would benefit all eligible Washoes along with tribal enterprises. They met with a representative from the Bureau of Indian Affairs on August 3, 1973. On August 10 the council passed a resolution requesting the assistance of a tribal operations specialist from Washington, D.C., and a representative from the Nevada Indian Agency to craft plans for utilization of the money.

No monetary compensation could ever rectify 120 years of injustices, bring back their lands, or heal the wounds. Still, the Washoes kept moving forward, dedicating close to half of the award to community welfare and tribal development. The remaining money was paid out in the form of per capita distributions to tribal members, and it is hard to imagine what that onetime payment meant to elders who had initiated the claim twenty years earlier. While the size of the judgment was certainly disappointing, the tribe had legitimized their claims and won federal recognition of their status as the original inhabitants of the eastern Sierra. In the coming years, successive generations of Washoes would work to make sure that recognition would be expanded to include Lake Tahoe as the center of their lands.

CHAPTER 9

THE JOURNEY HOME

> Lake Tahoe is the spiritual and cultural center of our world. Protecting the lake and surrounding homelands have been and continue to be a primary cause for my people.
>
> —Dr. Lisa Grayshield, Washoe

At noon on Saturday, July 26, 1997, President Bill Clinton began speaking at the Hyatt Hotel, on the eastern shore of Lake Tahoe. His keynote address, during a two-day summit meeting, highlighted the desperate need to protect Lake Tahoe. The summit included Vice President Al Gore, several cabinet members, U.S. senators and representatives from California and Nevada, as well as state, regional, and local leaders. The president reported that the Washoe Tribal chairman, Brian Wallace, had told him Washoes first asked the federal government for help at Tahoe well over a century earlier. Clinton assured listeners that the mail between the Washoes and Washington would begin traveling faster.[1]

Washoe elders Jo Ann Smokey Martinez and Theresa Smokey Jackson had offered the summit's opening invocation: "We pray that you will hear our voices and that they will not become just an echo in the Great Basin." Under Clinton's direction, federal officials did listen to Washoe voices. Vice President Gore spent significant time in meetings with community members and elders. By the end of the conference, the Washoes had a memorandum of understanding and assurances that they would have a role in managing the environment at the lake.

Secretary of Agriculture Dan Glickman established the Lake Tahoe Federal Advisory Commission, which included tribal representatives as well as other stakeholders, scientists, and government officials, all of whom had input on the use of millions of dollars of government moneys for environmental projects. Most heartening of all, President Clinton promised to return property for the tribe at Tahoe. It was a moment of pride, joy, and poignancy. Elder Adele James described it as "a good thing and a sad thing. We had a lot of elders that had passed on and had dreamed of getting the land back someday."[2]

The summit proved to be a watershed event. To fully understand its importance, the three decades leading up to it must be considered. As the Indian Claims Commission case wrapped up in the late 1960s, a new movement had emerged, one dedicated to acquiring land near Woodfords in Alpine County, California, for southern Washoes.

At the same time, the larger American sociopolitical landscape had begun to shift. The federal government's termination agenda spawned an unintended consequence: a renewed vigor among Native communities. New groups like the American Indian Movement, the National Indian Youth Council, and Indians of All Nations reminded Americans and the world at large that Indians had no intention of disappearing. These organizations helped to usher in a new era of Indian self-determination. The Washoes continued their quest to remain on and reclaim at least parts of their ancestral land.

In June 1966 the Washoe Tribal Council amended their constitution to create local community councils at Carson, Dresslerville, and Woodfords. Representatives from the respective community councils would then serve as members of the larger Washoe Tribal Council.

Members of the new Woodfords Council immediately set their minds to the task of acquiring public land for home sites. When Lorenzo Creel had made the land purchases that would become the Dresslerville, Carson, and Reno-Sparks Colonies forty-nine years earlier, members of the Hangalelti (southern Washoes) were disappointed. They did not want to relocate from their homes in the Woodfords Canyon to P'a·walu (central Washoe) land in the Carson Valley or Welmelti (northern Washoe) lands in Reno.

By the late 1960s, there were about 250 Washoes living near Woodfords. Because no land had been procured, many of these people were "squatting" on private lands. The majority of them lived in substandard housing with no running water, far from federal health and welfare centers.

At a Woodfords Community Council meeting in November 1966, the executive secretary of the Nevada Indian Affairs Commission, Alvin James, announced that the majority of Woodfords Washoes had signed a petition in favor of acquiring land from the public domain. They had also signed a petition calling for California Washoes to be placed under the jurisdiction of the Nevada Indian Agency instead of California. After much discussion, the community council chairman, Earl James, made a motion to accept both petitions, which council member Belma Jones seconded. The motion carried by a vote of four to nothing.[3]

A resolution from the Washoe Tribal Council the following year, 1967, called for action on both of the Woodfords petition items. The resolution acknowledged the "vastly sub-standard housing" of Woodfords Washoes but recognized their strong desire to remain in their southern lands. It stated, "These people do not want to relocate because this not only was the home of their ancestors, but has been their home all of their lives." The resolution suggested that Bureau of Land Management (BLM) lands be provided "for use as home sites for members of the Washoe Tribe." The tribal council also passed a subsequent resolution asking for a transfer in jurisdiction for California Washoes to Nevada. They requested help from the Bureau of Indian Affairs, the BLM, and the states of California and Nevada.[4] On June 5, 1967, the superintendent of the Nevada Indian Agency sent a letter to the commissioner of Indian affairs, supporting the request for a jurisdiction transfer. The commissioner approved, and on January 27, 1968, the transfer occurred.

The same year Nevada Democratic senator Alan Bible proposed a land-transfer bill. Bible grew up in Lovelock, Nevada, and earned a degree from the University of Nevada, Reno, and a law degree from Georgetown. He began work on Capitol Hill as an elevator attendant, a job he got from his mentor, the long-serving Nevada senator Pat McCarren. Following McCarren's death in 1954, Nevada voters elected Bible to three consecutive terms. As the chairman for a subcommittee on parks and recreation, he had a hand in creating close to one hundred national parks, monuments, and historical sites. He helped establish California's Point Reyes National Park, and he expanded Nevada's Toiyabe National Forest, among other projects.

In June 1968 Bible sent the Woodfords Community Council a letter with a copy of the proposed land-transfer bill, Senate Bill 2257. The council expressed their approval. Even with Senator Bible shepherding the bill, it took two years and several committee hearings to pass.[5]

On July 30, 1970, the U.S. Congress passed Public Law 91–362, "An Act to declare that the United States holds in trust for the Washoe Tribe of Indians certain lands in Alpine County, California." It was a short act, declaring that eighty acres in Alpine County would be held in trust by the United States for the Washoe Tribe. The money to purchase it would be "deducted from any appropriation that is made to satisfy a judgment by the Indian Claims Commission." Unfortunately, mirroring earlier government efforts to secure lands for the tribe, the acquisition was far from ideal. It was a rocky shelf unsuitable for farming. One tribal member, Fred Duman, said he would rather move to Alcatraz. But other community members did not see it that way. Belma Jones acknowledged that the land was not their first choice but said she would move to the property once it was ready. Community chairman Earl James admitted the land consisted of "rocks and brush" but thought it would make a good place for housing. At the very least, southern Washoes now had a place close to their ancestral homes.[6]

As more and more Native communities across the West began scoring victories, it became apparent that termination was dead. Indians had taken a strong hand in shaping their own futures. A period of self-determination had begun. Washoes started asserting their sovereign rights. An example of this can be found in their effort to gain control of regulating hunting and fishing in their Pine Nut Lands.

The issue of Washoe hunting and fishing rights can be traced back to the 1860s, during the Comstock era, when Euro-Americans began overfishing Lake Tahoe and overhunting the Pine Nuts. The fact that Nevada Indians did not technically fall within state jurisdiction forced legislators to be creative.

The Northern Paiutes, who had a large reservation that included Pyramid Lake, were in a perfect position to supply the growing American market with fresh fish. By the 1870s Paiutes were selling up to $10,000 worth of fish annually. Because the Nevada state legislature could not enforce their fishing and hunting laws on the reservation, they worked around Paiute sovereignty by putting in place strict regulations regarding the transport of fish from Pyramid on rail lines. This effectively put an end to the Native people's large-scale fish trade.[7]

For Washoes, who did not have reserved lands until 1917, there was no question that they *would* be subject to the state hunting and fishing laws. In the midst of the human deluge connected to the Comstock, Washoes did not have time or the ability to contest state hunting laws. It was not until the tribe regathered its strength following the initial wave of American colonization that it would bring the issue to the federal government's attention. The petition Washoes sent to the federal government in 1914 (which was discussed in chapter 6) included a request for special hunting and fishing rights.[8]

In response to the petition, the assistant commissioner of Indian affairs, E. B. Meritt, sent a letter requesting that the superintendent of the Carson Indian School "inform the office as to whether there is any action to be taken that lies within your authority which will be of assistance to them." Five days later, the superintendent responded, "I have talked the matter over with local authorities and I am informed that the State Fish and Game Laws, have been construed to apply to the Indians and white people alike, within the boarders [sic] of the State. Inasmuch as the Washoe Indians do not live upon an Indian Reservation, they have no right to the privilege of hunting and fishing without procuring a license." The superintendent went on to explain that the matter would likely be taken up by the Nevada state legislature the following January. He concluded, "If the Office so desires, I shall proceed to interview our assembly men looking toward that end."[9]

Action did not follow, and the problem persisted year after year.

Tribal council minutes from October 11, 1954, stated, "After inquiring whether the Indians had a right to hunt in their pine nut lands any time they want, it was found that individuals can hunt only during the hunting season. The matter was set aside until a committee or council members confer with the fish and game commission." More than twenty years would pass before the issue was finally addressed.[10]

In October 1975 state officials made it clear that they would enforce hunting regulations in the Pine Nuts. The Department of Fish and Game held a drawing for deer tags that year for a district that included the Pine Nuts and informed Washoes they could not hunt for deer if they did not get a tag.

In 1978 the tribal council created a Hunting and Fishing Ordinance that provided detailed regulations for tribal lands along with conservation practices. Robert Hunter, the superintendent of the Western Nevada Indian Agency, approved the ordinance on December 12, 1978. Washoe members Vernell Frank and Carl James had been hunting in the Pine Nuts for subsistence for years. In coordination with the tribe, Frank and James sued two Nevada officials for the right to hunt in the Pine Nut Lands free from state authority. The U.S. District Court for the State of Nevada heard the case: *Washoe Tribe of the States of Nevada and California, and Vernell Frank and Carl James v. Joseph Greenley, Director for the State of Nevada, Department of Wildlife, and William Parsons, Chief of Law Enforcement for the State of Nevada Department of Wildlife, individually and in their official capacities.* The case focused on the question of whether the State of Nevada possessed the right to regulate hunting in the Pine Nut Lands.

The court's "Finding of Fact," issued in April 1980, acknowledged that the Pine Nut Lands fell within the "aboriginal territory" of the tribe. It further concluded that hunting of deer, antelope, and rabbits along with the gathering of pine nuts constituted recognized "aboriginal use" of the lands. Moreover, Washoes had traditionally practiced strict conservation methods and, as evidenced by their 1978 hunting ordinance, were prepared to do so once again.

Part of the purpose for setting aside the Pine Nuts, the court explained, had been to provide "exclusive hunting and fishing grounds" for Washoes. The court held that the enforcement of Nevada hunting laws on the Pine Nut Lands would "infringe upon the exercise of the powers of self-government of the Washoe Tribe."[11]

The court decreed on April 16, 1980, "The Washoe Pinenut Allotments are not subject to the jurisdiction of the State of Nevada with respect to the hunting activities of members of the Washoe Tribe within such Allotments." The ruling went on: "Members of the Washoe Tribe of Nevada and California may hunt within the Washoe Pinenut Allotments subject to the jurisdiction of the Washoe Tribe of Nevada and California, and free of direct or indirect regulation by the State of Nevada." The adjudication specifically recognized the Washoes' right to exercise "powers of self government" on tribal lands.[12]

The State of Nevada appealed the ruling to the Ninth Circuit Court of Appeals. On April 15, 1982, the appeals court dismissed the case, explaining that because the State of Nevada had not been specifically named in the case, and because the state did not "intervene or otherwise enter an appearance in the district court," it had no legal standing to appeal. Peter Sferrazza, tribal attorney, hailed the ruling as "the first case to hold that states are without jurisdiction to regulate hunting and fishing by tribal members on off-reservation allotments." The outcome demonstrated that by the early 1980s, the Washoe Tribal Council had found a footing from which it could begin to meaningfully impact regional, state, and national politics.[13]

The same year that the appeals court dismissed Nevada's case, the tribe made another significant land acquisition. But, as in all its gains, the Washoes did not get all they wanted. In 1980, due to declining enrollments and the desire to cut costs, the Bureau of Indian Affairs closed the doors of the Stewart Indian School. Following the closure, maintenance of the school grounds and buildings, many of which had fallen into serious disrepair, became the job of a small handful of BIA employees. It quickly became apparent that the BIA could no longer afford the upkeep. They therefore issued a one-year revocable permit for the Washoe Tribe to manage the facilities and grounds. In return, tribal members could work the agricultural lands that had formerly been part of the school. The Washoe Tribal Council realized they had an opportunity to gain back a small piece of their ancestral lands and passed a resolution on April 14, 1981, asking that the former school grounds become part of the Washoe reservation.

At the same time, the governor of Nevada, Robert List, asked the secretary of the interior to turn over all former school buildings and land to the State of Nevada. On October 6, 1982, the U.S. Congress passed Public Law 97–288. Although the State of Nevada was awarded most of the former school buildings, the act granted to the Washoe Tribe close to 3,000 acres of land that had formerly encompassed them. The Washoe acquisition included the farmlands and a couple of the school buildings. Also included in the conveyance to the Washoes were two parcels in the Clear Creek watershed. Clear Creek forms high in the eastern Sierra and descends 4,000 feet below to the Carson Valley. Prior to American colonization, Clear Creek provided a significant passageway for Washoes traveling from the valley to Tahoe. Its rich riparian resources also drew hunters, fishers, and gatherers. The addition of these parcels provided a physical and symbolic link for Washoes to their history and culture. It also created space for twentieth-century weavers to gather willow for baskets.[14]

Although tribal holdings had increased significantly, the dream of regaining land at Lake Tahoe remained elusive. Individuals had been finding ways to spend summers there since the advent of Tahoe tourism in the 1870s. But by the late twentieth century, Lake Tahoe real estate values were among the highest in the nation, and for the tribe acquiring land there had proved impossible.

The presidential summit at Lake Tahoe in 1997 opened new doors. Suddenly, if only briefly, Washoes were thrust into the center of national attention. The most powerful politicians in the United States acknowledged the right of Washoes to control land at their ancestral lake. The memorandum of understanding signed between the Washoe Tribe and the U.S. federal government, represented by the Forest Service, reaffirmed a federal commitment to "a government-to-government" relationship with the tribe. It also promised a "stronger working relationship on issues affecting the Washoe Tribe in the Lake Tahoe Basin." More important, the tribe had a commitment from the president of the

United States to provide land for them at Lake Tahoe. The "presidential commitment" included tribal management of 350 acres known as "Meeks Creek Meadow" on the western shore of the lake.[15]

One of the plans for land acquisition centered on the meadow. Traditionally, Washoe families used the Meeks area for summer home sites. From there they could fish in the lake and surrounding tributaries, gather medicinal and edible plants, and hunt along the timberline to the west. The plan for Meeks Meadow coming out of the summit stated that the Washoes wanted to "revitalize heritage and cultural knowledge, including the care and harvest of traditional plants." The land around Meeks Meadow, which backs up to the Desolation Wilderness, had been more or less preserved. The only significant development had been made in 1921 when an American built a small resort at the lake's edge that consisted of cabins and a campground. In 1998 Washoes won a twenty-year lease in a competitive bid to control more than 350 acres of Meeks Meadow and run the resort. The tribe is able to use the land and occasionally holds tribal events such as cultural camps there.[16]

When Clinton committed the federal government to getting land for the Washoes at Lake Tahoe, he did not mean just in the form of a lease. He wanted the tribe to actually hold title to land in trust with the federal government. According to George Waters, a Washoe lobbyist, President Clinton wanted to use an executive order to transfer land. But recent federal legislation disallowed that kind of exchange. At the behest of President Clinton, and in order to honor federal commitments, Nevada senator Harry Reid, who had been a primary organizer of the summit, proposed legislation for the land conveyance. Similar to the ICC and the Bible bill for alpine lands, the tribe would have to wait. Partisan politics stalled the bill. It took five years, but finally in 2003 President George W. Bush signed Public Law 108–67, granting approximately 25 acres of Forest Service land "to be held in trust for the Washoe."

The act's "Findings and Purposes" make it clear that Washington officials had been listening in 1997. It states a primary purpose of the act to be the assurance that Washoes "have the opportunity to engage in traditional and customary cultural practices on the shore of Lake

Tahoe to meet the needs of spiritual renewal, land stewardship, Washoe horticulture and ethnobotany, subsistence gathering, traditional learning, and reunification of tribal and family bonds."[17]

Asked about management practices, Brian Wallace, the tribal chairman, emphasized that the tribe would keep the site in its natural state. While the land would technically be accessible to outsiders, non-Washoes would have to follow Washoe rules at the site. But Wallace stated, "We are not going to put up a barbwire fence. We've had enough of that in our lives."[18]

Even if they wanted to, they could not have put up a fence because the boundaries described in Public Law 108–67 were wrong. The tribe ended up with a steep hillside and unusable shoreline. It took another six years for the boundary issue to be fixed. The passage of P.L. 111–11 in 2009 corrected the boundaries by adding about 100 feet of shoreline at scenic, undeveloped Skunk Harbor. It had taken decades of work, a presidential summit, and two federal laws to get there, but the dream of returning to the lake's shore had become reality.

Another item that had been broached by Washoes during the presidential summit was their concern for the ongoing desecration of the sacred site Deʔek Wadapuš, "Rock Standing Gray" or "Cave Rock." President Clinton had instructed the Forest Service to work closely with Washoes in managing Tahoe lands. Moreover, the Forest Service was instructed to conduct environmental studies at Cave Rock and "assist the Washoe Tribe in long range planning for the area."[19]

Cave Rock towers more than 360 feet above Tahoe's eastern shore. It is clearly visible from most parts of the 72 miles of lake shoreline. Meeks Bay Resort, directly across the lake, allows a clear view of the monolith 12 miles away. The formation has long been the center of powerful forces in the Washoe world. Prior to the arrival of Euro-Americans, Cave Rock was used exclusively by shamans. Across the American West, archaeologists consistently find evidence of humans having lived in caves, using them for survival purposes.

Given its proximity to Tahoe's shore, Cave Rock would have made an ideal shelter or summer home site for Washoe families. But archaeological remains and the oral tradition prove that ancestral Washoes did not use the cave that way. The first archaeological excavation in the 1950s and another in 1997, done by teams of archaeologists from the University of California, Berkeley, revealed a clear absence of materials that characterize a habitation center. Archaeologists did find an inscribed mammal bone and basalt projectile points there. But those items were brought to the cave, not made there, and they support the oral history that the area was used for esoteric purposes.[20]

Washoe shamans maintained a relationship with the site after colonization and well into the twentieth century. It is impossible to know what shamans did there. They guarded their practices even from their closest associates. One of the few living Washoe elders to have helped a shaman work at the site, Darrel Bender, was told to "mind his own business" when he asked the shaman what he did there. All Bender could say is that it had something to do with acquiring or maintaining power. There was a prescribed ritual handed down through many generations; people of power had to offer prayers and ceremonies at the site in an attempt to commune with the resident powers.[21]

It was understood that these shamans typically worked for the health of their communities. Ministrations at the site were done to help protect the people and the land. But like the rest of Washoe country, Cave Rock was significantly altered to satisfy American development. To accommodate increasing traffic along Highway 50, the main roadway from San Francisco and Sacramento along Tahoe's south shore to Carson City, two tunnels were blasted below Cave Rock, the first in 1931, the second in 1957. Many Washoes were sickened by the destruction. Some objected strongly, but no one listened. Why would anyone listen to a small Indian community that had no "legal" right to the land?

Beginning in 1989 rock climbers secured the first of what would eventually be 350 anchors on the rock face, turning Cave Rock into a world-class climbing venue. In the early 1990s the budding climbing superstar Dan Osman built several routes. The site had become "a [climber's] refuge with the most gymnastic routes in the state." When the Washoe community became aware of the climbers' presence at Cave Rock, they protested. In 1992 the chairman, Brian Wallace, started speaking publicly about Washoe concerns. At about the same time, a

Boulder, Colorado–based climbing-advocacy group, the Access Fund, began paying careful attention. A battle was brewing.[22]

Washoe efforts to protect their sacred site seemed to get a boost when in 1996, Cave Rock was proposed as a National Register cultural property. Many climbers had already abandoned the site after learning of its significance to the tribe. Some had not. The federal agency charged with resolving the dispute, the U.S. Forest Service, took their first concrete action in February 1997 when the supervisor for Lake Tahoe, Robert Harris, issued a temporary ban on climbing while the matter was studied. While Washoes took hope from the action, it motivated climbers and the Access Fund to take action. Harris had retired soon after he put the ban in place. The new supervisor, Juan Palma, faced immediate pressure, in the form of protest letters from climbers and threatened legal action from the Access Fund. In May 1997 he rescinded the ban.[23]

In an effort to broker a compromise, the Forest Service held a series of five collaborative meetings, the first on January 22, 1998. The meetings were contentious, with climbers offering concessions if they were allowed to continue using the site and Washoes saying it was unfair to ask them to compromise their values. Asked why the Washoes would not enter into the give-and-take, leader Wallace said that they were "depicted as uncompromising because they refused to agree to further destruction." At the last meeting, on May 27, 1998, Washoe elder Ruth Abbie spoke: "We've tried to hang on to whatever we had. . . . We couldn't object to them destroying Cave Rock, this natural, pristine site. The government goes right in there and does what they want: build a road. That's progress. They never inquired of the Washoes. Do you understand how strongly the Washoes feel about that? When we try to fight for the little we have left, the sacred spots, well, it's just like talking in the wind."[24]

Some climbers who attended the meetings went on the record in support of closing the site for climbing. Others expressed a deep connection to climbing at the site, insisting they did not want to lose it. In an effort to compromise, climbers and the Access Fund proposed voluntary climbing bans if Washoe shamans came to Cave Rock, provided that did not occur more than a half-dozen times or so a year. Chairman Wallace, elder Abbie, and other Washoe participants made clear their position. The decision would be left to the Forest Service.

In the fall of 1998, Carol Shull, the keeper of the National Register, determined that Cave Rock was eligible for protection not only as a cultural site but also as a historic transportation district and an archaeological site. These new designations offered other legal justifications for a climbing ban. Paul Minault, an attorney for the Access Fund, responded forcefully to Shull's findings. In a letter to Juan Palma, he questioned the authenticity of Washoe claims at Cave Rock. Minault accused the tribe of wanting to prohibit climbing as an expression of their "resurgent political power."[25]

Supervisor Palma, who had attended two of the five meetings, made his decision public, in what would be the central part of a Draft Environmental Impact Statement, in January 1999. He chose to allow rock climbing, if it were managed carefully to reduce negative effects on the site. The DEIS, released later that year, explained Palma's reasoning. He believed the site had to be preserved in its physical state up to the year 1996, when it was designated a cultural property. Because most of the climbing routes had been installed prior to 1996, they were part of the rock's history and therefore worthy of protection. Washoes received the news as a bitter defeat, although there was still time before the final decision would be rendered. Palma would not be making the decision. He had accepted a job with the BLM, leaving the Tahoe basin.

Maribeth Gustafson, from the Pacific Southwest Regional Office in San Francisco, became the new supervisor in July 2000. She immediately started working through the case history on Cave Rock: viewing film of the collaboration meetings, interviewing parties from the opposing sides as well as state and federal historic preservation officials, and touring the site with the Forest Service archaeologist. In 2002 Gustafson issued the Final Environmental Impact Statement on Cave Rock. It reversed Palma's finding, proposing a ban on climbing at the site. Gustafson's definition of the historic period at Cave Rock differed from Palma's by more than thirty years. She calculated the appropriate dates to be "prehistory" to 1965, the year Henry Rupert, the most renowned of the Washoe shamans, died. The site was to be protected as a cultural property and maintained as it was at that time. Because rock climbing was an adverse activity, destructive to the rock face, it would not be allowed.

Throughout his life, Rupert had adapted to the numerous changes at Cave Rock, continuing to use the place, although never speaking of his association with it. When an anthropologist tried to explore Rupert's experience in the 1950s, Rupert did not deny his practices but would not discuss them in detail. Rupert told the anthropologist, "I am not allowed to brag about my work and tell people what I can do. You don't advertise this kind of work."[26]

The Final Environmental Impact Statement described Rupert as a man who had exemplified "the tension Native traditional practitioners maintain between tradition, experimentation, and innovation." His power had continued to resonate in the twenty-first century.[27]

Before the ban could go into place, protesting climbers would have their day in court. Although the Access Fund was not of one mind on the issue, with the staff voting unanimously not to appeal the closure, the fund's attorneys and board of directors chose to push on and immediately requested that the Forest Service Regional Office review the issue. Although agreeing to postpone the ban until the courts ruled on Gustafson's decision, the climbing group's appeal was rejected by the Forest Service. The case was taken to the federal district court in Reno.

Fund lawyers argued that closing the site to climbing was in violation of the First Amendment. In particular, they reasoned, the prohibition of rock climbing at a public site to protect Washoe religious practices violated the Establishment Clause of the First Amendment. Historically, First Amendment arguments won for litigants who wanted to use Native sacred sites, and so the Access Fund pursued the argument, even though Gustafson insisted the closure was because of Cave Rock's cultural value. Judge Howard McKibben found nothing illegal about Gustafson's decision. He also accepted the Forest Service's argument that they were prohibiting climbing at Cave Rock to protect a significant historical and cultural site, not to promote Washoe religion.

The Access Fund proceeded to appeal the case to the next level of review. On August 27, 2007, the Ninth Circuit Court of Appeals issued its decision. Access Fund attorneys had pressed the First Amendment argument and also contended that Gustafson had acted arbitrarily and capriciously in reversing Palma's finding. The appeals court agreed with the lower court that "there was no hint that they agency favored tribal religion over other religions," but that owing primarily to its Washoe history, Cave Rock was a cultural, historical, and archaeological monument. Gustafson's thorough documentation showed further that the decision had been neither arbitrary nor capricious. The Ninth Circuit Court therefore upheld the district court's decision. Cave Rock would be closed to climbing.[28]

Like so many of the Washoe victories, this was still only partially satisfying. The tunnels remained. Cave Rock continues to be open for noninvasive recreational activity. People who have no connection to the ancient power and significance of the site can hike to the top and explore the cave. Nevertheless, it was a victory. The people whose ancestors had used the lake and its surrounding lands for thousands of years had stopped the destruction of one of their most valued places.

The acquisition of tribal lands and the expansion of economic ventures characterize the late twentieth and the early twenty-first centuries. Today a growing Washoe administrative complex occupies space on both sides of Highway 395 in the Pine Nuts, near the Dresslerville community. The buildings include administrative offices, the tribal court, maintenance operations, and offices dedicated to expanding social, economic, and environmental service programs. A state-of-the-art health center in the Dresslerville community provides an array of professional health services for tribal members. Dr. Loren Simpson, an attending primary care physician at the Washoe Health Clinic, who is also a member of the tribe, chose to return to the community where he grew up. "I came back because I wanted my kids to grow up here too." With the addition of new technologies like a digital X-ray machine, Dr. Simpson and other physicians are able to provide comprehensive care as well as respond quickly to medical emergencies.[29]

The tribe's successes and growth cannot obscure the fact that significant challenges persist. Poverty remains prevalent on reserved lands.

A study in the early 1990s revealed that up to 20 percent of the eligible workforce was not employed. Close to a quarter of those who did work were earning less than $7,000 a year. The continuing economic challenges are manifested in many harmful ways. Substance abuse and violence pose particularly troubling problems in each of the Washoe communities. The presence of gangs grew in the 1990s. The root of the problem is the ongoing colonization: alienated youths growing up in isolated, impoverished communities, while traditional Washoe lands house hotels, casinos, and businesses earning remarkable profits and homes that denote tremendous affluence.[30]

To combat the alienation and suffering, the tribe embarked on an extensive educational campaign that includes curriculum from kindergarten to college. For the youngest children, the tribal Curriculum Committee created a Washoe coloring book, with a map showing the locations of the regions of the three Washoe bands and the center of the Washoe world, Lake Tahoe. The book offers page-length descriptions of topics ranging from Washoe basketry and Datsolalee to traditional stories such as "The Two Sisters Who Married the Stars." The illustrations to be colored include traditional Washoe people, structures, tools, and food sources.

Language retention forms the critical center of educational efforts. Woodfords community member and language teacher Beverley Caldera tells her grandchildren, "If you no longer have your language, then you no longer have the right to be called Washoe." In 2006 Caldera and a local kindergarten teacher collaborated to create a family-tree project for students. The children would populate a family tree with photographs and the Washoe terms for each of their relatives.[31]

It is impossible to determine what specific efforts were made toward language retention over the first several decades of American colonial activities in Washoe country. It is, however, clear that as early as the 1950s, individuals began experimenting with converting the spoken Washoe language into a written form. The current culture/language resource director for the tribe, Herman Fillmore, explained that Roma James began translating Washoe stories in the 1950s, and Marvin Dressler attempted to sound out Washoe words and write them down phonetically in English; some of Dressler's early attempts are kept in bound journals in tribal archives.[32]

In 1979 the tribe hired William Jacobsen, a linguistics professor, to begin teaching Washoe-language classes two nights a week. Early on, it became evident the community would have to wrestle with the question over whether to use an "official" written orthography or a more user-friendly phonetic rendering of the spoken language. This question has divided community members over the past couple of decades, at times intensely, but Washoes have not lost their focus on teaching each new generation how to speak and communicate in Washoe. Fillmore makes it clear that the priority is to help keep the spoken language alive. Rather than lose valuable time and effort arguing over which written form of the language to use, Fillmore and other teachers put most emphasis on speaking lessons. For example, Lisa Enos, who teaches a course called Let's All Speak the Same Language, does not allow students to use pen and paper because she wants students to speak and hear the language without relying on the written words.[33] There is a determined urgency to the language work being done today, for good reason. Without attention and significant effort, there is a risk that the Washoe language could cease to exist. It is hard to estimate how many fluent speakers of the language are currently living, but the number is certainly fewer than twenty.

One of the most successful and notable endeavors aimed at language retention emerged in the late 1990s when Laura Fillmore (Herman's mother) and others created a full-immersion school, where students learned all of their subjects in the Washoe language, with Washoe cultural values underscoring the school's curriculum. The school modeled itself after the incredibly successful Hawaiian immersion-school program. Laura, a non-Native woman who married Benny Fillmore, a member of the Washoe community, dedicated much of her university studies to Native-language revival and immersion-school opportunities. She also developed strong skills in grant writing, which served the immersion program well. From the beginning, the program relied on the knowledge and participation of many community members, particularly elders who could speak the language. Elders who played a critical role were Adele James, Herman Holbrook, Sylvia Andrews, Eleanor Smokey, Amy Barber, Daniel McDonald, Tina Wyatt, Steven James, and Wes Barber. Many students went through the program until it ended in 2003.[34]

Herman, a graduate of the immersion school, went on to gain a degree from the University of New Mexico in 2012. His desire to promote the priorities established by the immersion school, and to put his newly acquired knowledge to work for the Washoes, brought him home. Herman is quick to deflect attention from himself. He insists that the community is what is important: "There is strength in this community, and that is the basis for all of our revitalization efforts; students and community members are just as important, if not more important, than teachers." In a recent conversation, Herman explained that many people are presently involved in language-retention work. Their priority is to start with the children; language serves as the vehicle for helping Washoe youths to understand the value of their culture, the longevity of their people in the eastern Sierra, and the strength of their traditions. Herman along with elder Melba Rakow, Mischelle Dressler, Lisa Enos, and Kristin Burtt fight on a daily basis to make sure the Washoe language will continue to be spoken in the eastern Sierra. Among the southern Washoes elders, Dinah Pete, Madeline Henry, and Beverly Caldera are also hard at work keeping the language alive.[35]

The elders who offered the invocation for the 1997 Summit at Lake Tahoe, Jo Ann Smokey Martinez and her sister Theresa Smokey Jackson, taught elements of Washoe culture, including weaving, in Douglas County schools from 1988 to 2005. Nevada governor Bob Miller awarded the Smokey sisters the Governor's Excellence in Folk Arts Award for their work in education. It is clear that throughout the twentieth and now twenty-first centuries, members of the Washoe Tribe have worked and will continue to work to make sure future generations will know their culture and their language.[36]

In 2006 the coordinator of the youth educational program, Liz Garcia, described how a two-day journey to Lake Tahoe was one piece of a larger tribal initiative called the "Native Extreme Teen Challenge." At Tahoe the teenagers were instructed in archery and bow making.

As well as challenging them "spiritually, physically, educationally, and mentally," an object of the program is for the young people to be able to live five days off the land.[37]

The issue of cultural preservation has been a fundamental concern of Washoes since colonization began. It formed a core of the first significant tribal development plan created in 1973. In 2006 the tribe created the Tribal Historic Preservation Office, which is the tribal equivalent of a state historic preservation office. It manages all elements of cultural affairs. This includes collaboration and advisory work with local, state, and regional agencies. Darrel Cruz, the tribal historic preservation officer, works with an advisory council that is made up of elders and community members. One of the buildings controlled by the Washoes in the former Stewart Indian School campus serves as the Cultural Center and Archives building. There is another educational center, library, and archive repository on the Woodfords reservation.

In 1999 a grant from the Environmental Protection Agency provided funds for the creation of the Washoe Environmental Protection Department (WEPD). Utilizing the grant, the Washoes have been able to establish mechanisms for evaluating water resources, fire management, and range conservation. The approaches to environmental protections represent a balanced mix between traditional conservation practices and new technology-based initiatives.

A central concern for the WEPD is water. Like the entire American West, water in Washoe lands can be scare and is often overallocated. What water they control exists in the form of surface wetlands, groundwater, a small allocation of the Carson River, and unassigned rights to the Clear Creek watershed. Their share of the Carson's flow is used to water the Stewart Ranch, acquired in 1982. But because the allocation is minimal, combined with ongoing draught, water availability is precarious.

To protect surface- and groundwater sources, the WEPD initiated an extensive water-sampling program. The program included global positioning system and geographic information system mapping of wetlands. The technologically driven monitoring system has taken into account the many complicated factors involved in maintaining a modern wetlands with the various industrial and agricultural waste. In 2006 the Washoes released their "Wetland Protection and Mitigation Standards" in an effort to protect and reclaim watered areas. The plan included a provision for establishing "buffer" zones consisting of 250 feet on the edge of creek banks and all wetlands in general. The program also established the rule that for every acre of wetland on tribal lands that is compromised, another two acres of protected wetlands must be created.[38]

The tribe has had moderate success in the economic arena. The Washoe Development Group serves as the business arm of the tribal council. It manages seven distinct tribe-owned businesses, including two smoke-shop markets, the tribal ranch, and a Chevron gas station in Carson City. These entities have brought in marginal profits because of evolving challenges but remain valuable, as they continue to provide jobs for tribal members. A fairly new avenue of economic development centers on the construction and maintenance of renewable sources of energy. The Washoe Wisk'e'em "wind" project was made possible by a congressional act in 2010. The project calls for the creation of four small vertical wind turbines on tribal lands. In June 2011 two of the turbines were completed.[39]

A study of housing on reserved lands determined that almost 70 percent of those living on Washoe lands own their own homes. The Washoe Housing Authority's Mutual Assistance Program helped many of the owners to buy their homes without long-term mortgages. In fact, close to 80 percent of those who own homes on reservation lands do not have mortgages or equity loans against their property, and because of recent Housing and Urban Development funding, a new Dresslerville subdivision including twenty-three single-family detached homes is in the planning stages.[40]

As illustrated by the struggle with peyote, the challenge of administering the Pine Nuts, the prolonged Indian Claims Commission case, and land acquisitions, from its creation the Washoe Tribal Council has wrestled with complex problems. Because the form of governance created by the 1934 Indian Reorganization Act is not a traditional Washoe institution, a segment of the community continues to challenge decisions of the council. Those engaged in governing seek more efficient means of directing affairs. In a 2011 development plan, tribal administrators listed a growing bureaucracy that "gets in the way of progress" as one of their biggest challenges. It also listed "fragmentation" as an ongoing problem. Evidence of this can be found in recent one-term chairmanships and the recall of a tribal chair.[41]

In the spring of 2006, a group of more than one hundred Washoes made a strenuous two-day, fourteen-mile hike from Carson City, Nevada, to Lake Tahoe. Following a route established by their ancestors, the first day they walked up Kings Canyon to a camping site at Spooner Lake, seven thousand feet above sea level. Rueben Vasques, a thirteen-year-old resident of Dresslerville, said it felt like the ancestors were "walking with us," and nineteen-year-old Erick Enos noted the importance of following "in the footsteps of our ancestors." On the second day of the journey, as participants reached the lakeshore at Skunk Harbor, they offered prayers, like their ancestors generations before them.[42]

The presidential summit of 1997 set in motion a series of events that brought Washoe concerns to public light and prompted their reclamation of land on both the east and the west shores of Tahoe. Despite a century and a half of abuses, dislocations, and exploitation, the Washoes have continued to maintain their connection to the symbolic center of their lands. In the wake of the summit, elder Winona James expressed a sentiment that continues to unite Washoe people: "Our hearts are still with Tahoe." As former chairman Brian Wallace stated at the acquisition of the Skunk Harbor property: "This is not the end point; this is just the beginning of our journey back home."[43]

AFTERWORD

One evening in July 2008, I set out north along the base of the eastern Sierra on Foothill Road. I wound my way up Kingsbury grade, reached the summit, and began the descent toward Lake Tahoe. I followed Highway 50 on Tahoe's eastern shore, passing through the eastbound tunnel at Cave Rock, continuing past the dense second-growth pine forests. I was heading to Sand Harbor, a public beach on Tahoe's northeast shore, known for its white sand beaches and its annual Shakespeare festival.

My friend Art George Jr. had invited me to a production of *A Midsummer Night's Dream*. George, a Washoe man, played a role at the end of the production. He entered the stage in the final scene as the actors were waking from their fairy-induced slumber. There is no comparable character in Shakespeare's original play; Michael Walling, the director, had added the role. Walling, who is from England, explained his addition: "In America . . . you have living and breathing beside you, a culture which remains vibrant and alive, while retaining its deep indigenous roots in the landscapes of the continent."[1]

Once onstage George stoked a fire of sage and juniper. As smoke rose he offered prayers in the Washoe language. The historical significance of a Washoe man offering prayers on the shore of Tahoe may not have been apparent to all viewers, but a Native American praying over a fire with a sweeping view of the lake ringed by majestic mountains in the background had a palpable effect. The audience burst into sustained applause. When I met George after the play, a number of spectators and cast members lingered. A man approached George and said, "Hey, great job tonight." Art thanked him, turned to me, and said, "My part was easy—I wasn't acting." The fire George stoked helps to illustrate the rekindling of the Washoe presence at their ancestral lake. Washoes never left their beloved lake; it is just that now outsiders are beginning to recognize their ancestral connection and to a limited degree Washoe legal rights to their home lands. At the time of the performance, the tribe had just recently gained access to Meeks Meadow and Meeks Bay and acquired the property at Skunk Harbor. The acquisitions, the fulfillment of a long, painful journey, had been precipitated by the determination of Washoes who refused to leave their ancestral lands.

Washoe history, like that of all small western tribes, is important in its own right. But it also speaks to the larger understanding of the American West and the United States. The collective American memory is well established and hard to change. Many Americans associate the terms *colony* and *colonization* with the thirteen British colonies on the Atlantic slope, not with American usurpation of Native lands in the West. Hearing the term *Indian,* non-Natives might imagine a Plains warrior in full regalia, mounted on horseback, or Graham Greene in the movie *Thunderheart.* They might not think of their neighbor who happens to be Indian as part of the deep imperial and colonial history of the North American continent.

Over the past half century, scholars have begun to contextualize the vastly diverse experiences of Native people in American history. That work has borne fruit. Today, in the first chapter of some American history textbooks, a reader might encounter a Native creation story juxtaposed with the land-bridge theory. But no one would suggest there is not still work to be done.[2]

The Washoe story provides a ballast for the popular version of American history in the eastern Sierra world. The growth of the United States was not a simple progression of civilization into the "wilderness." That "wilderness" had been composed of complex, organized societies developed by Native peoples, including the Washoes, for thousands of years before Americans arrived.

From the impact of the first wave of California gold seekers to the presidential summit at Lake Tahoe in 1997, Washoes have worked to maintain a presence in their homeland. Although they still suffer from the long-term effects of colonization, they also continue to fight for a future that maintains their identity as the Waši·šiw, "the People from Here."

NOTES

PREFACE

1. Amy James, Washoe, interview by Jo Ann Nevers, Reno-Sparks Indian Colony, October 23, 1975 (Reno: Inter-Tribal Council of Nevada Archives Project, file 100), as cited in Jo Ann Nevers, *Wa She Shu: A Washo Tribal History* (Reno: Inter-Tribal Council of Nevada, 1976), 6–10.

INTRODUCTION

1. Dick Bender, who served as an interpreter for Captain Jim, gave information about the trip to Washington, D.C. See Dick Bender, "Washoe Indian's [sic] Timber Land of Nevada and Their Claims on the Pinenut Range," folder 254, box 2, Reno, Nev., Indian Agency Special Agent Land Correspondence, 1908–24, Record Group 75, National Archives and Records Administration, Pacific Region, San Bruno, Calif. See also Jo Ann Nevers, *Wa She Shu: A Washo Tribal History* (Reno: Inter-Tribal Council of Nevada, 1976), 57–61. Information on Epesuwa and reference to his meeting with the president can be found in *Life Stories of Our Native People: Shoshone, Paiute, Washo* (Reno: Inter-Tribal Council of Nevada, 1974), 13. Cimé Dimé means "Double Water"; the springs are located off Highway 395, just south of Minden, Nevada. Many elders identify this as an area where the T'agim Gumsabayʔ (pine nut harvest festival) was held.
2. Scott Stine, *A Way across the Mountain: Joseph Walker's 1833 Trans-Sierran Passage and the Myth of Yosemite's Discovery* (Norman: University of Oklahoma Press, 2015), 60–61.
3. The quote from Manuel Bender comes from Mary Adelzadeh, "Empowerment

in an Era of Self-Determination: The Case of the Washoe Tribe and US Forest Service Co-management Agreement" (master's thesis, University of Michigan, 2006), 50.
4. Ned Blackhawk, *Violence over the Land: Indians and Empires in the Early American West* (Cambridge, Mass.: Harvard University Press, 2006), 177.
5. John C. Frémont, *Narratives of Exploration and Adventure,* edited by Allan Nevins (New York: Longmans, Green, 1956), 344–60.
6. Historian Colin Calloway, in his work *One Vast Winter Count: The Native American West before Lewis and Clark* (Lincoln: University of Nebraska Press, 2003), observed that the modern American reliance on automobiles and oil may not be that different from Plains Indians' relationship to bison and horses.
7. Steven Michael Fountain, "Big Dogs and Scorched Streams: Horses and Ethnocultural Change in the North American West, 1700–1850" (Ph.D. diss., University of California, Davis, 2007), 3, 9.
8. Khal Schneider, "Making Indian Land in the Allotment Era: Northern California's Indian Rancherias," *Western Historical Quarterly* 41, no. 4 (2010): 431.
9. Adelzadeh, "Empowerment in an Era of Self-Determination," 57–65.
10. See Matthew Makley and Michael J. Makley, *Cave Rock: Climbers, Courts and a Washoe Indian Sacred Place* (Reno: University of Nevada Press, 2010).
11. See Caitlin Aimee Keliiaa, "*Washiw Wagayay Mangal:* Reweaving the Washoe Language" (master's thesis, University of California, Los Angeles, 2012).
12. The late Warren L. d'Azevedo spent much of his professional career working with the Washoes and published an incredible amount of work. See, for example, "The Washo Indians of California and Nevada," *University of Utah Anthropological Papers* 67 (1963): 1–25; "Current Status of Anthropological Research in the Great Basin," *University of Nevada, Desert Research Institute Social Sciences and Humanities Publications* (1966): 130–65; *Straight with the Medicine: Narratives of the Washoe Followers of the Tipi Way* (Reno: Black Rock Press, 1978; reprint, Berkeley: Heyday Books, 1985); "The Delegation to Washington: A Washoe Peyotist Narrative," *Indian Historian* 6, no. 2 (1979): 273–86; and "Washoe," in *The Handbook of North American Indians 11,* edited by William C. Sturtevant (Washington, D.C.: Smithsonian Institution, 1986), 466–96. Other anthropologists include James F. Downs, *The Two Worlds of the Washo: An Indian Tribe of California and Nevada* (New York: Holt, Rinehart, and Winston, 1966); Downs, "Washo Religion," *University of California Publications Anthropological Records* 16, no. 9 (1960): 370–92; Downs, "Effect of Animal Husbandry on Two American Indian Tribes: Washo and Navaho" (Ph.D. diss., University of California, Berkeley, 1961); and Jonathan Price, "The Washo Indians: History, Life Cycle, Religion, Technology, and Modern Life," *Nevada State Museum Occasional Papers* 4 (1980); Price, "Washo Economy" (master's thesis, University of Utah, 1962); Price, *Native Studies: American and Canadian Indians* (Toronto: McGraw-Hill-Ryerson, 1978).

13. Michael Green, *Nevada: A History of the Silver State* (Reno: University of Nevada Press, 2015).
14. James A. Clifton, "The Tribal History: An Obsolete Paradigm," *American Indian Culture and Research Journal* 3, no. 4 (1979): 81–100.
15. Nicholas Rosenthal, "Beyond the New Indian History: Recent Trends in the Historiography on the Native Peoples of North America," *History Compass* 4, no. 5 (2006): 965.
16. Blackhawk, *Violence over the Land*, 26.
17. Pekka Hämäläinen, *The Comanche Empire* (New Haven, Conn.: Yale University Press, 2008), 8, 1.
18. Patrick Wolfe, "Settler Colonialism and the Elimination of the Native," *Journal of Genocide Research* 8, no. 4 (2006): 388, 394. The estimate of $300 million comes from Green, *Nevada*, 130.
19. For a concise and useful description of extractive colonialism, see Nancy Shoemaker, "A Typology of Colonialism," *Perspectives on History: The Newsmagazine of the American Historical Association* (October 2015), https://www.historians.org.
20. James W. Nye, governor and ex officio superintendent of Indian affairs, to Caleb B. Smith, secretary of the interior, July 19, 1861, in *Annual Reports of the Commissioner of Indian Affairs* (Washington, D.C.: Government Printing Office, 1861), 111. The ethnographer was Stephen Powers. See his "The Life and Culture of the Washo and Paiutes," in *Contributions of the University of California Archaeological Research Facility, the Northern California Indians: A Reprinting of 19 Articles on California Indians Originally Published 1872–1877*, edited by Robert F. Heizer, no. 25 (Berkeley: University of California Department of Anthropology, 1975), 204. For information on Stephen Powers, see Don D. Fowler and Catherine S. Fowler, "Stephen Powers' 'The Life and Culture of the Washoe and Paiutes,'" *Ethnohistory* 17, no. 3 (1970): 117–49.
21. Quote from Bobbi Sykes taken from Linda Tuhiwai Smith, *Decolonizing Methodologies: Research and Indigenous Peoples* (1999; reprint, Dunedin: University of New Zealand Press, 2001), 24.
22. Waziyatawin Angela Wilson, *Remember This! Dakota Decolonization and the Eli Taylor Narratives* (Lincoln: University of Nebraska Press, 2005), 1.
23. For a good, concise discussion of the Cabazon case, see Nicholas Rosenthal, "The Dawn of a New Day? Notes on Indian Gaming in Southern California," in *Native Pathways: American Indian Culture and Economic Development in the Twentieth Century*, edited by Brian Hosmer and Colleen O'Neill (Boulder: University Press of Colorado, 2004), 91–110.
24. The quote from Chairman Miguel comes from Alysa Landry, "Ak-Chin Indian Community Files Suit over Water Right," *Indian Country Today*, April 27, 2017, https://indiancountrymedianetwork.com.
25. For a good, concise description of the Ak-Chin case, see Bonnie G. Colby, John

E. Thorson, and Sarah Britton, *Negotiating Tribal Water Rights: Fulfilling Promises in the Arid West* (Tucson: University of Arizona Press, 2005), 112–15.

26. Sam Howe Verhovek, "Reviving Tradition, Tribe Kills a Whale," *New York Times*, May 18, 1999, http://www.nytimes.com.

27. Joshua L. Reid, *The Sea Is My Country: The Maritime World of the Makahs* (New Haven, Conn.: Yale University Press, 2015).

CHAPTER 1: THE PEOPLE FROM HERE

1. For a glimpse of what the canyon holds, see "Lagomarsino Canyon: 10,000 Years of Rock Art," Nevada Rock Art Foundation, 2012, http://www.nvrockart.org.

2. A good place to start with Washoe stories is Grace Dangberg, "Washo Tales: Three Original Washo Indian Legends" (occasional paper, Nevada State Museum, Carson City, 1968), 40–42. The version of the creation story presented here comes directly from the tribe. Darrel Cruz, tribal historic preservation officer, provided the story in written form to me. For the story of creation and Nentushu, see Grace Dangberg, "Washoe Texts," *University of California Publications in American Archaeology and Ethnology* 22, no. 3 (1927): 439–41. The anthropologist James Downs wrote about the use of dual creation stories in his work *The Two Worlds of the Washo: An Indian Tribe of California and Nevada* (New York: Holt, Rinehart, and Winston, 1966), 60.

3. Omer Stewart's testimony appeared before the Indian Claims Commission, docket no. 288, *The Washoe Tribe of the States of Nevada and California, Plaintiff v. The United States, Defendant*, vol. 2 of testimony, transcripts from July 7, 1955, folder "III/2/7/I George Wright Collection Correspondence and Vol. II of Testimony," box 2, d'Azevedo, Warren L., Washoe Indians Research Papers, Collection 99-39, Special Collections Department, University of Nevada, Reno, 70–83. See also Susan Lindstrom, "A Contextual Overview of Human Land Use and Environmental Conditions," in *The Lake Tahoe Watershed Assessment* (South Lake Tahoe, Calif.: U.S. Department of Agriculture Forest Service, Lake Tahoe Basin Management Unit, 2000), 34.

4. Donald K. Grayson, *The Great Basin: A Natural Prehistory* (Berkeley: University of California Press, 2011), 300, http://www.jstor.org.skyline.ucdenver.edu.

5. Geoffrey Smith, "Footprints across the Black Rock: Temporal Variability in Prehistoric Foraging Territories and Toolstone Procurement Strategies in the Western Great Basin," *American Antiquity* 75, no. 4 (2010): 867.

6. Grayson, *Great Basin*, 302.

7. Ibid., 313–14.

8. In 1844 the American explorer John C. Frémont realized that the Washoe spoke a language different from their nearest neighbors. In the twentieth century

linguists designated the Washoe, along with eleven Californian Indian groups, Hokan speakers. What puzzles linguists is how the Hokan-speaking Washoe ended up in the middle of a region dominated by Uto-Aztecan speakers. One explanation places the Washoe in the region very early; the arrival of newcomers gradually created a Hokan island in a Uto-Aztecan sea. There have been studies exploring a possible connection between the Jiaque language, spoken in parts of Honduras, and Hokan, but at this point no definitive conclusions can be made. It is tempting to imagine in the distant past a unified Hokan speaking group that broke apart for various reasons, but that is pure speculation. Most linguists do agree that Hokan-speaking communities are some of the oldest in the Americas. The ten other Hokan-speaking groups are Karok, Shastan, Chimarkiko, Palaih-nihan, Yana, Pomoan, Esselen, Salinan, Chumashan, and Yuman. See William F. Shipley, "Native Languages of California," in *The Handbook of North American Indian*, edited by William C. Sturtevant (Washington, D.C.: Smithsonian Institution, 1978), 8:86–87. For information on the Jiaque language, see Joseph H. Greenberg and Morris Swedesh, "Jiaque as a Hokan Language," *International Journal of American Linguistics* 19, no. 3 (1953): 216–22. The foremost academic expert on Washoe language is William H. Jacobsen Jr. See his "Washoe Language," in *The Handbook of North American Indians*, edited by William C. Sturtevant (Washington, D.C.: Smithsonian Institution, 1986), 11:10. On the spread of Numic speakers, see Grayson, *Great Basin,* 314–19. The Uto-Aztecan language includes Aztecs, Hopis, and many other western tribal peoples from Oregon to Panama. The Washoes' nearest western neighbors, the Maidu, speak Penutian, which includes tribal communities all the way from Alaska to California.

9. For archaeological evidence, see Robert F. Heizer and Albert B. Elsasser, "Some Archaeological Sites and Cultures of the Central Sierra Nevada," *Reports of the University of California Archaeological Survey,* no. 21 (1953): 9, 19. See Stewart's testimony in The Indian Claims Commission, docket no. 288, *The Washoe Tribe of the States of Nevada and California, Plaintiff, v. The United States, Defendant,* vol. 2 of testimony, transcripts from July 7, 1955, folder "III/2/7/I George Wright Collection Correspondence and Vol. II of Testimony," box 2, Washoe Indians Research Papers, 70–83. Since their first contact with Americans, Washoes have spoken to the centrality of Lake Tahoe. See Earl James, Washoe, to Nicholas Allen, May 22, 1961, folder "90-37/I/14 Correspondence Jan.–July, 1961," box 1, George F. Wright Washo Claims Case Records, Collection 90-37/I, Special Collections Department, University of Nevada, Reno. See also Amy James, Washoe, interview by Jo Ann Nevers, Reno-Sparks Indian Colony, October 23, 1975 (Inter-Tribal Council of Nevada Archives Project, file 100), as cited in Jo Ann Nevers, *Wa She Shu: A Washo Tribal History* (Reno: Inter-Tribal Council of Nevada, 1976), 6–10. In an interview with the author, Washoe Community Council member Mahlon Machado explained, "Lake Tahoe is definitely one of the major spiritual bodies that we have. . . . If you refer to the aboriginal map it is the center of our

homelands. So Washoe people recognized it as something that was great and needed to be protected." He went on to state, "The Washoes believe it [the water] is part of them. . . . [W]hatever happens to the lake is going to happen to us. . . . [W]ater is moving; it is living." Mahlon Machado, interview with the author, tape recording, Woodfords, Calif., July 8, 2002. One of the earliest ethnographers to work with the Washoes, J. W. Hudson echoed the words of community members when he referred to Lake Tahoe as "their crown jewel with its rich fisheries and hunting grounds. The lake was once densely wooded with great pines . . . [a] veritable paradise for these people." Folder "99–39 Hudson, J. W., Correspondence and Field Notes ca. 1902," box 5, Washo Indians Research Papers, 242 (hereafter cited as Hudson Collection). Downs, *Two Worlds of the Washo,* 16, refers to Tahoe as "the center of the Washo world, geographically and socially."

10. Washoe elders and a small number of scholars also mention a fourth western group, the Tunglelti. Beverly Caldera, conversation with the author, longhand notes, Woodfords, Calif., July 25, 2006. Caldera remembered her grandfather referring to cousins who lived west of Tahoe as "Tunglelti."

11. For information on Washoe leadership from Washoe people in the 1930s, see Edgar E. Siskin, field notes, August 2, 1937, box 1, Edgar E. Siskin Papers, Collection 90-68, Special Collections Department, University of Nevada, Reno. See also Downs, *Two Worlds of the Washo,* 41; and Warren d'Azevedo, "Washoe," in *The Handbook of North American Indians,* edited by William C. Sturtevant (Washington, D.C.: Smithsonian Institution, 1986), 11:469. For information on elders, see Nevers, *Wa She Shu,* 27.

12. On *Maʔaš* lands, see d'Azevedo, "Washoe," 470–73. I also spoke with Art George Jr. regarding *Maʔaš* lands. Art George Jr., conversation with the author, longhand notes, Minden, Nev., July 28, 2002. The Washoes were not, of course, the only western indigenous community to conceive of family property. Anthropologist Wayne Suttles provided evidence that Northwest Coast Salish families owned individual "root plots." Similar to the Washoes, Salish individuals did not practice exclusivity to the degree that nonowners, or families whose land did not produce, had no access to resources. Kinship obligations and familial ties allowed for fair and regular access to productive resource areas. See Wayne Suttles, "Coast Salish Resource Management: Incipient Agriculture?," in *Keeping It Living: Traditions of Plant Use and Cultivation on the Northwest Coast of North America,* edited by Douglas Deur and Nancy J. Turner (Seattle: University of Washington Press, 2005), 185.

13. For information on water beings, see Downs, *Two Worlds of the Washoe,* 61–62.

14. For information on shamans and power, see Stanley A. Freed and Ruth S. Freed, "A Configuration of Aboriginal Washoe Culture," in *The Washoe Indians of California and Nevada,* edited by Warren L. d'Azevedo (Salt Lake City: University of Utah Press, Anthropology Publications, 1963), 41–43; James F. Downs, "Washo Religion," *University of California Publications: Anthropolog-*

ical Records 16, no. 9 (1960): 370; Edgar Siskin, *Washo Shamans and Peyotists: Religious Conflict in an American Indian Tribe* (Salt Lake City: University of Utah Press, 1983), 21; Don Handleman, "Aspects of the Moral Compact of a Washo Shaman," *Anthropological Quarterly* 45, no. 2 (1972): 88; and Downs, *Two Worlds of the Washoe*, 55–59. For information on Cave Rock, see Matthew S. Makley and Michael J. Makley, *Cave Rock: Climbers, Courts, and a Washoe Indian Sacred Place* (Reno: University of Nevada Press, 2010).

15. Siskin, *Washo Shamans and Peyotists*, 44. Darrel Cruz, tribal historic preservation officer, also helped explain this story while editing a draft of the manuscript.
16. Belma Jones, Washoe Project, interview by JoAnne Peden, tape "J," August 18, 1992, Markleeville, Calif., copy in possession of the author. Information on girls' training was given to anthropologist Edgar Siskin in the late 1930s by two Washoe men, George Snooks and Charlie Rube. See Siskin, folder "Field Notes, July 29, no year given (probably 1937)," box 1, Siskin Papers. See also d'Azevedo, "Washoe," 474.
17. Nevers, *Wa She Shu*, 18–20, 68–69; Jane Green Gigli, "Dat So La Lee, Queen of the Washoe Basket Makers," *Nevada State Museum Anthropological Papers*, no. 3 (1967): 1–27.
18. Darla Garey-Sage, "Washoe Women's Wisdom: Ethnobotany and Its Role in Contemporary Cultural Identity" (Ph.D. diss., University of Nevada, Reno, 2003), 220, 33. For information on *badópo*, see 220. D'Azevedo briefly mentions the prayer element connected to gathering as well as the conservation ethic in "Washoe," 477. See also Downs, *Two Worlds of the Washoe*, 17–26.
19. D'Azevedo, "Washoe," 486–87; Downs, "Washo Religion," 375–76.
20. For information on Washoe hunting tools, see d'Azevedo, "Washoe," 477; Downs, *Two Worlds of the Washoe*, 26; and John Price, "The Washo Indians: History, Life Cycle, Religion, Technology, and Modern Life," *Nevada State Occasional Papers* 4 (1980): 48. See also Hudson Collection, 247. It was Hudson who described the unique clutch of Washoe hunters as well as the method for crafting arrows. For information on the traditional beliefs about animals and their nature, see Downs, *Two Worlds of the Washoe*, 63.
21. Don D. Fowler and Catherine S. Fowler, "Stephen Powers's 'The Life and Culture of the Washo and Paiutes,'" *Ethnohistory* 17, nos. 3–4 (1970): 121. See also Hudson Collection, 247.
22. D'Azevedo, "Washoe," 477–78.
23. Downs, *Two Worlds of the Washo*, 26.
24. Darrel Cruz, Washoe tribal historic preservation officer, provided the information about hunting bighorns. The other hunting information comes from "Information given by Washoe Indians at Stewart, Nevada, on February 19, 1951," folder "90-37/I/4," box 1, Wright Washoe Claims Case Records.
25. The quote referring to antelope as sheep comes from Robert Lowie, "Ethnographic

Notes on the Washo," in *Publications in American Archaeology and Ethnology* 36 (Berkeley: University of California Press, 1940), 324–25. One nineteenth-century student of Washoe culture, J. W. Hudson, reported witnessing a charming ceremony conducted by "Old Tom." Hudson reported that Tom, in a trance state, "lay between two fires, into which he had caused certain herbs to charm the deer to him." Other anthropologists explained a similar practice. Stanley Freed and Ruth Freed identified an herb called *mugálu* that could be used to put deer to sleep. Downs also reported hearing about a sleeping medicine for deer. On charming, see Freed and Freed, "Configuration of Aboriginal Washo Culture," in *Washoe Indians of California and Nevada*, edited by d'Azevedo, 53; Downs, "Washo Religion," 379; and d'Azevedo, "Washoe," 478.

26. Siskin, folder "Field Notes, June 28, 1937," box 1, Siskin Papers. Siskin obtained information on hunting from Washoe "informant" George Snooks.

27. Downs, *Two Worlds of the Washo*, 26–30; Downs, "Washo Religion," 379; d'Azevedo, "Washoe," 477–78; Nevers, *Was She Shu*, 23. Downs, *Two Worlds of the Washo*, gives a comprehensive account of Washoe hunting practices. He also confirms that being attacked by a buck was a serious matter. "Having once been attacked by a young mule deer buck weighing far less than the writer, he agrees with his Washo informants that the possibility of attack was not one to be taken lightly" (29).

28. For information on the bear hunt, see Siskin, folder "Field Notes, June 28, 1937," box 1, Siskin Papers; and Downs, *Two Worlds of the Washoe*, 33.

29. Downs, *Two Worlds of the Washoe*, 29.

30. D'Azevedo, "Washoe," 478.

31. Information on boys' advancement to manhood taken from Downs, *Two Worlds of the Washoe*, 35–36.

32. Well into the twentieth century, equal numbers of newlyweds lived with the wife's family as with the husband's. See ibid., 38–42. The account of women's equal rights in the case of divorce comes from J. W. Hudson's unpublished manuscript, which can be found in the Hudson Collection, 240, 252–53.

33. Garey-Sage, *Washoe Women's Wisdom*, 214, describes Washoes' use of watercress.

34. James, interview by Nevers, as cited in Nevers, *Wa She Shu*, 6–10.

35. Nevers, *Wa She Shu*, 9. Downs also discussed the use of dams in *Two Worlds of the Washo*. John C. Frémont, in his journal, records the use of fish dams by the Washoe: "We followed the river for only a short distance along a rocky trail, and crossed it at a dam which the Indians made us comprehend had been built to catch salmon trout." John C. Frémont, *Narratives of Exploration and Adventure*, edited by Allan Nevins (New York: Longmans, Green, 1956), 346. For a detailed description of the fish weir, see Hudson Collection, 248.

36. D'Azevedo, "Washoe," 473; Downs, *Two Worlds of the Washo*, 12–16. Hudson describes the use of a swan's clavicle for hooks in Hudson Collection, 235.

37. "Information given by Washoe Indians at Stewart, Nevada, on February 19, 1951," folder "90-37/I/4," box 1, Wright Washoe Claims Case Records.

38. Hudson Collection, 238.
39. James, interview by Nevers, as cited in Nevers, *Wa She Shu*, 10; d'Azevedo, "Washoe," 474; Downs, *Two Worlds of the Washo*, 18–21.
40. Freed and Freed, "Configuration of Aboriginal Washoe Culture," in *Washoe Indians of California and Nevada*, edited by d'Azevedo, 48. See also Lowie, "Ethnographic Notes on the Washo," 321.
41. Steven Michael Fountain, "Big Dogs and Scorched Streams: Horses and Ethnocultural Change in the North American West, 1700–1850" (Ph.D. diss., University of California, Davis, 2007), 139, 145.
42. d'Azevedo, "Washoe," 470–73.
43. Garey-Sage, "Washoe Women's Wisdom," 126–27; d'Azevedo, "Washoe," 474. Herman Fillmore, interview conducted via e-mail, July 2014, digital copy in possession of the author and Mr. Fillmore.
44. Nevers, *Wa She Shu*, 10–11.
45. Downs, "Washo Religion," 382–83; Nevers, *Wa She Shu*, 10–11. See also Siskin, folder "Field Notes, June 28, 1937," box 1, Siskin Papers.
46. Bernice Auchoberry, interview by R. T. King, April 3, 1984, in *A Contribution to a Survey of Life in Carson Valley, from First Settlement through the 1950s* (Reno: Oral History Program, University of Nevada, Reno, Library, 1984), 17; Belma Jones, interview by JoAnne Peden, tape recording, tape "J," Woodfords, Calif., August 8, 1992, tape in possession of Barbara Jones.
47. Hudson's description of the caches in Hudson Collection, 235.
48. "Information given by Washoe Indians at Stewart, Nevada, on February 19, 1951," folder "90-37/I/4," box 1, Wright Washoe Claims Case Records; Nevers, *Wa-She-Shu*, 16–18.
49. Jones, interview by Peden.
50. Bertha Holbrook, Washoe, interview by Jo Ann Nevers, Fallon, Nev., October 22, 1974 (Inter-Tribal Council of Nevada Archives Project, file 108), as cited in Nevers, *Wa She Shu*, 16–17.
51. Nevers, *Wa She Shu*, 16–18.

CHAPTER 2: NEWCOMERS

1. Jedediah S. Smith, *The Southwest Expedition of Jedediah S. Smith: His Personal Account of the Journey to California, 1826–1827*, edited by George R. Brooks (Glendale, Calif.: A. H. Clark, 1977; reprint, Norman: University of Oklahoma Press, 1989), 169–73. Smith's group arrived in Washoe territory from the California coast, traversing the Sierra near modern-day Ebbets Pass. See also Gloria Griffen Cline, *Exploring the Great Basin* (1963; reprint, Reno: University of Nevada Press, 1988), 157.
2. When I asked Beverly Caldera, former chair of the language-school committee for the Washoe Tribal Council, she said that her grandsons use the word *mushege* when they refer to something scary, something wild like a

monster or a large bear. John A. Price described the Washoe use of *mushege* in "The Washo Indians: History, Life Cycle, Religion, Technology, Economy, and Modern Life," *Nevada State Museum Occasional Papers* 4 (1980): 4. Also, James F. Downs represented a translation of the word *mushege* in *The Two Worlds of the Washo: An Indian Tribe of California and Nevada* (New York: Holt, Rinehart, and Winston, 1966). C. Hart Merriam in "Vocabularies of North American Indians" listed *mah se se* (pronounced "shush'h"), which he translated as "stranger," in folder "Washo-shoo Vocabulary, 1923," box 5, d'Azevedo, Warren L., Washo Indians Research Papers, Collection 99–39, Special Collections Department, University of Nevada, Reno. Edgar Siskin referred to *musegeu* as "someone to be feared," in field notes, box 1, Edgar E. Siskin Papers, Collection 90–68, Special Collections Department, University of Nevada, Reno. For information on the word *da ba ah*, see Jo Ann Nevers, *Wa She Shu: A Washo Tribal History* (Reno: Inter-Tribal Council of Nevada, 1976), 45–46.

3. John C. Frémont, *Narratives of Exploration and Adventure*, edited by Allan Nevins (New York: Longmans, Green, 1956), 343; Ferol Egan, *Frémont: Explorer for a Restless Nation* (Reno: University of Nevada Press, 1985), 199.

4. S. A. Barrett, "The Washoe Indians," *Bulletin of the Public Museum of the City of Milwaukee* 2, no. 1 (1917; reprint, Milwaukee: Trustees of the Public Museum of the City of Milwaukee, 1978), 25. Barrett described a facility of communication between Washoes and Paiutes.

5. Martha Knack, "A Short Resource History of Pyramid Lake, Nevada," *Ethnohistory* 24, no. 1 (1977): 53.

6. Frémont, *Narratives of Exploration and Adventure*, 344–47.

7. Ibid., 351. See also Nevers, *Wa She Shu*, 39–40.

8. Frémont, *Narratives of Exploration and Adventure*, 352.

9. Ibid.

10. Ibid., 359. See also Nevers, *Wa She Shu*, 42.

11. Frémont, *Narratives of Exploration and Adventure*, 353.

12. Ibid., 360–61.

13. Blackhawk, *Violence over the Land: Indians and Empires in the Early American West* (Cambridge, Mass.: Harvard University Press, 2006), 276–77. James W. Nye, superintendent of Indian affairs, Nevada Territory, to Caleb B. Smith, secretary of the interior, July 19, 1861, in *Annual Reports of the Commissioner of Indian Affairs* (Washington, D.C.: Government Printing Office, 1861), 108–10.

14. Sutter took up residence in the Sacramento Valley in the late 1830s. He had soon established a small "barony" that he called New Helvetia. For a recent historical biography of Sutter, see Albert Hurtado, *John Sutter: A Life on the North American Frontier* (Norman: University of Oklahoma Press, 2006). See also Richard B. Rice, William A. Bullough, and Richard J. Orsi, *The Elusive Eden: A New History of California*, 2nd ed. (New York: McGraw-Hill, 1996), 154.

15. Historian James Rawls describes the process by which the "image" of California Indians changed under Spanish, Mexican, and American rule. The images applied by colonial powers facilitated Native exploitation. He argues that "it is by understanding how Anglo-Americans perceived the California Indians' lives that we most clearly unmistakably see the Indians' deaths." James Rawls, *Indians of California: The Changing Image* (Norman: University of Oklahoma Press, 1984), 200–201. For an excellent historical treatment of California Indians, see Albert Hurtado, *Indian Survival on the California Frontier* (New Haven, Conn.: Yale University Press, 1988). Missions sought to Christianize Indians and in turn create subjects for the Spanish monarchy. Spain did not have enough people to populate their American colonial lands in order to sufficiently hold their claims. Instead, they had to work to transform indigenous populations into Spanish citizens to keep enough feet on the ground to discourage French, English, Russian, and later American encroachments. The historiography of California missions demonstrates both the changing priorities of scholars and the divergent views of the mission system. Early reports on the missions based on travelers' accounts and Franciscan records tended to emphasize the "benevolent" Spanish intentions. Recently, the proposed sainthood of Junípero Serra, the "father" of California missions, has contributed to and brought more attention to alternative views of Serra and the mission system. Historian James Sandos described the "pain and anger" experienced by California Indians when the canonization debate, convened during the 1980s, ignored their perspective. Those who viewed Serra as less than saintly found Sherburne F. Cook's work on demographics and early California helpful. Cook published testimony from a mission Indian named Lorenzo Asesara who claimed, "The Spanish padres were very cruel to the Indians; they treated them very badly. . . . [T]hey made them work like slaves." Sherburne F. Cook's work *The Conflict between the California Indian and White Civilization* (Berkeley: University of California Press, 1976) remains a standard from which historians continue to draw insight. For literature on the canonization debate over Father Serra, see James A. Sandos, "Junípero Serra's Canonization and the Historical Record," *American Historical Review* 93 (December 1988): 253–69. See also Rev. Francis F. Guest's contribution to Rupert Costo and Jeannette Henry Costo, eds., *The Missions of California: A Legacy of Genocide* (San Francisco: Indian Historian Press for the American Indian Historical Society, 1987); and Robert Archibald, "Indian Labor at the California Missions: Slavery or Salvation?," *Journal of San Diego History* 24 (September 1978): 172–82.
16. Rice, Bullough, and Orsi, *Elusive Eden,* 154. A map of the Spanish and Mexican land grants in the nineteenth century reveals a predictable pattern of settlement near bodies of water. Sutter positioned his "fiefdom" on the confluence of the American and Sacramento Rivers.
17. Frémont, *Narratives of Exploration and Adventure,* 377–79.

18. M. Kat Anderson, *Tending the Wild: Native American Knowledge and the Management of California's Natural Resources* (Berkeley: University of California Press, 2005), 2–3.
19. Nevers, *Wa She Shu,* 43.
20. Poker Charlie apparently worked as an informant at times for Dr. S. L. Lee in Carson City, Nevada. For Poker Charlie on the Donner Party, see folder "Dr. S. L. Lee Personal 'Basket Catalog' PP 61–126," box 5, Washo Indians Research Papers. There is also a Washoe oral account of the Donner party in an interview conducted with a Washoe man by attorney George Wright. Unfortunately, Wright did not identify the man. Noble T. Murray to George Wright, March 23, 1963, folder "Correspondence Jan.–Mar. 1963," box 1, George F. Wright Washoe Claims Case Records, 90-37/I/20, Special Collections Department, University of Nevada, Reno. See also Nevers, *Wa She Shu,* 44.
21. Rice, Bullough, and Orsi, *Elusive Eden,* 113–29, 163.

CHAPTER 3: VIOLENT TRANSFORMATIONS

1. The account of the battle at the springs comes from Bernice Auchoberry, interview by R. T. King, April 3, 1984, in *A Contribution to a Survey of Life in Carson Valley, from First Settlement through the 1950s* (Reno: Oral History Program, University of Nevada, Reno, Library, 1984), 19.
2. Examples of stranger avoidance exist in the form of traditional narratives. One prevalent Washoe story recounts a social gathering in the T'a·gɨm ʔaša, where community members played games and sang songs. In the darkness surrounding the celebration, a giant monster-like figure, Hanawiywiy, crept toward the party. Nentushu (in this context Nentushu refers to an old woman and not the Creator) warned the people to keep quiet, but they continued to celebrate loudly. By not listening to their elders, people put themselves in great danger, unaware of the strange beast lurking nearby. Nentushu climbed into a storage pit and used a carrying basket to conceal herself. All the others "saw [Hanawiywiy] and there they died, their eyes turned white." On a recent trip to Cimé Dimé (Double Springs), Art George Jr. related a version of the "Hanawiywiy" story. He pointed out an area "where all the land looks like a big sink (no bushes or trees)." He explained that "one of the reasons all them bushes are cleared out is because of Hanawiywiy." After Hanawiywiy left, Nentushu found a lone surviving baby. She uprooted a sagebrush and twisted the roots around her cane and then carried the baby down into the hole where the sage roots had been and covered them with brush. When Hanawiywiy came back looking for more people to eat, he began pulling up bushes. When he came to the brush that hid Nentushu and the baby, he pulled with all of his might, but Nentushu gripped her cane tightly and Hanawiywiy gave up. The next day the monster

came back and ripped up all the remaining brush, but the old woman and the baby had escaped. This is a very popular Washoe story. The version produced here was taken from Grace Dangberg, "Washo Tales: Three Original Washo Indian Legends" (occasional paper, Nevada State Museum, Carson City, 1968), 40–42. Dangberg collected the stories from Bill Fillmore, who as a teenager witnessed the arrival of whites in *Washishiw* territory. Though published in 1968, the stories were recorded in 1920 and translated by Henry Moses Rupert. Rupert was widely known for his healing or doctoring powers and was featured in many anthropological works. See, for instance, Don Handelman, "The Development of a Washo Shaman," *Ethnology* 6 (1967): 444–64; Handelman, "Aspects of the Moral Compact of a Washo Shaman," *Anthropological Quarterly* 45, no. 2 (1972): 84–101; and Art George Jr., interview by the author, tape recording, Minden, Nev., July 17, 2006.

3. Thomas Frederick Howard, *Sierra Crossing: First Roads to California* (Berkeley: University of California Press, 1998), 51.

4. John A. Price, "Mormon Missions to the Indians," in *The Handbook of North American Indians*, edited by William C. Sturtevant (Washington, D.C.: Smithsonian Institution, 1986), 11:459. For the original boundaries declared by the Mormon Church, see Leonard J. Arrington, *Great Basin Kingdom: An Economic History of the Latter-day Saints, 1830–1900* (Cambridge, Mass.: Harvard University Press, 1958), 85.

5. Price, "Mormon Missions to the Indians," 459–60.

6. Myron Angel, ed., *History of Nevada* (Oakland: Thompson and West, 1881), 32. See also Sam P. Davis, ed., *The History of Nevada* (Reno: Elms, 1913), 225–26. Davis writes in more detail about the Settler government. Both Davis and Angel lived in Nevada for a good portion of their lives and provided their unique perspectives on the history of the state.

7. Angel, *History of Nevada*, 31.

8. William Cronon, *Changes in the Land: Indians, Colonists, and the Ecology of New England* (New York: Hill and Wang, 1983), 130–31.

9. The quote on land use comes from a book by Gilbert Malcolm Sproat, *The Nootka: Scenes and Studies of Savage Life*, originally published in 1868, as cited in Nancy J. Turner and Sandra Peacock, "Solving the Perennial Paradox: Ethnobotanical Evidence for Plant Resource Management on the Northwest Coast," in *Keeping It Living: Traditions of Plant Use and Cultivation on the Northwest Coast of North America*, edited by Douglas Deur and Nancy J. Turner (Seattle: University of Washington Press, 2005), 173–74.

10. Patricia Seed, *Ceremonies of Possession in Europe's Conquest of the New World, 1492–1640* (1995; reprint, New York: Cambridge University Press, 1997), 38–39.

11. J. D. C. Atkins, commissioner of Indian Affairs, *Annual Reports of the Commissioner of Indian Affairs* (Washington, D.C.: Government Printing Office, 1885), 3 (hereafter cited as *ARCIA* with the date in parentheses).

12. The office was established on March 11, 1824. Francis Paul Prucha, *Documents of United States Indian Policy*, 2nd ed. (Lincoln: University of Nebraska Press, 1990), 62. For a general history of the Bureau of Indian Affairs, see Theodore Taylor, *The Bureau of Indian Affairs* (Boulder, Colo.: Westview Press, 1984); Edward E. Hill, *The Office of Indian Affairs, 1824–1880: Historical Sketches* (New York: Clearwater, 1974); Robert M. Kvasnicka and Herman J. Viola, eds., *The Commissioners of Indian Affairs, 1824–1977* (Lincoln: University of Nebraska Press, 1979); and Alban W. Hoopes, *Indian Affairs and Their Administration with Special Reference to the Far West, 1849–1860* (Philadelphia: University of Pennsylvania Press, 1932).
13. Prucha, *Documents of United States Indian Policy*, 80.
14. Hill, *Office of Indian Affairs*, 1–3.
15. Quote from Holeman appeared in Hoopes, *Indian Affairs and Their Administration*, 141. Major G. W. Ingalls wrote a chapter, "Indians of Nevada," in *The History of Nevada*, edited by Davis, 37. For an account of violence in the Great Basin, see Ned Blackhawk, *Violence over the Land: Indians and Empires in the Early American West* (Cambridge, Mass.: Harvard University Press, 2008).
16. Jacob H. Holeman, Indian agent, Utah Territory, to Luke Lea, commissioner of Indian affairs, September 30, 1853, in *Annual Report of the Commissioner of Indian Affairs Transmitted with the Message of the President at the Opening of the First Session of the Thirty-Third Congress* (Washington, D.C.: Robert Armstrong, 1853), 204.
17. J. W. Hudson manuscript in folder "99–39 Hudson, J. W. Correspondence and Field Notes ca. 1902," box 5, d'Azevedo, Warren L., Washo Indians Research Papers, Collection 99–39, Special Collections Department, University of Nevada, Reno, 244.
18. James W. Nye, superintendent of Indian affairs, Nevada Territory, to Caleb B. Smith, secretary of the interior, July 19, 1861, in *ARCIA* (1861), 108–10; Major Henry Douglas, superintendent of Indian affairs, Nevada, to E. S. Parker, commissioner of Indian affairs, September 20, 1870, in *ARCIA* (1870), 96–100; Vernile DeWitt-Warr, "Destitute Nevada Indians," in *The History of Nevada*, edited by Davis, 135.
19. Quotes on atmosphere at Mormon Station taken from Michael J. Makley, *The Hanging of Lucky Bill* (Woodfords, Calif.: Eastern Sierra Press, 1993), 18–19.
20. For a description of the American movement away from English common law with regard to violence, see Richard Maxwell Brown, "Western Violence: Structure, Values, Myth," *Western Historical Quarterly* 24, no. 1 (1993): 4–20. Quote from Blackhawk comes from Blackhawk, *Violence over the Land*, 5. See also ibid. for an explanation of the Bear River Massacre.
21. Ingalls, "Indians of Nevada," in *The History of Nevada*, edited by Davis, 38.

22. For an account of the double murders, see ibid., 39. A summary of newspaper accounts can be found in Makley, *Hanging of Lucky Bill*, 42–43.
23. Sarah Winnemucca Hopkins, *Life among the Paiutes: Their Wrongs and Claims*, edited by Horace Mann (New York: G. P. Putnam's Sons, 1883), 61. See also Katherine Gehn, *Sarah Winnemucca: Most Extraordinary Woman of the Paiute Nation* (Phoenix: O'Sullivan, Woodside, 1975); and Catherine S. Fowler, "Sarah Winnemucca, Northern Paiute, 1844–1891," in *American Indian Intellectuals*, edited by Margot Liberty, Proceedings of the American Ethnological Society (St. Paul, Minn.: West, 1976). The quote regarding Ormsby's admission of the injustice comes from Makley, *Hanging of Lucky Bill*, 46.
24. For an account of the war, see Ferol Egan, *Sand in a Whirlwind: The Paiute Indian War of 1860* (New York: Doubleday, 1972). The casualty figures come from Russell R. Elliot with William D. Rowley, *History of Nevada*, 2nd ed. (Lincoln: University of Nebraska Press, 1987), 93.
25. Helen Nevers Enos, August 26, 1974, interviewed by Jo Ann Nevers (Inter-Tribal Council of Nevada Archives Project, file 110), as cited in Jo Ann Nevers, *Wa She Shu: A Washo Tribal History* (Reno: Inter-Tribal Council of Nevada, 1976), 52.
26. *Gold Hill (Nev.) Evening News*, October 21, 1872.
27. Quote from Hunt taken from Davis, *The History of Nevada*, 29.
28. Ibid., 39.
29. *San Francisco Herald*, July 17, 1855.
30. Elliot with Rowley, *History of Nevada*, 56–57.
31. Angel, *History of Nevada*, 42.
32. Dodge's quote taken from Hill, *Office of Indian Affairs*, 192. See also Nevers, *Wa She Shu*, 51.
33. Elliot with Rowley, *History of Nevada*, 62; Elliot Lord, *Comstock Mining and Miners* (Washington, D.C.: Government Printing Office, 1883), 24. Elliot Lord lived and wrote on the Comstock from 1879 to 1881. He provided a chart of Gold Canyon's fiscal report. He credited the decline to exhausted placers and a lack of water due to poor winters. The miners needed water to wash the sand. A description of the establishment of Johntown appears on page 33.
34. On blue earth and the Grosh brothers' assay, see George D. Lyman, *The Saga of the Comstock Lode: Boom Days in Virginia City* (1939; reprint, New York: Charles Scribner's Sons, 1949), 13–17. The letter to their father was described in Lord, *Comstock Mining and Miners*, 26. On the Grass Valley assay, see Angel, *History of Nevada*, 61; and Lyman, *Saga of the Comstock Lode*, 38–41.
35. Warren d'Azevedo, "Washoe," in *Handbook of North American Indians*, edited by Sturtevant, 11:494–95.
36. Lyman, *Saga of the Comstock Lode*, 47.

37. Quotes from Twain taken from Michael J. Makley, *The Infamous King of the Comstock: William Sharon and the Gilded Age in the West* (Reno: University of Nevada Press, 2006), 17.
38. Michael J. Makley, *John Mackay: Silver King in the Gilded Age* (Reno: University of Nevada Press, 2009), 20; Elliot with Rowley, *History of Nevada*, 55–56.
39. Elliot with Rowley, *History of Nevada*, 68.

CHAPTER 4: THE CHAOS OF DESTRUCTION

1. Pacific Coast Annual Mining Review and Stock Ledger, vol. 2, in *Journal of Commerce Mining Review* (1862). The account of environmental destruction comes from J. Ross Browne, *A Peep at Washoe and Washoe Revisited, 1863, 1864, and 1869* (Balboa Island, Calif.: Paisano Press, 1959), 179. J. Ross Browne was an author, reporter, and government agent for the Treasury Department who traveled around the West in the 1860s and recorded his experiences. The final quote from the opening paragraph regarding Washoe families having no place to go comes from Art George Jr., conversation with the author, longhand notes, Minden, Nev., July 28, 2005.
2. M. Kat Anderson, *Tending the Wild: Native American Knowledge and the Management of California's Natural Resources* (Berkeley: University of California Press, 2005), 84.
3. For a thorough treatment of the *Johnson v. M'Intosh* case, see Walter Echohawk, *In the Courts of the Conqueror: The 10 Worst Indian Law Cases Ever Decided* (Golden, Colo.: Fulcrum Press, 2010), 55–84.
4. Anderson, *Tending the Wild*, 86–87.
5. Belma Jones, interview by JoAnne Peden, tape recording, tape "J," Woodfords, Calif., August 8, 1992, tape in possession of Barbara Jones. For an account of the contested Carson River, see Grace Dangberg, *Conflict on the Carson: A Study of Water Litigation in Western Nevada* (Minden, Nev.: Carson Valley Historical Society, 1975).
6. Dan DeQuille [William Wright], *The Big Bonanza* (Hartford, Conn.: American, 1876; reprint, New York: Alfred A. Knopf, 1953), 291.
7. Ronald M. James, *The Roar and the Silence: A History of Virginia City and the Comstock Lode* (Reno: University of Nevada Press, 1998), 53–56.
8. The reference to DeQuille's quote regarding the tombs of Tahoe's forests comes from Susan Lindstrom, with contributions by Penny Rucks and Peter Wigand, "A Contextual Overview of Human Land Use and Environmental Conditions," in *Lake Tahoe Watershed Assessment,* edited by Dennis D. Murphy and Christopher M. Knopp (Washington, D.C.: Pacific Southwest Research Station, USDA Forest Service, 2000), 1:47.
9. Ibid., 57.

10. For information on Mackay, see Michael J. Makley, *John Mackay: Silver King in the Gilded Age* (Reno: University of Nevada Press, 2009).
11. Grant H. Smith, *The History of the Comstock Lode* (Reno: Nevada State Bureau of Mines and the Mackay School of Mines, 1943), 247. For further information on lumbering at Tahoe, see Douglas H. Strong, *Tahoe: An Environmental History* (Lincoln: University of Nebraska Press, 1984); and J. Makley, *A Short History of Lake Tahoe* (Reno: University of Nevada Press, 2011), 29–37.
12. M. Jake Vander Zanden et al., "Historical Food Web Structure and Restoration of Native Aquatic Communities in the Lake Tahoe (California-Nevada) Basin," *Ecosystems* 6, no. 3 (2003): 276.
13. *Mountain Democrat* (Placerville, Calif.), July 4, 1856; *Territorial Enterprise*, May 19 and July 14, 1860, as cited in Bob McQuivey, "Summary of Lake Tahoe Basin Resources (1854–1976)," 2–3, http://ndep.nv.gov.
14. *Reese River Reveille*, December 5, 1865, as cited in McQuivey, "Summary of Lake Tahoe Basin Resources," 5.
15. Susan Lindstrom, "A Contextual Overview of Human Land Use and Environmental Conditions," in *The Lake Tahoe Watershed Assessment* (South Lake Tahoe, Calif.: U.S. Department of Agriculture Forest Service, Lake Tahoe Basin Management Unit, 2000), 69.
16. *Territorial Enterprise*, June 26, 1872; *Virginia Evening Chronicle*, July 8, 1872, as cited in McQuivey, "Summary of Lake Tahoe Basin Resources," 13.
17. *Gold Hill (Nev.) News*, March 18, 1864; *Virginia Daily Union*, April 30, 1864, as cited in McQuivey, "Summary of Lake Tahoe Basin Resources," 3; "An Act Relating to Wild Game and Fish," November 21, 1861, and "An Act to Amend an Act Entitled 'An Act Relating to Wild Game and Fish,'" February 20, 1864, as cited in McQuivey, "Summary of Lake Tahoe Basin Resources," 2.
18. "An Act to Provide for the Preservation of Fish in This State," March 5, 1877, as cited in McQuivey, "Summary of Lake Tahoe Basin Resources," 20; *Genoa (Nev.) Weekly Courier*, April 17, 1885; *Carson (Nev.) Morning Appeal*, July 26, 1885, as cited in McQuivey, "Summary of Lake Tahoe Basin Resources," 58.
19. *Genoa (Nev.) Weekly Courier*, March 25, 1898; the *Gardnerville (Nev.) Weekly Courier*, April 6, 1900, as cited in McQuivey, "Summary of Lake Tahoe Basin Resources," 78–79. For information on Nevada state laws and their effect on Paiutes, see Martha Knack, "The Effects of Nevada State Fishing Laws on the Northern Paiutes of Pyramid Lake," *Nevada Historical Quarterly* 25, no. 4 (1982): 259.
20. For information on early agriculture in the Carson Valley, see Dangberg, *Conflict on the Carson*, 3–5; and James F. Downs, *The Two Worlds of the Washo: An Indian Tribe of California and Nevada* (New York: Holt, Rinehart, and Winston, 1966), 75.
21. James W. Nye, governor and ex officio superintendent of Indian affairs, to Caleb B. Smith, secretary of the interior, July 19, 1861, in *Annual Reports of*

the Commissioner of Indian Affairs (Washington, D.C.: Government Printing Office, 1861), 111 (hereafter cited as *ARCIA* with the date in parentheses).

22. Warren Wasson, acting Indian agent, to James W. Nye, governor of Nevada Territory and ex officio superintendent of Indian affairs for Nevada, July 13, 1861, in *Letters Received, Nevada Superintendency, 1861–1880,* NA microfilm publications 234, roll 538.
23. Jacob T. Lockhart, Indian agent, Nevada, to W. P. Dole, commissioner of Indian affairs, March 12, 1862, ibid.
24. Lockhart to Dole, June 27, 1864, and July 1, 1865, ibid.
25. For biographical information on Hubbard G. Parker, see Myron Angel, ed., *History of Nevada* (Oakland: Thompson and West, 1881), 86.
26. Hubbard G. Parker, superintendent of Indian affairs, Nevada, to Dennis Cooley, commissioner of Indian affairs, October 23, 1865, in *Letters Received,* roll 538.
27. Parker to Cooley, September 10, 1866, in *ARCIA* (1866), 117.
28. Theodore T. Dwight to Lewis Bogy, January 9 and January 20, 1867, ibid., roll 539.
29. Parker wrote the letter indicating everything was fine in December 1868. See Parker to Taylor, December 10, 1868, ibid. See also Parker to Ely Samuel Parker, September 20, 1869, in *ARCIA* (1869), 142.
30. Parker to Ely Samuel Parker, September 20, 1869, in *ARCIA* (1869), 142.
31. Major Henry Douglas, superintendent of Indian affairs, Nevada, to Ely Parker, April 5, 1870, in *Letters Received,* roll 539 (emphasis added).
32. J. W. Powell and G. W. Ingalls, special commissioners, to commissioner of Indian affairs, December 18, 1873, in *ARCIA* (1874).
33. A. J. Barnes, agent commissioner of Indian affairs, 1876, in *ARCIA* (1876), 115.
34. *ARCIA* (1870).

CHAPTER 5: SURVIVAL

1. James F. Downs, *The Two Worlds of the Washo: An Indian Tribe of California and Nevada* (New York: Holt, Rinehart, and Winston, 1966), 32–33. Downs noted, "The Washoe considered the bear a very special, if not sacred, animal possessed of enormous supernatural power." It is of no small significance that one of Rupert's earliest dreams involved a bear. For information on Rupert's life, see Don Handelman, "The Development of a Washoe Shaman," in *Native Californians: A Theoretical Retrospective,* edited by John Lowell Bean and Thomas Blackburn (Menlo Park, Calif.: Ballena Press, 1976), 381. In the late 1930s a graduate student in anthropology from Yale University, Edgar E. Siskin, began working with the Washoe. During his three summers in Washoe country, Siskin put together copious amounts of information, much of which is housed in the

Special Collections Department at the University of Nevada, Reno. Among his collection are his handwritten field notes. He lists one of his informants as "C. R." His notes refer to C. R. as "Charlie." It is likely that C. R. is Charlie Rube. Charlie Rube was Rupert's older brother-in-law. As Rube explained about bears: "If you talk about bear to anyone, the ground communicates your intentions to bear or the bear reads your mind. He concentrates on what you're thinking and know. People among the Washoe can do the same thing, mostly doctors." For Rube's full description of the sacred nature of bears in Washoe culture, see Edgar E. Siskin, field notes, June 25, 1937, Edgar E. Siskin Papers, Collection 90–68, box 1, Special Collections Department, University of Nevada, Reno.
2. The account of Dr. S. L. Lee can be found in the folder "Dr. S. L. Lee Personal Basket Collection," 13, box 5, in d'Azevedo, Warren L., Washo Indians Research Papers, Collection 99–39, Special Collections, University of Nevada, Reno.
3. Umeek, Richard Atleo, a Nuu-chah-nulth hereditary chief, writes about an imaginary evolutionary scale in the preface to Douglas Deur and Nancy Turner, eds., *Keeping It Living: Traditions of Plant Use and Cultivation on the Northwest Coast of North America* (Seattle: University of Washington Press, 2005), viii. See also Umeek [E. Richard Atleo], *Tsawalk: A Nuu-chah-nulth Worldview* (Vancouver: UBC Press, 2004).
4. Margaret Connell Szasz, *Education and the American Indian: The Road to Self-Determination since 1928*, 3rd ed. (Albuquerque: University of New Mexico Press, 1999), 9–10.
5. H. Price, commissioner of Indian affairs, *Annual Reports of the Commissioner of Indian Affairs* (Washington, D.C.: Government Printing Office, 1881), 3 (hereafter cited as *ARCIA* with the date in parentheses); J. D. C. Atkins, commissioner of Indian affairs, *ARCIA* (1885), 3–4.
6. W. D. C. Gibson, superintendent, commissioner of Indian affairs, September 7, 1891, in *ARCIA* (1892).
7. Handelman, "Development of a Washoe Shaman," 382.
8. Ibid., 381.
9. Edgar Siskin, *Washo Shamans and Peyotists: Religious Conflict in an American Indian Tribe* (Salt Lake City: University of Utah Press, 1983), 27–34.
10. James F. Downs, "Washo Religion," *University of California Publications: Anthropological Records* 16, no. 9 (1960): 370.
11. For a brief version of this story, see ibid., 367.
12. Stanley A. Freed and Ruth S. Freed, "A Configuration of Aboriginal Washoe Culture," in *The Washoe Indians of California and Nevada*, edited by Warren L. d'Azevedo (Salt Lake City: University of Utah Press, Anthropology Publications, 1963), 44. Freed and Freed claimed Hank Pete had told them the story of Welewkushkush. Hank Pete, the son of a Washoe leader during the late nineteenth and early twentieth centuries, also known as Captain Pete, was elected to the first Washoe Tribal Council in 1936.

13. Quote from Frank Rivers taken from Jo Ann Nevers, *Wa She Shu: A Washoe Tribal History* (Reno: Inter-Tribal Council of Nevada, 1976), 67; Winona James, interview by R. T. King, June 14, 1984, *A Contribution to a Survey of Life in Carson Valley, from First Settlement through the 1950s* (Reno: Oral History Program, University of Nevada, Reno, Library, 1984), 8, 29.
14. Bell Cordova to Frederick Snyder, superintendent of the Carson Indian School, December 16, 1919, and response, December 31, 1919; letter from Susie Corbett to Superintendent (not named), n.d., and response, July 27, 1920, folder "Application for Outing Girls, 1911," box 262, Carson Indian School Administrative Files, 1909–1923, Application for Outing Girls, Asbury, Special Agent, Record Group (RG) 75, National Archives and Records Administration (NARA), Pacific Region, San Bruno, Calif.
15. Siskin, *Washoe Shamans and Peyotists,* 175.
16. Handelman, "Development of a Washoe Shaman," 385. See also Freed and Freed, "Configuration of Aboriginal Culture," in *Washoe Indians of California and Nevada,* edited by d'Azevedo, 43. Handelman and Freed and Freed worked with Rupert, and it is likely he explained his power dream to them. The versions vary, but it is unclear if this is because Rupert altered his description or if Freed and Freed or Handelman interpreted it differently. Freed and Freed described the voice in the dream as a "talking deer," but Handelman claims the voice came from a snake who was "warning against the indiscriminate taking of life; previously Henry had killed wildlife, insects, and snakes without much concern." Rule 9C in "Rules and Regulations" for the guidance of the Court of Indian Offenses, Nevada Agency, in folder "Walker River Agency Correspondence, 1906–1932," box 252, Walker River Agency Correspondence, RG 75, NARA, Pacific Region, San Bruno, Calif.
17. Frederick E. Hoxie, *A Final Promise: The Campaign to Assimilate the Indians, 1880–1920* (Lincoln: University of Nebraska Press, 1984), 70–76; Emily Greenwald, *Reconfiguring the Reservation: The Nez Perces, Jicarilla Apaches, and the Dawes Act* (Albuquerque: University of New Mexico Press, 2002); Francis Paul Prucha, *The Great Father: The United States Government and the American Indians* (Lincoln: University of Nebraska Press, 1990), 666–70; Clifford E. Trafzer, *As Long as the Grass Shall Grow and Rivers Flow: A History of Native Americans* (New York: Harcourt College, 2000), 328–30; Thomas R. Berger, *A Long and Terrible Shadow: White Values, Native Rights in the Americas since 1492* (Seattle: University of Washington Press, 1991), 102–4. For an economic interpretation of the Dawes Act, see Leonard A. Carlson, *Indians, Bureaucrats, and Land: The Dawes Act and the Decline of Indian Farming* (Westport, Conn.: Greenwood Press, 1981); William T. Hagan, "Private Property, the Indian's Door to Civilization," *Ethnohistory* 3, no. 2 (1956): 126–37.
18. Francis Paul Prucha, *Documents of United States Indian Policy: The History of a Political Anomaly* (Berkeley: University of California Press, 1994), 171–74.

19. Siskin, field notes, August 2, 1937, box 1, Siskin Papers.
20. Dick Bender gave information about the meetings. See Dick Bender, "Washoe Indians' Timber Land of Nevada and Their Claims on the Pinenut Range," folder 254, box 2, Reno, Nevada, Indian Agency Special Agent Land Correspondence, 1908–24, RG 75, NARA, Pacific Region, San Bruno, Calif. See also Nevers, *Wa She Shu,* 57. Information on Epesuwa and reference to his meeting the president can be found in *Life Stories of Our Native People: Shoshone, Paiute, Washo* (Reno: Inter-Tribal Council of Nevada, 1974), 13. Cimé Dimé means "Double Water"; the springs are located off Highway 395, just south of Minden, Nevada. Many elders identify this as an area where the T'agim Gumsabay? (pine-nut harvest festival) was held.
21. Statement of Dick Bender, Washo interpreter, folder 254, Special Agent Land Correspondence, 1908–24, RG 75, NARA, Pacific Region, San Bruno, Calif.
22. Nevers, *Wa She Shu,* 60–61.
23. Heather Cox Richardson, *Wounded Knee: Party Politics and the Road to an American Massacre* (New York: Basic Books, 2010).
24. Russell R. Elliot with William D. Rowley, *History of Nevada,* 2nd ed. (Lincoln: University of Nebraska Press, 1987), 80–84, 124.
25. Lorenzo D. Creel to Colonel Dorrington, April 1, 1917, folder 254, Special Agent Land Correspondence, 1908–24, RG 75, NARA, Pacific Region, San Bruno, Calif.
26. Letter from H. F. Bartine on behalf of Dick Bender and Captain Jim to the Washoes, April 27, 1892, Captain Jim Manuscript Collection, Nevada Historical Society, Reno.
27. Creel to Dorrington, April 1, 1917, folder 254, Special Agent Land Correspondence, 1908–24, RG 75, NARA, Pacific Region, San Bruno, Calif.
28. Khal Schneider, "Making Indian Land in the Allotment Era: Northern California's Indian Rancherias," *Western Historical Quarterly* 41, no. 4 (2010): 430–31.
29. William E. Casson, special allotting agent, and James K. Allen, superintendent of Stewart Indian School, to the commissioner of Indian affairs, May 26, 1903, folder "Washoe Indians—Relief, 1902–1925," box 275, Carson Indian School Administrative Files, 1909–1923, RG 75, NARA, Pacific Region, San Bruno, Calif.
30. Land Circular no. 320, *Leasing Indian Allotments Free from Departmental Control,* July 19, 1909, Robert G. Valentine, commissioner of Indian affairs, folder "61788—1909, Carson, 313," box 57, Records of the Bureau of Indian Affairs Central Classified Files, 1907–1939, Carson, 22074–1909–313, pt. 2, 82772–1911–313, RG 75, NARA, Washington, D.C.
31. Calvin H. Asbury, superintendent, Carson Indian School, to the commissioner of Indian affairs, March 17, 1905, folder "19910–1910, Carson, 313," ibid. Information on Asbury taken from "Peyotism in Montana," *Montana: The Magazine of Western History* 33, no. 2 (1983): 11–12.

32. Asbury, superintendent, Carson Indian School, to commissioner of Indian affairs, March 4, 1910, folder "19910-1910, Carson, 313," box 57, Records of the Bureau of Indian Affairs Central Classified Files, 1907–1939, Carson, 22074-1909-313, pt. 2, 82772-1911-313, RG 75, NARA, Washington, D.C.
33. Asbury to commissioner of Indian affairs, June 1, 1909, folder "42409-1908, Carson, 313," box 56, Records of the Bureau of Indian Affairs Central Classified Files, 1907–1939, Carson, 17938-1908-313 to 22074-1909-313, pt. 1, RG 75, NARA, Washington, D.C.
34. Ibid.
35. J. H. Dortch, chief clerk, Bureau of Indian Affairs, to Asbury, June 25, 1909, ibid.; Asbury, superintendent, Carson Indian School, to the commissioner of Indian affairs, June 30, 1909, ibid.
36. Asbury to commissioner of Indian affairs, December 27, 1911, folder "Washoe Indians—Relief, 1902-1925," box 275, Carson Indian School Administrative Files, 1909-1923.
37. Richard Barrington to Asbury, April 9, 1910, folder "Relief of Washoe Indians—197," box 275, Carson Indian School Administrative Files, 1909-1923 [1925], Allotments Relief of Washoe Indians.
38. Asbury to commissioner of Indian affairs, May 10, 1911, ibid.
39. Harry Fillmore, Washoe, to Asbury, special Indian agent, Reno, May 20, 1915, folder "459, Gardnerville," box 11, Reno Indian Agency Records of Agency and Nonagency Indians, RG 75, NARA, Pacific Region, San Bruno, Calif.
40. Asbury to Harry Fillmore, Gardnerville, Nev., May 21, 1915, ibid.
41. Asbury, superintendent, Carson Agency, to commissioner of Indian affairs, January 28, 1908, folder "7918-1908 Carson 056," box 9, Records of the Bureau of Indian Affairs Central Classified Files, 1907–1939, Carson, 7918-1908-056 to 9803A-1936-068, RG 75, NARA, Washington, D.C.
42. James Finch, secretary to governor of Nevada, to Francis G. Newlands, Nevada senator, December 9, 1909, folder "Washoe Indians Relief, 1902-1925," box 275, Carson Indian School Administrative Files, 1909-1923 [1925], Allotments Relief of Washoe Indians.
43. E. E. Roberts, Nevada congressman, to Robert G. Valentine, commissioner of Indian affairs, December 17, 1911, folder "Relief of Washo Indians—1917," ibid.

CHAPTER 6: WASHOE COLONIES

1. Donald Worster, *Rivers of Empire: Water, Aridity, and the Growth of the American West* (1985; reprint, Oxford: Oxford University Press, 1992).
2. While a realist in terms of water supply, Powell was an idealist when it came to administering that water. Powell had witnessed the meteoric rise of railroad monopolies and their equally swift demise, both marked by corruption,

inefficiency, and dubious relationships between politicians and capitalists. Powell worried that the massive hydraulic infrastructure he envisioned would follow a similar fate if westerners did not act quickly. He imagined a cooperative of western farmers pooling their capital and labor to create the canals, dams, and reservoirs needed to irrigate the West. That way water and the mechanisms created to control it would be owned and operated by local communities, not distant bureaucracies. Donald Worster, *Rivers of Empire: Water, Aridity, and the Growth of the American West* (New York: Oxford University Press, 1985), 132–35.

3. On Newlands, see William D. Rowley, *Reclaiming the Arid West: The Career of Francis G. Newlands* (Bloomington: Indiana University Press, 1996). On the Carson irrigation project, see Grace Dangberg, *Conflict on the Carson: A Study of Water Litigation in Western Nevada* (Minden, Nev.: Carson Valley Historical Society, 1975). For a description of the relationship between Francis Newlands and his father-in-law, the powerful banker, land magnate and senator William Sharon, see Michael J. Makley, *The Infamous King of the Comstock: William Sharon and the Gilded Age in the West* (Reno: University of Nevada Press, 2006).

4. Kate A. Berry, "Of Blood and Water," *Journal of the Southwest* 39, no. 1 (1997): 93–94; on Powell's survey of the Lahontan Valley, see 89.

5. Statistics come from the "Alpine Decree Findings of Fact," issued by U.S. District Court, October 28, 1980.

6. *Annual Reports of the Department of the Interior for the Fiscal Year Ended June 30, 1904: Indian Affairs, Part 1, Report of the Commissioner, and Appendixes* (Washington, D.C.: Government Printing Office, 1905), 60.

7. Even if Washoes wanted "reclaimed lands," it is likely that there would have been bureaucratic infighting. Anthropologist Martha Knack described conflicts of interest within the Department of the Interior that stretched well into the twentieth century. She also noted the larger irony that at least five entities under its management contributed to the largest encroachments on Indian lands in the 1900s. See Martha C. Knack, "Federal Jurisdiction over Indian Water Rights in Nevada," in *Battle Born: Federal-State Conflict in Nevada during the Twentieth Century*, edited by A. Costandina Titus (Dubuque, Iowa: Kendall/Hunt, 1989), 131–32.

8. C. H. Asbury to C. F. Hauke, July 9, 1911, folder "42409-1908, Carson, 313," box 56, Records of the Bureau of Indian Affairs Central Classified Files, 1907–1939, Carson, 17938-1908-313 to 22074-1909-313, pt. 1, Record Group (RG) 75, National Archives and Records Administration (NARA), Washington, D.C.

9. Asbury to commissioner of Indian Affairs, April 16, 1912, folder "Washoe Indians 1912–1914," box 270, Carson Indian School Administrative Files, 1909–1923, "H" Washoe Indians, RG 75, NARA, Pacific Region, San Bruno, Calif.

10. Maurice L. Zigmond, "Gotlieb Adam Steiner and the G. A. Steiner Museum," *Journal of California and Great Basin Anthropology* 1, no. 2 (1979): 324.

11. Dixie Westergard, "Dat So La Lee," Nevada Women's History Project, http://www.unr.edu/nwhp.
12. "Abe Cohn, Jewish Agent for Dat-So-La-Lee and Her Magnificent Indian Baskets," Jewish Museum of the American West, http://www.jmaw.org.
13. For general information on the Arts and Crafts movement in the Progressive Era, see Gwendolyn Wright, "The Progressive Housewife and the Bungalow," in *Thinking through the Past,* edited by John Hollitz (Boston: Houghton Mifflin, 2005), 2:115. For more specific information on women and the Arts and Crafts movement, see Margaret Jacobs, "Shaping a New Way: White Women and the Movement to Promote Pueblo Indian Arts and Crafts, 1900–1935," *Journal of the Southwest* 40, no. 2 (1998): 187–215, quote on 188.
14. Jo Ann Nevers, *Wa She Shu: A Washo Tribal History* (Reno: Inter-Tribal Council of Nevada, 1976), 68–69.
15. Marvin Cohodas, "Louisa Keyser and the Cohns: Mythmaking and the Basket Making in the American West," in *The Early Years of Native American Art History,* edited by Janet Catherine Berlo (Seattle: University of Washington Press, 1992), 102.
16. Dr. S. L. Lee's inventory, folder "Dr. S. L. Lee Personal Basket Collection," box 5, d'Azevedo, Warren L., Washo Indians Research Papers, Collection 99-39, Special Collections Department, University of Nevada, Reno. Information on Scees Bryant Possock comes from "Washoe Basket Weavers," *Online Nevada Encyclopedia,* a publication of Nevada Humanities, http://www.onlinenevada.org.
17. Information on Captain Pete's election taken from the *Nevada Appeal,* December 12, 1912.
18. Oley O. Haugner to Asbury, May 17, 1912, folder "Destitute [Indians] Carson, 36 B," box 33, Agency General Subject Records, 1906–1925, Records Related to Health Social Services and Biological Development, RG 75, NARA, Pacific Region, San Bruno, Calif.
19. Asbury to Captain Pete, April 5, 1912, folder "Relief of Washoe Indians—197," box 275, Carson Indian School Administrative Files, 1909–1923 [1925], Allotments Relief of Washoe Indians, RG 75, NARA, Pacific Region, San Bruno, Calif.
20. Oley Haugner, on behalf of Captain Pete, to Asbury, December 11, 1913, folder "Destitute [Indians] Carson, 36 B," box 33, Agency General Subject Records, 1906–1925, Records Related to Health Social Services and Biological Development, RG 75, NARA, Pacific Region, San Bruno, Calif.
21. Asbury to Captain Pete, December 12, 1913, ibid.
22. Asbury to Haugner, December 13, 1913, ibid.
23. M. Merrill to Asbury, December 2, 1913, folder "36 D Destitute Woodfords," box 33, ibid.
24. Asbury to Mrs. M. Merrill, December 8, 1913, ibid.
25. Merrill to Asbury, December 9, 1913, and his response, December 11, 1913, ibid.

26. Dr. E. T. Krebs to Colonel S. H. Day, Carson City, Nev., December 13, 1913, folder "210 Washoe Indian File," box 14, Nevada Reno Indian Agency General Records of Agency and Nonagency Indian Tribal Groups, RG 75, NARA, Pacific Region, San Bruno, Calif.
27. "Report on Washoe Allotments, 1917," Lorenzo Creel, special supervisor, to Colonel L. A. Dorrington, special agent, Nevada, folder "254," box 27, Special Agent Land Correspondence, 1908–24, ibid.
28. *Annual Reports of the Department of the Interior*, 74–75.
29. Asbury to Cato Sells, commissioner of Indian affairs, June 20, 1913, folder "262 Washoe Land Lease General," box 3, Nevada Investigative Records of Colonel L. A. Dorrington, Special Agent, 1913–1923, Special Agent at Large, Reno, RG 75, NARA, Pacific Region, San Bruno, Calif. The commissioner, Cato Sells, who was to gain notoriety by banishing books that referred to the Asian origins of the indigenous peoples of America, responded a month later.
30. Sells to Asbury, July 21, 1913, ibid.
31. "Notice," ibid.
32. Mr. and Mrs. Merrill to Asbury, November 26, 1913, folder "264 Woodfords Grazing Lease," box 3, ibid.
33. Asbury to L. M. Jacobsen, Gardnerville, Nevada, December 24, 1913, folder "262 Washo Land Lease General," box 3, Nevada Investigative Records, ibid.; Lease Contract Folder 553, "lease cards," box 1, Reno, Nevada, Indian Agency Special Agent Land Correspondence, 1908–24, ibid.
34. Meritt to Asbury, December 16, 1914, folder "254 List of Allottees and Money Due," Reno, Nevada, Indian Agency Special Agent Land Correspondence, 1908–24, ibid. On the difficulty of collecting payment, see Nevers, *Wa She Shu*, 71–72.
35. Dick Bender, "Washoe Indian's Timber Land of Nevada and Their Claims on the Pinenut Range," folder 254, box 2, Reno, Nevada, Indian Agency Special Agent Land Correspondence, 1908–24, Record Group 75, NARA, Pacific Region, San Bruno, Calif.
36. "Washoe Basket Weavers," *Online Nevada Encyclopedia*, a publication of Nevada Humanities, http://www.onlinenevada.org.
37. Petition from Washoe Tribe to the Senate and House of Representatives, Washington, D.C., March 28, 1914, folder "Washoe Indians, 1912–1914," Carson Indian School Administrative Files, 1909–1923, "H" Washoe Indians, box 270, ibid.
38. Asbury to the commissioner of Indian affairs, October 8, 1914, ibid.
39. Meritt, assistant commissioner of Indian affairs, to Captain Pete, November 11, 1914, ibid.
40. Russell R. Elliot with William D. Rowley, *History of Nevada*, 2nd ed. (Lincoln: University of Nebraska Press, 1987), 234. See also Fred L. Israel, *Nevada's Key Pittman* (Lincoln: University of Nebraska Press, 1963).

41. Susan Wise Ford, "Lorenzo D. Creel and the Purchase of Land for Washoe Colonies, 1917" (master's thesis, University of Nevada, Reno, 1989), 105–6.
42. Charles J. Kappler, ed., *Indian Affairs Laws and Treaties*, vol. 4, *(Laws) Compiled to March 4, 1927* (Washington, D.C.: Government Printing Office, 1919), 73.
43. Finding Aid, Lorenzo D. Creel Collection, Special Collections Department, University Nevada, Reno.
44. Creel to James E. Jenkins, superintendent of Reno Indian Agency, July 1, 1922, folder "82–1/II/1 Correspondence, 1/1922–5/22," ibid.
45. Quote from Sells taken from Francis Paul Prucha, *The Great Father: The United States Government and the American Indians* (Lincoln: University of Nebraska Press, 1990), 770. For information on Sells, see Lawrence Kelly, "Cato Sells (1913–21)," in *The Commissioner of Indian Affairs, 1824–1977*, edited by Robert M. Kvasnicka and Herman J. Viola (Lincoln: University of Nebraska Press, 1979), 243–49. Historian Frederick Hoxie has suggested that by 1920, the assimilative federal agenda had changed. Many politicians, bureaucrats, and influential citizens no longer believed Natives could fully assimilate (if they ever genuinely did). In the nineteenth-century era of military conflicts and American victories, Indian administrators promised to offer the vanquished complete membership in the United States. In Hoxie's view, this promise went unfulfilled and subtly changed so that by the 1920s, "full membership" into American society was no longer offered. Hoxie's premise helps explain the often contradictory nature of early-twentieth-century policies. Driven by earlier commitments to complete assimilation but tempered with the lack of "results," administrators like Sells contributed to a confusing policy. Frederick Hoxie, *The Final Promise: The Campaign to Assimilate the Indians, 1880–1920* (Lincoln: University of Nebraska Press, 1984). Hoxie's work has been scrutinized over the years, and other historians have come to question the distinctions he made in the assimilative agenda. Michael D. Green, for example, questioned whether American officials ever intended to "fully" accept Indians as Americans. Green suggested that Hoxie's assertion grants early assimilative figures like Henry Dawes and Richard Henry Pratt along with collective American culture right after the Civil War too much credit and wondered how different the eras described by Hoxie really were. See Michael D. Green, "Assimilation and Racism in American Indian Policy," *Reviews in American History* 13, no. 2 (1985): 227–31.
46. Creel to Dorrington, March 22, 1917, folder "Carson," box 2, Nevada Investigative Records of Colonel L. A. Dorrington.
47. Steve Achard and Conrad Buedel, *Lost Legacy of the Carson Valley: The Rise and Fall of the H. F. Dangberg Ranching Empire* (Minden, Nev.: Steve Achard and Conrad Buedel, 2011), 28–29.
48. Grace Dangberg, *Carson Valley: Historical Sketches of Nevada's First Settlement* (Carson Valley, Nev.: Carson Valley Historical Society, 1972), 7–8.

49. Achard and Buedel, *Lost Legacy of the Carson Valley,* 202–3.
50. Creel to Dorrington, Reno, March 22, 1917, folder "Carson, " box 2, Nevada Investigative Records of Colonel L. A. Dorrington.
51. Ibid.
52. Creel to Dorrington, June 30, 1917, folder "Washoe Indians Relief, 1902–1925," box 275, Carson Indian School Administrative Files, 1909–1923 [1925], Allotments Relief of Washoe Indians, RG 75, NARA, Pacific Region, San Bruno, Calif.
53. Douglas County Book of Deeds, "Book P," October 27, 1913–February 1, 1918, 780, 781. On Newlands and Dangberg, see Rowley, *Reclaiming the Arid West;* and Dangberg, *Conflict on the Carson.*
54. Winona James, interview by R. T. King, June 14, 1984, in *A Contribution to a Survey of Life in Carson Valley, from First Settlement through the 1950s* (Reno: Oral History Program, University of Nevada, Reno, Library, 1984), 27.
55. Creel to Dorrington, March 22, 1917, folder "Carson," box 2, Nevada Investigative Records of Colonel L. A. Dorrington.
56. Myron Angel, ed., *History of Nevada* (Oakland: Thompson and West, 1881), 37.
57. Creel to Dorrington, March 22, 1917, folder "Carson," box 2, Nevada Investigative Records of Colonel L. A. Dorrington.
58. Ford, "Creel and the Purchase of Land," 121.
59. Creel to Dorrington, Reno Nevada, March 22, 1917, folder "Carson," box 2, Nevada Investigative Records of Colonel L. A. Dorrington.
60. Achard and Buedel, *Lost Legacy of the Carson Valley.*
61. Nevers, *Wa She Shu,* 79; Ford, "Creel and the Purchase of Land," 114.
62. Creel to Jenkins, Reno, Nevada, July 1, 1922, folder "82-1/II/1 Correspondence, 1/1922–5/22," Creel Collection. For information on Fred Dangberg's gambling debts, see Achard and Buedel, *Lost Legacy of the Carson Valley,* 202–6.

CHAPTER 7: PREJUDICE AND PERSISTENCE

1. Douglas County, Ordinance no. 6, April 5, 1917. H. C. Jepsen, county clerk and ex officio county treasurer, clerk of the First Judicial District Court, Douglas County, Nevada, sent a copy of the ordinance to the Department of the Interior on February 14, 1922. He claimed in the letter that Ordinance no. 6 was "the only ordinance in Douglas County pertaining to Indians." The letter can be found in folder "170 Law and Order; Special Dresslerville (Washoe People)," box 28, Bureau of Indian Affairs, Carson Indian School Superintendent Program and Administrative Records, 1930–1951, Record Group (RG) 75, National Archives and Records Administration (NARA), Pacific Region, San Bruno, Calif.
2. John Dressler, "Recollections of a Washo Statesman" (Reno: Oral History Project, University of Nevada, Reno, Library, 1972), 128; Bernice Auchoberry,

interview by R. T. King, April 3, 1984, in *A Contribution to a Survey of Life in Carson Valley, from First Settlement through the 1950s* (Reno: Oral History Program, University of Nevada, Reno, Library, 1984), 13.

3. Jo Ann Nevers, *Wa She Shu: A Washoe Tribal History* (Reno: Inter-Tribal Council of Nevada, 1976), 76–77.
4. Superintendent, Reno Indian Agency, to William Johnson, September 15, 1924, folder "Washoe Indians—Relief, 1902–1925," box 275, Carson Indian School Administrative Files, 1909–1923 [1925], Allotments Relief of Washoe Indians, RG 75, NARA, Pacific Region, San Bruno, Calif.
5. Edward B. Scott, *The Saga of Lake Tahoe: A Complete Documentation of Lake Tahoe's Development over the Last One Hundred Years* (Crystal Bay, Nev.: Sierra Tahoe, 1964), 211–20.
6. Belma Jones, interview by JoAnne Peden, tape recording, tape "G," Woodfords, Calif., August 8, 1992, tape in possession of Barbara Jones.
7. Winona James, interview by R. T. King, June 14, 1984, in *Contribution to a Survey of Life,* 32.
8. Fred Dressler, interview by R. T. King, April 10, 1984, ibid., 195–97. See also Auchoberry, interview by King, ibid., 8.
9. Similar to the Washoe, communities like the Tohono O'odhams (Papagos) of Arizona worked to meet twentieth-century America on their own terms. They did take characteristically "American" jobs in mines and on railroads, but they built their work cycles in a way that honored tradition and permitted a "high degree of control over the direction of cultural adaptation." Frederick Hoxie, "From Prison to Homeland: The Cheyenne River Indian Reservation before World War I," in *The Plains Indians of the Twentieth Century,* edited by Peter Iverson (Norman: University of Oklahoma Press, 1985), 58, 78.
10. Lorenzo Creel to Malcolm McDowell, July 6, 1922, folder "US Indian Service Correspondence, June 1922–1926," box 8, Creel Collection, Special Collections Department, University Nevada, Reno. See also Creel to the superintendent for Indian affairs, October 7, 1922, folder "4 U.S. Indian Service Dressler Colony 1922," ibid.
11. Creel to James E. Jenkins, superintendent, Reno Indian Agency, May 11, 1922, folder "US Indian Service Correspondence, January 1922–May 1922," ibid. The folder contains both a rough draft of Creel's letter to Jenkins and the copy he sent. The rough draft includes quotes from the letter Jenkins sent to Creel. For information on Jenkins's assault on Washoe traditions, see Nevers, *Wa She Shu,* 81–82.
12. Superintendent of Reno Indian Agency to Oley O. Haugner, December 24, 1924, folder "Washoe Indians—Relief, 1902–1925," box 275, Carson Indian School Administrative Files; Governor Boyle to Colonel Dorrington, March 25, 1920, ibid.
13. John H. Oberly, commissioner of Indian affairs, report to the secretary of the

interior, 1888, *Annual Reports of the Commissioner of Indian Affairs* (Washington, D.C.: Government Printing Office, 1888).

14. C. H. Asbury, superintendent, Carson Indian School, to Mr. Flanigan, Pyramid Land and Stock Co., May 29, 1911, and Asbury to C. W. Atherton, March 29, 1911, folder "Application for Outing Girls, 1911," box 262, Carson Indian School Administrative Files.

15. Jesse B. Mortsolf, superintendent, Carson Indian School, to commissioner of Indian affairs, April 28, 1914, folder "47941–1914, Carson, 824," box 104, Records of the Bureau of Indian Affairs Central Classified Files, 1907–1939, Carson, 47941–1914–824 to 36429–1935–917, RG 75, NARA, Washington, D.C.

16. Frederick Snyder, superintendent, Carson Indian School, to commissioner of Indian affairs, October 4, 1926, and Mrs. Daisy Joe (Aggie's cousin) to Frederick Snyder, September 20, 1926, folder "A3397–1926, Carson, 824," ibid.

17. Belma Jones, interview by Jo Anne Peden, tape recording, tape "G," August 8, 1992, and tape "I," February 14, 1992, Woodfords, Calif., tapes in possession of Barbara Jones.

18. James, interview by King, in *Contribution to a Survey of Life*, 8, 29.

19. Laurence M. Hauptman, "The Indian Reorganization Act," in *The Aggressions of Civilization: Federal Indian Policy since the 1880s*, edited by Sandra L. Cadwalader and Vine Deloria Jr. (Philadelphia: Temple University Press, 1984), 134.

20. Frederick Hoxie, "The Reservation Period, 1880–1960," in *The Cambridge History of the Native Peoples of the Americas*, vol. 1, *North America*, pt. 2, edited by Bruce G. Trigger and Wilcomb E. Washburn (Cambridge: Cambridge University Press, 1986), 224–25.

21. Ibid., 133.

22. R. David Edmunds, Frederick Hoxie, and Neal Salisbury, *The People: A History of Native America* (Boston: Houghton Mifflin, 2007), 379–80. See also Peter Iverson, *"We Are Still Here": American Indians in the Twentieth Century* (Wheeling, Ill.: Harlan Davidson, 1998), 89–91; and Hauptman, "The Indian Reorganization Act," 136–37.

23. John Collier, *From Every Zenith: A Memoir and Some Essays on Life and Thought* (Denver: Sage Books, 1963), 115; Kenneth R. Philp, *John Collier's Crusade for Indian Reform, 1920–1954* (Tucson: University of Arizona Press, 1977), 7–9; Lawrence C. Kelly, *The Assault on Assimilation: John Collier and the Origins of Indian Policy Reform* (Albuquerque: University of New Mexico Press, 1983), 15–17. See also Hauptman, "The Indian Reorganization Act," 132–48. Hauptman points to the growing tendency of scholars to emphasize Collier's paternalism combined with his "naïve and often romantic perceptions of modern Indian life" (133). See also Elmer R. Rusco, *A Fateful Time: The Background and Legislative History of the Indian Reorganization Act* (Reno: University of Nevada Press, 2000). See also Philp, *Collier's Crusade for Indian Reform*.

24. Alida C. Bowler, superintendent, to John Collier, commissioner of Indian

affairs, November 1, 1934, folder "9532–1936, Carson, 066," box 9, Records of the Bureau of Indian Affairs Central Classified Files, 1907–1939, Carson, 7918–1908–056 to 9803A-1936–068, RG 75, NARA, Washington, D.C. Steven J. Crum described Bowler's background and noted she had no familiarity with Nevada communities when she took the assignment. See Steven J. Crum, *Po'I Pentun Tammen Kimmappeh / The Road on Which We Came: A History of the Western Shoshone* (Salt Lake City: University of Utah Press, 1994), 92.

25. William Zimmerman Jr., assistant commissioner, to Bowler, November 24, 1934, folder "9532–1936, Carson, 066," box 9, Records of the Bureau of Indian Affairs Central Classified Files, 1907–1939, Carson, 7918–1908–056 to 9803A-1936–068, RG 75, NARA, Washington, D.C.

26. John H. Holst, supervisor in charge, to Collier, February 14, 1934, "Report on Indian Self Government Conferences—Carson Jurisdiction," ibid.

27. Bowler to Collier, June 11, 1935, folder "9532–1936, Carson, 066," ibid.

28. In the words of Harry Whiteman, a Crow delegate to the Plains Indian Congress in 1934, "We [Crow] acquired our present rights by continually wedging our way to better things and we are going to keep them." Frederick Hoxie, *Parading through History: The Making of the Crow Nation in America, 1805–1935* (Cambridge: Cambridge University Press, 1995), 340–42.

29. In June 1966 the Washoe Tribal Council amended their constitution, reaffirming that the Washoe Tribe would not exercise jurisdiction of the Reno-Sparks Colony. It also set tribal membership at "at least one-fourth (1/4) degree Washoe Indian blood." The size of the governing council was increased to nine members, and it was stipulated that at Carson Colony, Dresslerville, and Woodfords, local community councils would provide a governing body. Three members from the Dresslerville Colony, two from Woodfords and Carson Colonies, one from the Reno Sparks Colony, and one tribal member not residing on any tribal lands would constitute the Washoe Tribal Council. For a copy of the amended constitution, see George E. Fay, ed., "Charters, Constitutions and By-Laws of the Indian Tribes of North America, Part XII: The Basin-Plateau Tribes," in *Occasional Publications in Anthropology* (Greeley: Museum of Anthropology, University of Northern Colorado, 1971).

30. Tribal Council minutes, February 15, 1937, folder "#064 Washoe Tribe Minutes, 1936–1941," box 7, Western Nevada Agency, Carson, Tribal Council Minutes/Resolutions, 1940–1974, RG 75, NARA, Pacific Region, San Bruno, Calif.

31. For a comprehensive account of the Peyote religion among the Washoe, see Edgar Siskin, *Washo Shamans and Peyotists* (Salt Lake City: University of Utah Press, 1983). See also Omer C. Stewart, "Washo-Northern Paiute Peyotism: A Study in Acculturation," *University of California Publications in American Archeology and Ethnography* 40, no. 3 (1944): 63–142.

32. Most histories addressing the spread of the Peyote religion in North America identify two Lipan Apache men, Pinero and Chiwat, as having introduced

Comanche and Kiowa Indians in Oklahoma to the ritual use of the herb. They were certainly not the only individuals promoting the practice. Quanah Parker, a Comanche man, helped spread the Peyote faith during the late nineteenth and early twentieth centuries. On one occasion, Parker asked the Oklahoma territorial government why the freedom of religion established by the Constitution did not apply to the Peyote faith. Parker's efforts generated the momentum that ultimately culminated in the incorporation of the Native American Church in Oklahoma in 1918, though Parker did not live to see it. Hoxie, "Reservation Period," 206–10.

33. David F. Aberle, *The Peyote Religion among the Navaho*, 2nd ed. (Norman: University of Oklahoma Press, 1982), 9; Stewart, "Washo-Northern Paiute Peyotism," 64.
34. Warren L. d'Azevedo, *Narratives of Washoe Followers of the Tipi Way: Straight with the Medicine* (Berkeley, Calif.: Heyday Books, 1978), 4.
35. Ibid., 6.
36. Siskin, *Washo Shamans and Peyotists*, 97; d'Azevedo, *Washoe Followers of the Tipi Way*, 14 (quote).
37. Statement of Francis La Flesche testifying before a congressional committee in 1918 in *Major Problems in American Indian History*, edited by Albert Hurtado and Peter Iverson (Lexington, Mass.: D. C. Heath, 1994), 412–13.
38. D'Azevedo, *Washoe Followers of the Tipi Way*, 14, 3–4. Another example often described as a pan-Indian movement exists in the Ghost Dance of the 1880s and 1890s. The Ghost Dance began among the Northern Paiutes living near the Walker River in Nevada after Wovoka, known to Euro-Americans as Jack Wilson, had a vision. Wovoka's message spread, and soon Plains communities like the Lakotas had adopted a form of the vision and dance. Both the Ghost Dance and the Peyote religion incorporated certain elements of Christianity, demonstrating that as the American government worked to suppress Native cultures, people found ways to reinvent tradition with Christian elements. Statement of La Flesche testifying before a congressional committee in 1918 in *Major Problems in American Indian History*, edited by Hurtado and Iverson, 412–13.
39. Bowler to E. A. Farrow, superintendent, Paiute Agency, Cedar City, Utah, December 21, 1936, folder "027," box 3, Intoxicants, Drugs, and Peyote, RG 75, NARA, Pacific Region, San Bruno, Calif.
40. Farrow to Bowler, December 24, 1935, and Bowler to Farrow, January 22, 1937, ibid.
41. Siskin, *Washo Shamans and Peyotists*, 100–103; Stewart, "Washo-Northern Paiute Peyotism," 94.
42. Petition of Washoe Indians against peyote use sent to Bowler, April 19, 1937, and her response, April 21, 1937, folder "027," box 3, Intoxicants, Drugs, and Peyote, RG 75, NARA, Pacific Region, San Bruno, Calif.

43. Bowler to the director in the Bureau of Standards, August 27, 1938, ibid.
44. Quote from Fillmore taken from Siskin, *Washo Shamans and Peyotists,* 128; Stewart, "Washo-Northern Paiute Peyotism," 73.
45. D'Azevedo, *Washoe Followers of the Tipi Way,* vii, 52.
46. Ray Fillmore, tribal chairman, to Collier, "The Progress Made by the Washoe Tribe and Their Appreciation," December 24, 1938, folder 064, "Washoe Tribe Minutes, 1936–1941," box 7, Western Nevada Agency, Carson, Tribal Council Minute/Resolutions, 1940–1974, RG 75, NARA, Pacific Region, San Bruno, Calif.
47. "Rehabilitation of Landless Indians," annual report, 1938, folder "4415–1939, Carson 031, 2 of 2," box 3, Records of the Bureau of Indian Affairs Central Classified Files, 1907–1939, Carson, 52523-1938-031 to 4415-1939-031, RG 75, NARA, Washington, D.C.
48. President Roosevelt to the Indian tribal councilmen in Nevada, November 16, 1939, folder "5722-1938, Carson, 013," box 1, Records of the Bureau of Indian Affairs Central Classified Files, 1907–1939, Carson, 12541-1939-010 to 13374-1936-031, RG 75, NARA, Washington, D.C.
49. Willie Smokey, transcript from the Fifth Inter-Tribal Conference, November 1940, folder "Minutes, Fifth Inter-Tribal Conference of Council Representatives Carson Jurisdiction, November, 1940," box 6, Carson Indian School Minutes, RG 75, NARA, Pacific Region, San Bruno, Calif.
50. Ray Fillmore to the Committee on Indian Affairs, September 7, 1941, and Collier to Fillmore, September 20, 1941, folder "5722-1938, Carson, 013," box 1, Records of the Bureau of Indian Affairs Central Classified Files, 1907–1939, Carson, 12541-1939-010 to 13374-1936-031, RG 75, NARA, Washington, D.C. For an example of the divide between Collier and Thomas, see Philp, *Collier's Crusade for Indian Reform,* 201–2.

CHAPTER 8: CARRYING IT

1. Washoe Tribal Council Minutes, November 4 and December 2, 1943, folder "#064 Washoe Tribe Minutes, 1941–1943," box 7, Western Nevada Agency, Carson, Tribal Council Minutes/Resolutions, 1940–1974, Record Group (RG) 75, National Archives and Records Administration (NARA), Pacific Region, San Bruno, Calif.
2. Ibid.
3. Washoe Tribal Resolution, April 7, 1949, folder "#064, Washoe Tribe Resolutions, 1939–1960," ibid. The proposed individual relinquishment agreement would have created a share-stock certificate program in which all enrolled Washoes could claim four shares in a tribal corporation. All allotment holders

would have received an additional share for every forty acres held had the program been implemented.
4. Washoe Tribal Council Minutes, April 3, 1942, and Don Foster, superintendent, Carson Indian Agency, to commissioner of Indian affairs, April 17, 1942, folder "#064 Washoe Tribe Minutes, 1941–1943," ibid.
5. Peter Iverson, *"We Are Still Here": American Indians in the Twentieth Century* (Wheeling, Ill.: Harlan Davidson, 1998), 116 (emphasis added).
6. For the most comprehensive account of termination-era policy, see Donald Fixico, *Termination and Relocation: Federal Indian Policy, 1945–1960* (Albuquerque: University of New Mexico Press, 1986), on specifically the ICC, 28–29; R. David Edmunds, Frederick Hoxie, and Neal Salisbury, *The People: A History of Native America* (Boston: Houghton Mifflin, 2007), 408; and Iverson, *"We Are Still Here,"* 115–17.
7. Edmunds, Hoxie, and Salisbury, *The People*, 408; Fixico, *Termination and Relocation*, 33.
8. Edmunds, Hoxie, and Salisbury, *The People*, 406.
9. Ibid., 399–401; Iverson, *"We Are Still Here,"* 132–33; Fixico, *Termination and Relocation*, 134–57.
10. Fixico, *Termination and Relocation*, 94.
11. George F. Wright, attorney at law, to Hank Pete, Washoe councilman, March 31, 1948, folder "90-37/I/1 Correspondence, 1948," box 1, George F. Wright Washo Claims Case Records, Collection 90-37/I, Special Collections Department, University of Nevada, Reno.
12. Washoe Tribal Council Minutes, April 21, 1948, folder "#064 Washoe Tribe Minutes, 1945–1950," box 7, Western Nevada Agency, Carson, Tribal Council Minutes/Resolutions, 1940–1974, RG 75, NARA, Pacific Region, San Bruno, Calif.
13. Pete to Wright, May 10, 1948, and Wright to Pete, May 20, 1948, and Pete to Wright, July 1, 1948, folder "90-37/I/1 Correspondence 1948," box 1, Wright Washo Claims Case Records.
14. H. M. Knutson to Wright, November 8, 1948, ibid.
15. Washoe Tribal Council Minutes, July 20, 1948, folder "#064 Washoe Tribe Minutes, 1945–1955," box 7, Western Nevada Agency, Carson, Tribal Council Minutes/Resolutions, 1940–1974, RG 75, NARA, Pacific Region, San Bruno, Calif.
16. E. P. Carville, attorney at law, to Wright, May 4, 1949, folder "90-37/I/2 Correspondence, 1949," Wright Washo Claims Case Records.
17. Wright to Pete, May 16, 1949, and Wright to C. T. Busha, attorney at law, May 16, 1949, ibid.
18. Wright to Washoe Tribal Council, August 23, 1949, Wright to Busha, August 23, 1949, and Busha to Wright, August 10, 1949, ibid.
19. Carnegie Smokey, secretary, Washoe Tribe, to Wright, January 7, 1950, folder "90-37/I/3, Correspondence 1950," ibid.

20. Busha, to Wright, January 31, 1950, E. Reeseman Fryer, superintendent, to Wright, February 7, 1950, and D. S. Myer, commissioner of Indian affairs, to Wright, June 5, 1950, ibid.
21. Busha to Wright, July 15 and September 25, 1950, ibid.
22. Busha to Wright, February 5, 1951, and Wright to Busha, February 6, 1951, folder "90-37/1/4 Correspondence, 1951," ibid.
23. Busha to Wright, February 5, 1951, and "Information Given by Washoe Indians at Stewart, Nevada, on February 19, 1951," ibid.
24. Washoe Tribal Council Minutes, April 5, 1951, folder "#064 Washoe Tribe Minutes, 1945–1955," box 7, Western Nevada Agency, Carson, Tribal Council Minutes/Resolutions, 1940–1974, RG 75, NARA, Pacific Region, San Bruno, Calif.
25. Burton Ladd to Wright, July 3, 1951, John Lewis Smith to Wright, February 15, 1951, Busha to Wright, June 27, 1951, and Wright to Busha, July 8, 1951, folder "90-37/1/4 Correspondence 1951," Wright Washo Claims Case Records.
26. Docket no. 288 before the Indian Claims Commission and Smith to Wright, August 16, 1951, ibid.
27. Wright to John Lewis Smith, March 12, 1952, folder "90-37/I/5 Correspondence, 1952," ibid.
28. Smith to Wright, June 4, 1953, and Order for Consolidation issued by Edgar E. Witt, chief commissioner, and William M. Holt, associate commissioner, November 19, 1953, ibid.
29. Response of Defense before the Indian Claims Commission, Docket no. 288, *The Washoe Tribe of the States of Nevada and California, Plaintiff v. The United States of America, Defendant,* April 14, 1955, filed by Perry W. Morton, assistant attorney general, and Ralph A. Barney, attorney, folder "90-37/I/8 Correspondence, Jan.–May, 1955, Wright Washo Claims Case Records. On the Southern Paiute case, see Martha Knack, *Boundaries Between: The Southern Paiutes, 1775–1995* (Lincoln: University of Nebraska Press, 2004), 245–48.
30. Tribal Council minutes, December 15, 1952, folder "#064 Washoe Tribe Minutes, 1945–1955," box 7, Western Nevada Agency, Carson, Tribal Council Minutes/Resolutions, 1940–1974, RG 75, NARA, Pacific Region, San Bruno, Calif.
31. Tribal Council minutes, June 19, 1955, ibid.
32. Tribal Council minutes, August 27, 1955, ibid.
33. Before the Indian Claims Commission, Docket no. 288, *The Washoe Tribe of the States of Nevada and California, Plaintiff v. The United States, Defendant,* vol. 2 of testimony, transcripts from July 7, 1955, folder "III/2/7/I George Wright Collection Correspondence and Vol. II of Testimony," box 2, d'Azevedo, Warren L., Washoe Indians Research Papers, Collection 99-39, Special Collections Department, University of Nevada, Reno, 70–83.
34. Deposition of Richard Barrington, Washoe elder, ibid. See also an address prepared by George Wright and delivered for the Centennial Celebration at Carson City, Nevada, October 31, 1964, "Richard E. Barrington," ibid. See also Jo

Ann Nevers, *Wa She Shu: A Washoe Tribal History* (Reno: Inter-Tribal Council of Nevada, 1976), 86.

35. Wright to Smith and Nicholas Allen, September 27, 1955, folder "90-37/I/9 Correspondence, June, Dec. 1955," box 1, Wright Washo Claims Case Records.
36. Wright to Roy James, Washoe Tribal chair, Barrington, and Omer Stewart, February 25, 1958, folder "III/2/7/3 George Wright Papers—Correspondence," box 2, Washo Indians Research Papers. See also Wright to Oren George, February 25, 1958, ibid.
37. H. D. Rosenthal, *Their Day in Court: A History of the Indian Claims Commission* (New York: Garland, 1990), 266-67.
38. Earl James, Washoe Tribal Council member, to Nicholas Allen, September 8, 1959, folder "90-37/I/12 Correspondence, 1959," box 1, Wright Washo Claims Case Records.
39. "Statement of Chief Commissioner to Members of the Bar and Others at Calendar Conference," September 21, 1960, and James to Wright, September 25, 1960, ibid.
40. James to Allen, May 22, 1961, folder "90-37/I/14 Correspondence, Jan.-July, 1961," ibid.
41. "Rules for Appraisal of Indian Lands," folder "90-37/II/39 Case Notes," box 3, ibid.
42. Washoe Tribal Resolution, April 13 and 14, 1961, folder "Washoe Tribe Resolutions, 1958-1963," box 7, Western Nevada Agency, Carson, Tribal Council Minutes/Resolutions, 1940-1974, RG 75, NARA, Pacific Region, San Bruno, Calif.
43. Memorandum to Appraisers and Allen, February 23, 1963, folder "90-37/I/20 Correspondence, Jan.-Mar., 1963," box 1, Wright Washo Claims Case Records.
44. Fred W. Richards, tribal secretary, to Wright, March 12, 1963, ibid.
45. An address prepared by George Wright for the Centennial Celebration at Carson City, Nevada, October 31, 1964, "Richard E. Barrington," Washoe elder, folder "III/2/7/1 George Wright Collection Correspondence and Vol. II of Testimony," box 2, Washo Indians Research Papers.
46. Barrington to Wright, October 10, 1963, folder "90-37/I/22 Correspondence, May-Dec., 1963," box 1, Wright Washo Claims Case Records.
47. Before the Indian Claims Commission, *The Washoe Tribe of the States of Nevada and California, Plaintiff v. The United States of America, Defendant*, Docket no. 288, decided October 31, 1969, "Findings of Fact," folder "90-37/II/32 Washoe Vs. U.S. Findings of Fact, Oct. 31, 1969," box 3, ibid.

CHAPTER 9: THE JOURNEY HOME

1. Ed Vogel, "Tribe's Long Journey Back to Tahoe Begins," *Las Vegas Review-Journal*, August 3, 1997, B1.

2. Sean Whaley, "Gore Vows to Protect Lake," *Las Vegas Review-Journal*, July 26, 1997, A1; Holly Atchison, "Washoe Language Circle, Elders Bask in Memories of Summit," *Record-Courier* (Carson Valley, Nev.), August 13, 1997.
3. Woodfords Community Council minutes, November 18, 1966, folder "#064 Washoe Tribe—Woodfords Resolutions, 1974," box 8, Western Nevada Agency, Carson, Tribal Council Minutes/Resolutions, 1940–1974, Record Group (RG) 75, National Archives and Records Administration (NARA), Pacific Region, San Bruno, Calif.
4. Washoe Tribal Resolutions 67-W-8, 67-W-9, and 67-W-10, folder "Washoe Tribe Resolutions, 1965–1967," box 7, Western Nevada Agency, Carson, Tribal Council Minutes/Resolutions, 1940–1974, RG 75, NARA, Pacific Region, San Bruno, Calif.
5. Washoe Tribal Resolution 72-WF-1, folder "Washoe Tribe—Woodfords Resolutions, 1974," box 8, Western Nevada Agency, Carson, Tribal Council Minutes/Resolutions, 1940–1974, RG 75, NARA, Pacific Region, San Bruno, Calif. Information on Senator Bible taken from a *New York Times* obituary, published September 14, 1988, http://ndep.nv.gov.
6. Jerry Belcher, "Alpine County's Indians Win Their Own Reservation," *San Francisco Sunday Examiner and Chronicle*, September 20, 1970, A4.
7. Martha Knack, "The Effects of Nevada State Fishing Laws on the Northern Paiutes of Pyramid Lake," *Nevada Historical Society Quarterly* 15, no. 4 (1982): 257–59.
8. Petition from Washoe Tribe to the Senate and House of Representatives, Washington, D.C., March 28, 1914, folder "Washoe Indians, 1912–1914," Carson Indian School Administrative Files, 1909–1923, "H" Washoe Indians, box 270, RG 75, NARA, Pacific Region, San Bruno, Calif.
9. E. B. Meritt, assistant commissioner of Indian affairs, to J. B. Mortsolf, superintendent, Carson Indian School, November 11, 1914, and Mortsolf to commissioner of Indian affairs, November 16, 1914, folder "Washoe Indians, 1912–1914," box 270, Carson Indian School Administrative Files, 1909–1923, RG 75, NARA, Pacific Region, San Bruno, Calif.
10. Washoe Tribal Council minutes, October 11, 1954, folder "#064 Washoe Tribe Minutes 1945–1950," box 7, Western Nevada Agency, Carson, Tribal Council Minutes/Resolutions, 1940–1974, RG 75, NARA, Pacific Region, San Bruno, Calif.
11. "Findings of Fact," April 16, 1980, for the case *Washoe Tribe of the States of Nevada and California, and Vernell Frank and Carl James, Plaintiffs, v. Joseph Greenley, Director of the State of Nevada Department of Wildlife, and William Parsons, Chief of Law Enforcement for the State of Nevada Department of Wildlife, individually and in their official capacities,* folder "97-04/III/4/2 Washoe Pinenut Case, April 1980," box 6, Warren d'Azevedo Papers, Collection 97-04, Special Collections Department, University of Nevada, Reno, 2–4.

12. "Declaratory Judgment," April 16, 1980, for ibid., 2.
13. Quote from Peter Sferrazza taken from Edward C. Johnson, "Issues: The Indian Perspective," in *The Handbook of North American Indians,* edited by William C. Sturtevant (Washington, D.C.: Smithsonian Institution, 1986), 11:596.
14. "An Act to declare that the United States holds certain lands in trust for the Washoe tribe of Nevada and California and to transfer certain other lands to the administration of the United States Forest Service," Public Law 97–288, 97th Cong., October 6, 1982. See also Washoe Tribe of California and Nevada, "Clear Creek Stormwater Management Plan," prepared by the Washoe Environmental Protection Department, December 2008, http://www.washoetribe.us.
15. Lake Tahoe Presidential Forum, Actions to Protect Lake Tahoe, status report, March 1998, http://www.fs.usda.gov.
16. Ibid., 36. In 2005 I had the opportunity to visit a Washoe culture camp held at the Meeks Resort. Washoe elders were working with children, teaching them flint knapping and weaving techniques, among other things. Information on Meeks Meadow taken from Michael Makley, "Saving Lake Tahoe: An Environmental History of a National Treasure" (unpublished manuscript), 141.
17. "An Act to direct the Secretary of Agriculture to convey certain land in the Lake Tahoe Basin Management Unit, Nevada, to the Secretary of the Interior, in trust for the Washoe Indian Tribe of Nevada and California," Public Law 108–67, 108th Cong., August 1, 2003.
18. Quote from Brian Wallace taken from Gregory Crofton, "Washoe Tribe Returns to Tahoe Roots with Land Transfer," *Tahoe Daily Tribune,* August 13, 2003.
19. Lake Tahoe Presidential Forum, Actions to Protect Lake Tahoe, status report, March 1998, http://www.fs.usda.gov, 35.
20. "Notes and News," *American Antiquity* 23, no. 3 (1958): 331–32; Edward B. Scott, *The Saga of Lake Tahoe: A Complete Documentation of Lake Tahoe's Development over the Last One Hundred Years* (Crystal Bay, Nev.: Sierra Tahoe, 1964), 256; *Cave Rock Management Plan Final Environmental Impact Statement* (hereafter cited as *FEIS*) (Sacramento: Jones & Stokes, 2002), chaps. 3, 1, 13–15. Cave Rock is the only Washoe spiritual site that has been archaeologically tested and ethnographically studied. Additionally, it was the first excavated site in Douglas County to receive a Smithsonian number (DO-1/University of California at Berkeley; DO-8/Nevada State Museum).
21. Darrel Bender, videotaped interview with Michael Makley, Carson City, Nev., June 6, 1998, in possession of author.
22. *FEIS,* chaps. 3, 8; Paul McHugh, "The Battle over Cave Rock," *San Francisco Chronicle,* September 25, 2003.
23. Matthew S. Makley and Michael J. Makley, *Cave Rock: Climbers, Courts, and a Washoe Indian Sacred Place* (Reno: University of Nevada Press, 2010), 47–49.
24. Ibid., 67.
25. Ibid., 67–70.

26. Don Handelman, "Aspects of the Moral Compact of a Washo Shaman," *Anthropological Quarterly* 45, no. 2 (1972): 96; James F. Downs, "Washoe Religion," *University of California Publications Anthropological Records* 16, no. 9 (1960): 369.
27. Maribeth Gustafson, "Record of Decision for Cave Rock Management Direction," July 8, 2003, 7; *FEIS,* chaps. 2, 7–9.
28. Makley and Makley, *Cave Rock,* 87–92.
29. Sherry Smokey, "Wa She Shu: We Were Always Here," *Carson Magazine* (Fall 2006): 28.
30. Warren d'Azevedo, "The Washoe People in the Twentieth Century," paper presented to the third annual Wa-She-Shu-Edu, Festival of Native American Arts and Culture, Tallac Historic Site, Lake Tahoe, Calif., July 30, 1993, 13.
31. Smokey, "Wa She Shu," 26.
32. Herman Fillmore, phone interview by the author, December 7, 2017, longhand transcripts in possession of the author.
33. Ibid.; Caitlin Aimee Keliiaa, "*Washiw Wagayay Mangal:* Reweaving the Washoe Language" (master's thesis, University of California, Los Angeles, 2012), 35–37.
34. Keliiaa, "*Washiw Wagayay Mangal,*" 53.
35. Fillmore, interview.
36. Smokey, "Wa She Shu," 22–23.
37. Don Cox, "Washoe Tribe Youth Follow Ancient Path, Test Endurance during Carson-to-Tahoe Trek," *Reno Gazette Journal,* June 25, 2006, A1, A3.
38. Washoe Tribe of Nevada and California Comprehensive Economic Development Strategy, Narrative/Profile, 2011, http://info.washoetribe.us, 15–22.
39. Ibid., 35–36, 43–45.
40. Ibid., 39–40.
41. Ibid., 47.
42. Cox, "Washoe Tribe Youth Follow Ancient Path," A1, A3.
43. Quote from Brian Wallace taken from Crofton, "Washoe Tribe Returns to Tahoe Roots."

AFTERWORD

1. Michael Walling, "A Local Habitation," *Lake Tahoe Shakespeare Festival, 2008 Season,* 14.
2. Historian David Rich Lewis suggested that most American children imagine Indians in the form of "Plains Indians—mounted warriors in feathers and leathers." See David Rich Lewis, "Native Americans in the 19th-Century West," in *A Companion to the American West,* edited by William Deverell (Malden, Mass.: Blackwell, 2004), 144.

INDEX

Abbie, Ruth, 175
Access Fund, 175–78
Ak-Chin, 15–16
Ak-Chin Farms, 16
Akimel O'odham, 15
Algonquian, 10
Allard, L. P., 143
Allen, James K., 88
Allen, Nicholas, 159
All-Pueblo Council, 128
Alpine County, California, 165, 167
American Indian Defense Association (AIDA), 128, 129
American Indian Movement, 165
American River, 61
Anaconda Mining Company, 8
Anderson, M. Kat, 3
Andrews, Sylvia, 181
animal bosses, 23, 29, 80, 84
antelope charming, 29, 80, 84
Antelope Valley, California, 62
anthropologists, 19; longevity of Washoes in the Sierra and, x; Spirit Cave Mummy and, 20; Washoe precontact population estimates by 71; work with tribal communities, 9
Arapaho, 6
Arts and Crafts movement, 94, 99, 101
Asbury, Calvin H., 102, 108, 111, 117, 126; correspondence with Captain Pete and, 103–4; emphasis on need for assimilation and, 97–98; Epesuwa's second trip to Washington, D.C., and, 92; land relinquishment requests by, 90; leasing of the pine nut allotments, 106–107; petition from Washoes and, 109–10; question of Washoe reservation, 90, 97; Washoe health care and, 104–5; Washoe trespassing claims and, 88–89, 91
Atkins, J. D. C., 49
Auchoberry, Bernice: pine nut festival ceremony and pine nut gathering, information on, 35, 122; Ordinance no. 6 and, 119

Bannock, 33
Barber, Amy, 181
Barber, Wes, 181
Barrington, Richard E.: criticism of allotments, 90; deposition for Indian Claims Commission case and, 157–58; testimony in Indian Claims Commission case, 161–62
Bartine, Horace F., 86, 87
Bartleson-Bidwell party, 39
bears: power and, 30; Henry Rupert association with, 76–77; Washoe hunting of, 30
Beleliwe, 80
Bender, Darrel, 174
Bender, Dick, 94, 157; petition for rights on Pine Nut Lands, 108; problems with allotment and, 90–91; trip to Washington, D.C., with Epesuwa, 85–87
Bender, Manuel, 3

BIA. *See* Bureau of Indian Affairs
Bible, Alan, 166
Bicose store, 101
Blackhawk, Ned, 5, 11, 42, 52
Bowler, Alida, 129–30, 135–36, 155
Boyle, Emmet, 125
Browne, John Ross, 60
Buchanan, James, 56
Bureau of Indian Affairs (BIA), 90, 128, 145, 157, 163, 166, 170
Burtt, Kristin, 181
Busha, C. T., Jr., 148–54, 159, 162

Cabazon, 15
Cahuilla, 15, 17
Caldera, Beverley, 179, 181, 194n10, 197–98n2
California gold rush, ix, 2, 7, 47, 61, 87. *See also* gold
California Trail, 50
California v. Cabazon Band of Mission Indians, 15
Captain Jim, 87; trip to Washington, D.C., 1, 77, 84–86. *See also* Epesuwa
Captain Joe, 85
Captain Pete, 94, 102–4, 106, 109–10, 120
Carlisle Indian School, 78, 157
Carson City, Nevada, 4, 55, 64, 77, 79, 83, 85, 87, 88, 98, 99, 107, 110, 118, 154, 174, 183, 184
Carson Indian School, 77, 79, 81, 83, 88, 92, 104, 105, 118, 126, 127, 129, 135, 157, 168. *See also* Stewart Indian School
Carson Morning Appeal, 68
Carson River, 5, 8, 47, 57, 63, 96, 112, 138, 212; purchase of Washoe colonies and, 115–17. *See also* Watasému
Carson Tahoe Lumber and Fluming Company (CTLFC), 64
Carson Valley, xi, 4, 8, 50, 54, 56, 102, 119, 121, 122, 130, 140, 143, 147, 165, 171; center for Euro-American agricultural growth, 70; Lorenzo Creel's visit to, 112–18; named after Kit Carson, 48
Carson Valley Agency, 57
Carson, Christopher "Kit," 42, 48

Carville, Edward P., 148
Casson, W. E., 88
Cave Rock: legal proceedings and, 9, 17, 152, 173–78; proposal to create a park and, 151; Henry Rupert's association with, 76, 83; sacred site, 24, 81. *See also* De?ek Wadapuš
Ceese (basket weaver), 102. *See also* Possock, Scees Bryant
Central Pacific Railroad, 73
Cheyenne, 6
Chief Grey Horse, 136. *See also* Lancaster, Ben
Clinton, Bill, 7, 164, 165, 172, 173
Codhas, Marvin, 101
Cohn, Abram, 99
Cohn, Amy, 99–101
Cohn's Emporium, 99–100
Collier, John, 128–31, 137, 140, 143, 144, 145
colonization, 13; American, 43, 44, 46, 51, 84, 95, 104, 168, 171, defined, 14–15; Spanish and, 11, 34, 41. *See also* extractive colonialism; settler colonialism
Comanche, 12, 133
Comstock silver rush, ix, 2, 4, 13, 42; initial rush, 58–65; news of, 58–59
Corbett, Susie, 82
Cordova, Pedro, 82
Creel, Lorenzo Dow: background of, 111; defense of Washoe colonies, 123–24; Washoe colonies and, 111–18, 165
Crow, 6, 111; Indian Claims Commission and, 131
Crum, Steve, 17
Cruz, Darrel, 182

Dabuda, 98–99. *See also* Datsolalee; Keyser, Louisa
Dangberg, Frederika, 113
Dangberg, Hennrich August, 113
Dangberg, Henry Fred, 113, 117
Dangberg, H. F., 69, 109, 112, 113, 115
Datsolalee, 4, 26, 94; relationship with Amy Cohn and, 98–101. *See also* Dabuda; Keyser, Louisa

Dawes Act, 6, 7; Washoe use of, 77, 83–88
DaɁaw, x. *See also* Lake Tahoe
DaɁaw Ɂaga, x
decolonization, 12
degikup (basketry style), 4, 100
Deidesheimer, Philip, 63
Department of the Interior, 49, 97, 148, 149
DeQuille, Dan, 63
Derby Canal, 96
Deseret, 47
Detutudi (Washoe shaman), 25
Dexter, Jean, 19
DeɁek Wadapuš, 9, 24, 151, 173. *See also* Cave Rock
Dick, Lena Frank, 101
di mash ("my face"), 34
di MaɁaš ("my pine nut lands"), 34
Dodge, Frederick, 57
Donner Lumber and Boom Company (DLBC), 65
Donner Party, 45
Dorrington, L. A., 111, 112, 114
Dortch, J. H., 90
Double Springs, 46, 52, 77. *See also* Simee Dimeh
Double Springs Flat, 1, 35
Douglas County, 114, 119, 120, 181
Douglas County Council of Defense, 120
Douglas, Henry, 52, 74,
dreams: Henry Rupert and, 76–77, 80, 82–83, 84, 208n16; significance for Washoes, 24, 29, 35, 80, 81
Dressler, John, 38, 119
Dressler, Marvin, 179
Dressler, Mischelle, 181
Dressler, William F., 116, 117, 122
Dresslerville Colony, 117, 124, 130, 137, 138, 161, 165, 178, 183, 184
Duman, Fred, 167
Duncan, Pete, 76, 85
Dwight, Theodore T., 73,

Eisenhower, Dwight, 146
Enos, Erick, 184
Enos, Helen Nevers, 46, 55
Enos, Lisa, 180, 181
Epesuwa, 1, 54, 89; lobbying of the Nevada governor and, 91–92; use of the Dawes Act 6–7, 76, 77, 84–87; victim of witchcraft, 77. *See also* Captain Jim
extractive colonialism: defined, 12–13; logging and, 64

Faletti Ranch, 138
Fallon, Nevada, 20, 97
Farrow, E. A., 135
Fillmore, Benny, 180
Fillmore, Bill, 103–4, 105
Fillmore, Harry, 91
Fillmore, Herman, 35, 179
Fillmore, Laura, 180
Fillmore, Ray, 131, 136, 137, 140
Finch, James, 91, 92
fishing: development of commercial operations at Lake Tahoe, 1, 2, 65–66; important traditional fishing sites, 8, 64; Indian Claims Commission Act and, 152–53, 162; as *MaɁaš* lands, 23; overfishing of Tahoe, 66–70; Paiutes and, 51, 67; scapegoating of Washoes in regional newspapers, 66–68; Washoe customs, 32–33, 151, 167–70; Washoes working as guides, 4
Flathead, 145
Fort McDermitt Paiute community, 139
Fountain, Steve, 6, 33
Frank, Johnnie, 141
Frank, Vernell, 169
Frémont, John C., 5, 12, 39–44, 48, 59, 153
Fryer, E. Reeseman, 150

Garcia, Liz, 181
Gardnerville, Nevada, 102, 107, 119
Gelvin, Ralph, 147
Genoa, Nevada, 48, 53, 55, 56, 57, 76, 96, 107, 109
Genoa Weekly Courier, 68
George, Anna, 89
George, Art, Jr., 1, 185, 200n2

George, Spotted, 97
Gilbert, Aggie, 127
Glenbrook, Nevada, 64
Glickman, Dan, 165
gold, ix, 2, 7, 12, 13, 45, 47, 57, 59, 60, 61, 62, 87, 117, 186. *See also* California gold rush
Gold Canyon, 57–58
Gold Hill Evening News, 67
Gore, Al, 7, 164
Gould, Jay, 65
Grayshield, Lisa, 164
Great Basin, 33, 34, 47, 48, 50; anthropological cultural region, x; characterized as desolate, 3, 6, 14, 42; eastern boundary of Washoe territory, ix, x, 2, 41, 43; first humans in, 18, 20–22; as region of study, 11, 17; Indian Claims Commission Act and, 154; water beings and, 24
Great Salt Lake, 47
Green, Michael, 10
Greene, Graham, 186
Grorud, Albert A., 152
Grosh, Allen, 57
Grosh, Hosea, 57
Gustafson, Maribeth, 176–78

Hämäläinen, Pekka, 12
Hangalelti, 88, 89, 98, 105, 121, 165; traditional range defined, 23, 32
Harris, Robert, 175
Haugner, Oley O., 102–4, 125
Hauke, C. F., 97
Heidtman property, 138
Heizer, Robert, 157
Henry, Madeline, 181
Highway 50, 174, 185
Highway 395, 7, 46, 178
Hoag, Jay H., 153, 154
Hobart, Walter Scott, 64
Hokan language, x, 21, 22
Holbrook, Charles, 69
Holbrook, Herman, 181
Holeman, Jacob, 50–52
Holst, John, 130
Homestead Act, 83

Honey Lake, California, 33, 44
Hoover, Herbert 128, 145
horseless Indians, 6, 33–34
House Concurrent Resolution 108, 146
Houssman, William, 115
Hudson, J. W., 51, 194n9
Humboldt River, 5, 50
Humboldt Sink, 51
Humboldt Valley, 86
Hunt, Garland, 55
Hunter, Robert, 169
hunter-gatherers, stereotypes of, 2–3
Huron, 49
Hyde, Orson, 56

Indian Claims Commission (ICC), 144, 147, 149, 150, 151, 155, 156, 172. *See also* Indian Claims Commission Act
Ickes, Harold, 128
Incline, Nevada, 64
Indian Appropriation Act of 1916, 111
Indian Claims Commission Act, 144. *See also* Indian Claims Commission
Indian Reorganization Act (IRA), 7, 128–31, 137, 138, 139, 140, 143, 183
Indians of All Nations, 165
Ingalls, G. W., 50, 53, 75
Intercourse Act of 1834, 56
IRA. *See also* Indian Reorganization Act
Iroquois, 12, 145

Jacobs, Margaret, 99
Jacobsen, William H., xvii, xviii, 180, 193n8
Jacobson, L. M., 107
Jake, Leslie, 161, 162
James, Adele, 165, 181
James, Alvin, 166
James, Benny, 115
James, Carl, 169
James, Earl, 159, 160, 166, 167
James, Maggie Mayo, 102
James, Roma, 131, 179
James, Ronald, 148, 156
James, Steven, 181
James, Winona, 81, 122, 127, 184
Jenkins, James E., 123–25

John, Susie, 76
Johnson v. M'Intosh, 61
Johnson, William, 120
Johnston, Albert Sydney, 56
Johntown gold camp, 57
Jones, Belma, 94; memories of Carson Indian School, 127; on pine nut harvesting, 35; preparation for winter, 36; on summers at Lake Tahoe, 121–22; on Washoe girls' training, 25; Woodfords land purchase and, 166–67

Keyser, Charlie, 99
Keyser, Louisa, 4, 26, 98; Arts and Crafts movement and, 94; relationship with Amy Cohn and, 98–101. *See also* Dabuda; Datsolalee
Kings Canyon, 184
Kizer, Delaney, 156
Klamath, 145
Knack, Martha, 17
Knutson, H. M., 148
Krebs, E. T., 104, 105
Kroeber, Alfred, 156

Ladd, Burton A., 152
Lagomarsino Canyon, 18, 20
Lahontan cutthroat trout, 65
Lahontan Dam, 96
Lahontan, Lake, 65
Lahontan Valley, 96, 97
Lake Lahontan. *See* Lahontan, Lake
Lake Tahoe. *See* Tahoe, Lake
Lakota, 6, 12, 123
Laman, 47
Lamanites, 47
Lancaster, Ben, 133, 135–37. *See also* Chief Grey Horse
Lane, Franklin K., 111
Lange, H., 115
Lea, Luke, 50
Lee, Simeon Lemuel, 77, 99–100
Lehi, 47
Lenúka, "Captain Jim," 54, 84, 108
Lincoln, Abraham, 59, 86
Lindstrom, Susan, 19

List, Robert, 171
Lockhart, Jacob, 71–73
logging, destruction of Lake Tahoe forests, 2, 63–65, 70
Lowie, Robert, 156

Machado, Mahlon, 18, 193n9
Mackay, John, 65
Maidu, 33
Makah, 16–17
Markleeville, California, 42, 107
Marshall, James, 61
Martis archaeological complex, 20
Mast, B. G., 69
Maxwell, Gemima, 89
Mayo, Sarah Jim, 102, 108
MaʔAš, 23, 34, 194n12
McCarren, Pat, 167
McDonald, Daniel, 181
McKibben, Howard, 177
McMarlin, John, 54
Meeks Bay, 8–9, 172–73
Mélo (Washoe interpreter for Frémont), 42
memorandums of understanding, 7–8, 164, 171
Menominee, 145
Meriam, Lewis, 127
Meritt, E. B., 110, 168
Mexico, 44, 45, 133
Miguel, Robert, 15
Miller, Bob, 181
Miller, Leman, 105
Minault, Paul, 176
Minkey, Si-sa, 85
Miwok, 33
Mormons: colonization of Washoe lands, 47, 48, 55–57, 112; establishment of supply stations and, 47
Mormon Station, 48, 50, 51, 52, 53, 54, 55, 56
Mortsolf, Jesse B., 126
"Moses" (nickname for Henry Rupert), 83
Moses Street, Carson City, Nevada, 83
Mountain Democrat, 66
Murray, Noble T., 160, 161

mushege (wild due to madness), 39, 197n2
Myer, Dillon, 145, 150

National Congress of American Indians, 156
National Indian Youth Council, 165
Nentushu, 19
Nephi, 47
Nephites, 47
Nevada, 4, 10, 45, 54, 55; colonization and, 15; Comstock Lode and, 13, 62; creation of Washoe colonies and, 111; Intertribal Council and, 139–40; Mormon claims to, 47–48, 50; Natives and, 3; Public Law 280 and, 146–47, 156; statehood, 59; state legislative acts related to Washoes, 67–69; territory creation of, 57; textbooks and history of, 10; U.S. congressional delegation and, 85–87; Washoes and, 13, 72, 74, 81, 92, 97, 113–15, 118, 125, 132, 147, 151, 161
Nevada Indian Superintendency, 123
Nevada State Parks Commission, 20
Nevers, Jo Ann, xiv, 60
New Indian History, 11–12
Newlands, Francis, 91, 96, 115
Newlands Project, 96. *See also* Truckee-Carson project
Ninth Circuit Court of Appeals, 9, 16, 132, 152, 170, 178
Nissenan, 33
Nixon, Richard, 113
Numaga, 54, 55, 91
Numic language, 22, 33, 193n8
Nye, James W., 14, 42, 52, 70, 71

Oberly, John, 126
Odawa, 49
Office of Indian Affairs, 49
Old Red Ledge, 58
Ophir Mining Company, 63
Ordinance no. 6, Douglas County, Nevada, 119–20, 215n1
Ormsby, William, 54–56

Osman, Dan, 174
outing program, 126–27

Pacific Wood, Lumber, and Flume Company (PWLFC), 65
Paiute, 3, 10, 51, 129; fishing practices, 40; Indian Claims Commission Act and, 152–54; Northern, 5, 22, 55, 91, 96, 151; relationship with Washoe, 22, 24, 39, 54, 57, 73, 74, 92, 97, 118, 130; selling fish to Americans, 66–67, 168; Southern, 11, 17, 34, 50
paleo-Indians, 20
Palma, Juan, 175, 176, 178
Papago, 15, 216n9. *See also* Tohono O'odham
Parker, Hubbard G., 71–74
P'a·walu, 35, 48, 70, 89, 91, 97, 109, 165; traditional range defined, 23, 31, 51, 76
Pete, Dinah, 181
Pete, Hank, 131, 132, 147, 150, 151, 207n12
Pete, Molly, 104, 105
peyote, 88, 132–37
Piggot, Michael, 87, 108
pine nut festival, 34–35, 86. *See also* T'agim Gumsabay?
Pine Nut Mountains, 2, 77, 103
Pine Nut Stock Growers Association, 107, 142
piñon pine nuts, 34; importance to Washoe people, 1, 6
Pittman, Key, 110–11
Possock, Scees Bryant, 102. *See also* Ceese
Powell, John Wesley, 75, 95, 96
Pratt, Richard Henry, 78, 79
presidential summit at Lake Tahoe, 8, 164–71, 173, 184
Price, Hiram, 79
Public Law 91-362, 167
Public Law 93-135, 163
Public Law 97-288, 171
Public Law 108-67, 172–73
Public Law 280, 146, 156
Pyramid Lake War, 51, 55
Pyramid Lake, Nevada, 4, 39, 40, 51, 57, 65, 67, 74, 129, 131, 139, 168

Rakow, Melba, 181
Reclamation Act, 95–96
Reese, John, 48, 49
Reid, Harry, 7, 172
Reid, Joshua L., 17
Reno-Sparks Indian Colony, 118, 119, 130, 132, 165
Reno, Nevada, 4, 62, 96, 117, 118, 120, 148, 177
Richards, Fred, 161
Rivers, Frank, 81
Roberts, E. E., 92
Roosevelt, Franklin, 128, 139, 140, 144
Rosenthal, Nicholas, 11
Rube, Charlie, 80, 84, 85, 157, 207n1
Runs After, Olney, 123
Rupert, Henry, 76–84, 93, 142, 176–77

Sallee, Tom, 148, 150, 151
Sand Harbor, Nevada, 185
San Francisco, California, 58, 64, 66, 81, 98, 113, 146, 147, 154, 174, 176
San Francisco Herald, 54, 56
Schneider, Khal, 7
Sells, Cato, 106, 107, 112
Seminole, 49, 111
Senate Bill 2257, 167
settler colonialism, 12–13, 70
Sferrazza, Peter, 170
shamanism, 24–25, 30, 33, 77, 80–85, 124, 134, 137; Cave Rock and, 173–77
Sharon, William, 64
Shawnee, 49
Shoshone, 10, 17, 53, 123, 139; Northern, 33; Western, 3, 11, 22, 50
Shull, Carol, 176
Sierra Nevada Mountains, 6, 51; arrival of strangers in, 39, 41; distinct from Rocky Mountains, 2; as western boundary for Washoe territory, ix, x, 1, 22
Sierra Nevada Wood and Lumber Company (SNWLC), 64
Simee Dimeh, 46. *See also* Double Springs
Simme Dimeh Summit, 7
Simpson, Loren, 178

Siskin, Edgar, 136
Skunk Harbor, Lake Tahoe, 173, 184, 186
Smith, Jedediah, 38–39
Smith, John Lewis, Jr., 148
Smokey, Carnegie, 149–50
Smokey, Eleanor, 181
Smokey, Willie, 119, 131, 133, 140, 141, 142
Smokey Jackson, Theresa, 164, 181
Smokey Martinez, Jo Ann, 164, 181
Snyder, Frederick, 127
Spanish, 5, 11, 33, 43, 44
Spanish colonization, 11, 13, 34, 41
Spirit Cave Mummy, 20
Sproat, Gilbert Malcolm, 48
Stanford, Leland, 65
Steiner, Gotlieb Adam, 98
Steward, Julian, 156, 158
Stewart, Omer, 19, 136, 137, 155–58
Stewart, William, 79, 86, 87
Stewart Indian School, 79, 82, 126, 127, 170, 182. *See also* Carson Indian School
Susanville, California, 22
Sutter, John, 43, 61
Sykes, Bobbi, 14

Tʼa·gɨm ʔaša, 34, 87. *See also* Pine Nut Mountains
Tʼagɨm Gumsabayʔ, 34–35, 86. *See also* pine nut festival
Tahoe, Lake, xi, 39, 101, 116, 185; Cave Rock and, 9, 80, 175–78; as center of Washoe homelands, x, 18–19, 164, 179, 193n9; colonization of, 1, 2, 13, 63–65, 78; early humans and, 20–21; Indian Claims Commission Act and, 151–63; overfishing of 67–69; presidential summit and, 7–8, 164–65, 181, 187; seasonal cycle and, 22, 31, 121; tourist trade and, 4; Washoe land acquisition and, 17, 171–72, 184
Thomas, Elmer, 140
Thunderheart, 186
Tlingit and Haida Indians of *Alaska v. United States* (1968), 162
Tohono Oʼodham, 15, 216n9. *See also* Papago

Torison, James, 85
Treaty of Guadalupe Hidalgo, 45
Truckee-Carson project, 96, 97. *See also* Newlands Project
Truman, Harry, 144, 145
Twain, Mark, 42, 58, 59, 63
Tzimél Dimé, 46

Union Mill and Mining Company, 115
United States Forest Service, 8; Cave Rock case and, 171–77
Utah, 50, 55, 57, 70, 75, 95, 135, 159; Mormon claims to, 47; Office of Indian Affairs and, 49
Ute, 2, 11, 12, 24, 33, 34, 50; Indian Claims Commission settlement and, 150
Uto-Aztecan language, 22, 193n8

Valentine, Robert, 88, 92
Vasques, Rueben, 184
Virginia and Truckee Railroad, 64
Virginia City, Nevada, 2, 4, 66, 67; establishment of, 57–59; need for lumber, 63
Virginia Daily Union, 67

Wagotom (Washoe shaman), 85
Walker River, 51, 57
Walker River Paiutes, 139
Wall, Myron, Jr., 161
Wallace, Brian, ix, xi, 164, 184; Cave Rock case and, 173–76
Walling, Michael, 185
Washiw Wagayay Mangal, 9
Washoe: complaints about trespassing on allotments, 88–91; connection to Lake Tahoe, x, 9, 18, 159, 163, 193n9; fishing practices and, 32–33; John C. Frémont encounter, 39–42; girls' ceremony, 27–28; girls' training, 25–27; hunting practices, 28–31; Indian Claims Commission Act and, 147–63; land purchase of 1917 and, 111–18; pine nut festival and, 34–35; presidential summit and, 8, 164–71, 173, 184; seasonal cycle of, 21, 31–37; Jedidiah Smith encounter, 38–39; use of the Dawes Act, 6–7, 77, 83–88; work as ranch hands, 4, 75, 76, 120; work in the tourist trade, 4, 9, 94, 121
"Washoe," word used to define Comstock region, 58
Washoe Constitution, 131
Washoe Development Group, 183
Washoe Environmental Protection Department (WEPD), 182
Washoe Johnny, 85
Washoe Nation, 7
Washoe Tribe of the States of Nevada and California, Plaintiff v. The United States, Defendant, The (1951), 152–53
Washoe Valley, 55
Washoe Wiske'em project, 183
Wasson, Warren, 71
Watasému, 31, 42. *See also* Carson River
Waters, George, 172
Watkins, Arthur V., 159–60
wegéleyú, 29, 77; defined, 24; Henry Rupert and, 79–82
Welewkushkush, 80–81
Welmelti, traditional range defined, 23
WEPD. *See* Washoe Environmental Protection Department
Williams, James, 54
Wilson, Waziyatawin Angela, 15
Wilson, Woodrow, 108
Winnemucca, Sarah, 54–55
Wolfe, Patrick, 13
Woods, John, 52
Worster, Donald, 95
Wright, George F.: Indian Claims Commission case and, 148–62; services retained by the Washoe, 147
Wyatt, Tina, 181

Zimmerman, William, Jr., 129, 145

www.ingramcontent.com/pod-product-compliance
Lightning Source LLC
Chambersburg PA
CBHW032213230426
43672CB00011B/2533